Dr. Kockelmans has published two books and several articles in the realm of philosophy of science; one of the books, a study on the special theory of relativity, was awarded the gold medal of *Teylers Tweede Genootschap* in 1956. His most recent publications are in the area of contemporary continental European philosophy and include, in addition to many articles, two books an Heidegger's philosophy and two books on Husserl's phenomenology. Duquesne University Press has published his books, *Martin Heidegger* and *Phenomenology and Physical Science*, while *A First Introduction to Husserl's Phenomenology* is in preparation.

Edmund Husserl's
Phenomenological Psychology
A Historico-Critical Study

DUQUESNE STUDIES
Psychological Series

4

Edmund Husserl's

Phenomenological Psychology

A Historico-Critical Study

Joseph J. Kockelmans, Ph.D.

DUQUESNE UNIVERSITY PRESS
Pittsburgh, Pa.
Editions E. Nauwelaerts, Louvain

DUQUESNE STUDIES
Psychological Series

Adrian van Kaam, Ph.D., and Edward Hogan, Ph.D., editors

Volume One—*Stephen Strasser*, PHENOMENOLOGY AND THE HUMAN SCIENCES. *A Contribution to a New Scientific Ideal.* XIII and 339 pages. Price: $6.00.

Volume Two—*Aron Gurwitsch*, THE FIELD OF CONSCIOUSNESS. XIV and 427 pages. Price: $7.95.

Volume Three—*Adrian van Kaam*, EXISTENTIAL FOUNDATIONS OF PSYCHOLOGY. XIV and 386 pages. $7.95.

This work was translated
from the Dutch by
Bernd Jager and Revised
by the Author.

Library of Congress Catalog Card Number 67-27995
© 1967, by Duquesne University
PRINTED IN THE UNITED STATES OF AMERICA
BY KINGSPORT PRESS, INC., KINGSPORT, TENNESSEE

PREFACE

Edmund Husserl first spoke publicly about a new phenomenological psychology some forty years ago. He conceived this new psychology as a discipline destined to play an important role in the already established empirical psychology as well as in philosophy. The influence of Husserl's ideas was responsible for the extensive phenomenological psychological movement which subsequently took hold in many countries. A careful analysis of this phenomenological movement as it developed makes one quickly aware of the presence of a number of clearly distinguishable currents, all in fact claiming Husserl as their origin. However one soon realizes that only a few psychologists employ Husserl's concepts without major modifications. What is typical in this picture is that many psychologists talk about phenomenology without offering any real clarification of the meaning of the term they are using, and furthermore where phenomenological literature is concerned, there is also frequently a lack of clear-cut distinction between Husserl's thought and that of other phenomenologists such as Scheler, Heidegger, Sartre, Jaspers, Merleau-Ponty and others.

There is, however, a basis for understanding this confusion which exists; what has happened is that in psychology, as well as in sociology and anthropology, the different trends of thought have developed without clearly formulated philosophical premises. One must take into account here also the fact that it has been virtually impossible for most authors to see phenomenological problems in their historical perspective because until just recently Husserl's thought was open to only the privileged few who had access to his manuscripts. Any knowledge concerning his thought, which perforce came through via secondary sources then, was characterized by considerable divergence on a number of points. These, certainly, are some of the important factors which give rise to difficulties when one considers the question of what must be understood by phenomenological psychology. It seems obvious that a reasonable solution to the problem will not be found by constructing some sort of largest common denominator comprising all the existing phenomenologies, and using it as a point of departure for the description of phenomenological psychology. Instead, what suggests itself as the way to a meaningful formulation is a careful historical investigation of the essential differences underlying the various phenomenologies toward the end of finding a firm basis from which to operate while attempting to determine the essential characteristics of phenomenological psychology. Fortunately it is now possible to make a start on the important historico-critical task which remains to be undertaken; thanks to the indefatigable efforts of the scholars of the Husserl Archives, there is access today to the complete text of Husserl's last work and to all of his other important contributions to phenomenological psychology from 1920 to 1930.

The specific task to which I address myself in this book is that of presenting a historico-critical appraisal of Husserl's own development as far as phenomenological psychology is concerned. Toward this aim I have allowed myself to be guided by the following questions: how did Husserl arrive at his views regarding phenomenological psychology? What task did he envision for this new discipline? What are its essential aspects? How does this psychology relate to empirical psychology on the one hand, and to philosophy on the other? Only after these questions have been answered will it be possible to appraise Husserl in the light of recent developments; only then will one be able to see the perspectives his thought has opened up for present day psychology and to comprehend the true pattern of his thinking.

It must be stated at the outset that this book does not pretend to solve all questions related to Husserl's view on psychology.

It is my hope, however, that the study will make at least a substantial contribution toward the elucidation of some of the more persistent problems of phenomenological psychology.

CONTENTS

LIST OF ABBREVIATIONS

References to Husserl's publications are all to the German edition of his works as indicated below. The list also includes all the English translations that are known to me. However, in view of the fact that the most important texts of Husserl that are dealt with in this book were not yet available in translation references have not been made to these translations even where that would have been possible.

Phil. d. Arithm.　*Philosophie der Arithmetik. Psychologische und logische Untersuchungen.* Erster Band. (Halle a.S.: C.E.M. Pfeffer, 1891).

L. U.　*Logische Untersuchungen,* 3 vol. (Halle a.S.: Max Niemeyer, 1921–1922).

Die Idee　*Die Idee der Phänomenologie. Fünf Vorlesungen* (1907). Herausgegeben und eingeleitet von Walter Biemel. (Husserliana, Band II). (The Hague: Martinus Nijhoff, 1950).
The Idea of Phenomenology. Trans. William P. Alston and George Nakhnikian. (The Hague: Martinus Nijhoff, 1964).

Phil. str. W.　"Philosophie als strenge Wissenschaft", in *Logos,* 1 (1910–1911) 289–341.
"Philosophy as Rigorous Science", in Quentin Lauer, *Edmund Huserl: Phenomenology and the Crisis of Philosophy.* (New York: Harper and Row, 1965), pp. 69–147. See also: *Cross Currents,* 6 (1956), pp. 228–246, 324–344.

Ideen　*Ideen zu einer reinen Phänomenologie und phänomenologischen Philosophie.*

Ideen I   *Erstes Buch: Allgemeine Einführung in die reine Phänomenologie.* Herausgegeben von Walter Biemel. (Husserliana, Band III). (The Hague: Martinus Nijhoff, 1950). *Ideas. General Introduction to Pure Phenomenology.* Trans. W. R. Boyce Gibson. (New York: Collier Books, 1962).

Ideen II   *Zweites Buch: Phänomenologische Untersuchungen zur Konstitution.* Herausgegeben von Marly Biemel. (Husserliana, Band IV). (The Hague: Martinus Nijhoff, 1952).

Ideen III   *Drittes Buch: Die Phänomenologie und die Fundamente der Wissenschaften.* Herausgegeben von Marly Biemel. (Husserliana, Band V). (The Hague: Martinus Nijhoff, 1952).

Erste Philos.   *Erste Philosophie. Erster Teil: Kritische Ideengeschichte* (1923–1924). Herausgegeben von Rudolf Boehm. (Husserliana, Band VII). (The Hague: Martinus Nijhoff, 1956). *Zweiter Teil: Theorie der phänomenologischen Reduktion* (1923–1924). Herausgegeben von Rudolf Boehm. (Husserliana, Band VIII). (The Hague: Martinus Nijhoff, 1959).

Phän. Psych.   *Phänomenologische Psychologie* (1925). Herausgegeben von Walter Biemel. (Husserliana, Band IX). (The Hague: Martinus Nijhoff, 1962).

Phenomenology   "Phenomenology", in *Encyclopaedia Britannica,* 14th edition. London, 1927, vol. 17, col. 699–702.

F. tr. L.   *Formale und transzendentale Logik. Versuch einer Kritik der logischen Vernunft.* (Halle a.S.: Max Niemeyer, 1929).

Cart. Med.   *Cartesianische Meditationen und Pariser Vorträge.* Herausgegeben und eingeleitet von Prof. S. Strasser. (Husserliana, Band I). (The Hague: Martinus Nijhoff, 1950). *Cartesian Meditations. An Introduction to Phenomenology.* Trans. Dorion Cairns. (The Hague: Martinus Nijhoff, 1960).

Krisis   *Die Krisis der europäischen Wissenschaften und die transzendentale Phänomenologie. Eine Einleitung in die phänomenologische Philosophie.* Herausgegeben von Walter Biemel. (Husserliana, Band VI). (The Hague: Martinus Nijhoff, 1954).

Erf. u. Urt.   *Erfahrung und Urteil. Untersuchungen zur Genealogie der Logik.* Redigiert und herausgegeben von Ludwig Landgrebe, (Hamburg: Claassen, 1954).

INTRODUCTION

Since the turn of the century the scientific world has undergone some far-reaching changes. For the most part these changes have been determined by the fact that a number of the sciences began consciously to free themselves from the influence of physics as the model-science. Also, we see how attempts have been made in the realm of the sciences of man to apply empirical methods to the study of man *as a person*. Using Strasser's term these sciences can be covered in the expression 'positive anthropology.' Among them psychology and sociology play a predominant role. In this particular context psychology is no longer delineated as the science which studies man's behavior inasfar as in this behavior man manifests himself as a psychophysical unity,[1] but as that science which investigates the different modes of man's orientation toward the cultural, religious, historical, social, economical, and technical world. As such, psychology, as is true for all other empirical sciences of man, should not be confused with the earlier 'sciences of the mind,' the *Geisteswissenschaften,* for the empirical sciences of man are not concerned with the 'objective mind,' but seek to understand man *as a person*. In this way a real separation has been effected between the empirical sciences of man and the physical sciences. It remains possible, of course, to make man the subject of investigation in natural science. But such an approach is not the only one possible, and, furthermore, it is impossible following that approach to make man *as a person* the subject of investigation. On the other hand, however, we want to make it clear here once and for all that the empirical sci-

1. Ph. Kohnstamm, J. Linschoten, M. Langeveld, B. Kouwer, D. Van Lennep en B. Palland, *Inleiding in de psychologie*, Groningen, 1955, pp. 3–4.

ences of man mentioned above remain *genuinely* empirical
sciences, inasfar as they make use of empirical methods of
investigation. For, the empirical sciences of man which study man
as a person, also organize man's experience in such a fashion
that it can give rise to inductive conclusions. These inductive
conclusions can, in turn, be subjected to the critical appraisal
of a community of scholars. The difference between the physical
sciences and these empirical sciences of man, therefore, is not so
much accounted for in terms of the methods used; first and foremost this difference must be seen in the divergent ways man
himself can be viewed. The physical sciences consider man as a
creature produced by and wholly accounted for in terms of
surrounding nature. In this view man is seen as a link in the
chain of cosmic evolution, as an organism dependent upon, and
determined by, a biological substratum, whereas in the empirical
sciences of man, man is viewed under the aspect of the
originator and elaborator of a world in which he lives, works
and dwells.[2]

To account fully for the far-reaching changes in the scientific
world since the turn of the century, we must take into consideration a number of factors. One important and undeniable factor
is Husserl's phenomenology. Husserl's influence on the scientific revolution could be the subject of a separate study. As we
have made some attempt in that direction as far as the physical
sciences are concerned, in a previous publication,[3] we shall limit
ourselves here to the meaning of Husserl's work for empirical
psychology.

If one wishes to shed light on the meaning of Husserl's
philosophy for contemporary psychology, it clearly does not
suffice to quote isolated statements and expressions from his
major publications, however important such a procedure could
admittedly be. For there does exist a close relationship between empirical psychology and philosophy. This relationship

2. S. Strasser, *Phenomenology and the Human Sciences,* Pittsburgh, 1963, p.
6.

3. Joseph J. Kockelmans, *Phenomenology and Physical Science,* Pittsburgh,
1966.

is and remains problematic mostly because it is usually only implicitly determined. If we were able to make this relationship explicit, probably then it would be possible to determine the scientific status of psychology. But this task is a very difficult one in Husserl's view. Furthermore, the scientific status of empirical psychology itself is far from being simple to determine. For the empirical psychology in question is no longer the experimental laboratory psychology of Wundt; it also encompasses genetic, social, and clinical, as well as industrial, and psychopathological psychologies. All of these disciplines are concerned with the understanding of man and his world. Yet, psychology is not a purely descriptive discipline either and, as such, is not fully divorced from the experimental sciences. It is incorrect and unjust to deny psychology its character as a scientific discipline and to call it a philosophical theory of man with practical implications. It is equally unjust to make psychology a category under literature. The problems arising out of these issues become in themselves still more complicated by the fact that empirical psychology began as an ally of the natural sciences. This inheritance had prevented psychology, except rarely, from divorcing itself from physiology.

Scientific psychology originated in the seventeenth century in an atmosphere pervaded by the dualistic spirit of Descartes. It therefore failed originally to understand its own specific identity. Once delivered from the grasp of philosophy, psychology fell into the hands of the already maturing natural sciences. While under the influence of the natural sciences, psychology uncovered a great number of facts about human and animal behavior. These facts, however, were understood only within the narrow perspective arising from a naive naturalistic point of view. These facts never became "phenomena" in the original meaning of the word, and failed, therefore, to fit into a real and significant explanation in the strict sense.[4]

Before returning to Husserl and the importance of his work

4. F. J. J. Buytendijk, "Die Bedeutung der Phänomenologie Husserls für die Psychologic der Gegenwart," in *Husserl et la Pensée Moderne* (Ed. H. L. Van Breda et J. Taminiaux), Den Haag, 1959, 78–98, pp. 78–82.

for empirical psychology, we should look in greater detail at the foundations of naturalistic objectivism in psychology. This objectivism requires every truly empirical science to make a clear distinction between the subject and the object of study. At the basis of this distinction is the old habit of making a contrast between the independently existing, spatio-temporal world, and pure consciousness. When this separation is pursued to its ultimate conclusions it becomes clear that man-as-a-person can never become the object of a purely empirical investigation; for as such man precisely is the subject of investigation. The experimenter organizes his experiences methodically with the aid of a scientific apparatus which, indeed, is able to yield scientifically useful results. A closer look at this scientific apparatus yields a number of important ingredients. First of all, we notice a set of fixed rules which guide the whole observational process. We find a preference for measuring instruments by means of which further objectivity is achieved. We also notice a carefully defined group of categories, concepts, and models. Furthermore, the language used to describe the whole experimental process is restrained by a set of precise definitions which are guided completely by mathematico-logical devices. Finally, there are the statistical methods, the hypotheses, and verification principles. This scientific apparatus is, in essence, the same for all sciences. In psychology it is preferable to work with animals rather than with human beings because an objective interpretation of the scientific facts is easier there. Generally speaking psychology is solely designed for the study of facts. The question of whether these facts are freely realized remains irrelevant for psychology ultimately; psychology must remain mute in the face of values and teleology on the ground that these aspects of human life, too, remain outside the scope of its methods. In short, the method of this psychology is characterized by an objectifying reduction of phenomena; all experience is strained through the narrow pores of a tight methodological filter, so that of the previous richness of the phenomena, the only thing that remains intact is that which can be described and dealt with exactly by means of the methods characteristic of the natural sciences.[5]

This objectivism has been fostered in part by the hope that the comprehensive unity of all the sciences and the unity of our human view on the world could, thus, be saved notwithstanding the progressive specialization in the different sciences. Without any doubt, the unity of the sciences in the sense of a comprehensible coherence of the results of all kind of investigations is a great good. The greatest philosophers have always searched for a radical justification of such a unity of our scientific view on the world.[6] It is not possible to attain this desired and desirable unity through the reduction of all empirical sciences to one single empirical science, through reduction of all objectivity to the objectivity of physics. Nor do we serve the quest for unity well by substituting one single verification-principle for all other forms of verification, by disregarding all scientific languages in favor of one universal scientific language. Method, conceptual system, and language cannot be considered as neutral and purely technical aids by means of which it would be possible to express and describe everything whatsoever in a univocal way, albeit true that pure ambiguity is equally inconceivable because the scientific character which every science pursues as an ideal makes fixed demands upon all of them. Objectivism puts a one-sided stress on the empirical character of psychology, because it sees in physics (taken as it factually developed in history) the one ideal for all empirical sciences; all sciences must model themselves after physics as far as scientific experience, methods and language are concerned. However, such objectivism makes it impossible for psychology to be a genuine science of real human beings in a real world. Objectivism, in fact, asks us to understand the predicate 'scientific' to mean 'in accordance with the demands of logic and mathematics as these are understood and used by physics.'

5. R. Müller-Freienfels, *De voornaamste richtingen in de hedendaagse psychologie* (Trans. P. Ronge), Utrecht, 1938, pp. 17–26.
6. Joseph J. Kockelmans, *op. cit.*, pp. 70–91.

But such an interpretation would make it forever impossible to make scientific use of all experiences which are grounded in the self-awareness of a *free* human being. It follows that man cannot become the theme of an objective science, unless he is examined and studied in exactly the same manner as a crystal would be in the laboratory of the physicist or chemist.[7]

It seems clear, without further elaboration, that such a view is unacceptable. In fact, many psychologists have been aware of this for a long time and have searched for new ways to approach man scientifically without having to reduce him to a thing. It is possible to deny physics its supremacy as the model-science for all other sciences without declaring in the same breath that psychology can, therefore, never hope to be a science. Scientific is not identical with physical. The view that objectivity can be reached only in the way it is done in physics, is based on an objectivistic prejudice and ultimately founded in a completely unacceptable, epistemological position. Objectivism is a degenerate form of the laudable striving for objectivity, taken in the sense of the freedom from prejudices and, thus, of the striving towards intersubjective truth.[8]

We are aware that on many occasions the case against objectivism has been sorely overstated. This is probably why the criticisms against objectivism have fallen on so many deaf ears among the logicians. Many an orator, inveighing against the evils of a psychology modeling itself after the physical sciences, has been led astray by his own eloquence. Leaving a clearly defensible position, he seems to plead for a psychology freed from logic, from general methodology, and mathematics. One must agree with the logicians that such a psychology ceases to be a scientific psychology. The criticism can be directed only against the view that mathematics, logic, and scientific method can be employed solely in the manner in which physics has made use of them. Psychology can free itself from the dominance of physics and still be a scientific psychology: it can bind itself by laws of logic and general methodology, even afford mathematics (pro-

7. S. Strasser, *op. cit.*, pp. 10–20.
8. *Ibid.*, pp. 21–26.

vided it is understood in a not too one-sided way as the science of the quantitative in the narrow sense of this term) a central position within its framework without imitating physics.

Furthermore, while turning away from physics as the model-science, contemporary psychology has moved toward a closer association with philosophy in the hope of a closer articulation of the specifically human realm. This articulation can only succeed, however, by taking one's starting point in a careful analysis and description of the psychological phenomena them-selves. This contention will be worked out in more detail in the succeeding pages. Suffice it to say that everything said in the foregoing can be proved only in a theory of science which itself must be based in a general epistemology. This epistemology in turn presupposes a philosophical anthropology which itself again is founded in an ontology.

Husserl's great contribution to the sciences of man in general, and to psychology in particular, has been the opening of new possiblilities. He has pointed out, first of all, that a mere de-scription of facts alone does not yet yield scientific and psycho-logical knowledge, even if such a description is in continuous harmony with immediately given phenomena. Neither can lists of statistical data be thought to constitute, by themselves, a truly scientific psychology. Whether we treat facts statistically or describe them in another way, we still have only facts. And facts, as such, can only form points of departure for a scientific study; they never can form the whole of it. It is true, of course, that it is of the greatest importance for educators, sociologists, or judges to know what is factually happening in the world. Yet, facts and correlations between them do not give us a scientific, theoretical knowledge of man's behavior. In and of themselves they are blind, incapable of giving us insight. Psy-chology is not merely a collection of those facts. A true psy-chology is concerned with finding the structures of meaning which underlie all forms and manners of man's Being-in-the world. James and the proponents of Gestalt psychology, in their own ways, have contributed to this view; even Wundt prepared part of the way.

Husserl is also greatly indebted to Franz Brentano. Continuing along the paths opened up by the latter, Husserl became convinced that we can come to a clear understanding of the nature and task of psychology only when we become fully aware of the immensely important fact that all human behavior is intentional behavior. Psychology must make real intentionality the starting point of its research. For, in the natural attitude man experiences himself in the life-world in which he dwells only through the intentional relationships which he maintains with the real things in the world around him. These intentionalities must form the subject of careful intentional noetico-noematic analyses which in turn must be followed by careful and exact descriptions. In these analyses and descriptions we are not primarily concerned with the factuality of facts. We are, rather, concerned with the essential structures underlying these facts and which, ultimately, constitute their genuine meaning. That is why, for a psychologist, a set of reductive procedures is of the utmost importance.

Psychological research should first of all be free from all theoretical prejudices whatsoever. To guarantee this is the task of a first form of reduction. Husserl notes that we need a further reduction to free us of the innate limitations of our naive and natural way of looking at things. For this mode of looking at things does not allow us to bring to light the underlying meaning-structures of the phenomena, because of the preoccupation with factual facts characteristic of our natural attitude. To perform this change in attitude is in Husserl's view the task of the phenomenological-psychological reduction. Furthermore, our prescientific experience of the life-world (*Lebenswelt*) has been modified through culture, science and philosophy, and religion. This necessitates the use of another special reduction, whose task is to make a transition possible from the cultural world in which we actually are living to the more original life-world. From what has been said we should not draw the conclusion that there will be no room for experimentation in psychology. There are, however, certain new requirements regarding experimentation which follow from the previous discussion. Psychological experiments should work with real life situations within which it will be possible for the experimental subject to stand out to the world in a *meaningful* relationship. Using the data provided by the experiment, we must make use of noetico-noematic analyses to get at *what* it is that the person experiences and *how* he sees it. Experimentation even remains of prime importance here. For the results of the phenomenological analyses will be richer the more the experience in question is more fully understood because of its being observed in a variety of situations. Phenomenological psychology even requires a repeated return to the things themselves; it tries to get the right view on the exemplary case. Thus, it tries to justify the value of the free variation which forms a necessary prerequisite to the ideation (*Wesensschau*). Phenomenological psychology needs a step by step controlled progression from simple experiences, via the experimentally verified scientific phenomena, to the *pure* phenomena. In such experimentation, our first concern is not with numbers and correlations, however useful and important they may be otherwise. The focus is on the meaning-structures and especially on the genesis of the meaning of the phenomena concerned, which are to be studied objectively without prejudices and theories. It is self-evident that experiments able to serve this purpose, must be chosen with extreme care.

Phenomenological psychology can also be of great importance to psychotherapy, as we can quickly gather from the number of publications that make use of this approach. In the area of psychotherapy, we become especially aware of the task of psychology in view of the crisis in which man finds himself today. A physical psychology is not equipped to deal with this predicament. Only a psychology closely allied with philosophy can meet the needs of man in crisis; it is phenomenological psychology which makes such a close relationship between psychology and philosophy possible.[9]

The foregoing consideration implies a great number of

9. F. J. J. Buytendijk, *art. cit.,* pp. 82–96.

problems. Not all that we have said has been unequivocally expressed by Husserl. He has, however, clearly pointed in the direction which we have taken up here. Our study will concern itself, initially, with Husserl's own view on phenomenological psychology. We shall be particularly concerned with Husserl's own development as a phenomenological psychologist. Only by so doing can we make the task and the nature of phenomenological psychology understandable, and grasp at the same time its relationship to empirical psychology and to transcendental philosophy. Only at the end of this study will it be possible to return to the theme of this introduction. At that time we shall have at our disposition the information needed to justify our position. It will then become clear how certain of our present remarks imply a criticism of Husserl's work.

The problems discussed in this book are relevant to psychology, but also to pedagogy and philosophy. For the benefit of these latter we have inserted a brief survey of the history of psychology. This survey is not intended to be a new or profound contribution to psychology's history. It is aimed only at providing those basic facts which will help place Husserl's psychological work in the appropriate historical context. The psychologists among my readers can turn to the second chapter of the book without loss of continuity.

1 SHORT SURVEY OF THE HISTORY OF PSYCHOLOGY UP TO THE TWENTIETH CENTURY

Introduction

In this chapter we shall deal with the history of psychology up to the beginning of our century. This seems to be a highly problematic task. For one can legitimately ask the question of whether or not a scientific psychology existed before the nineteen-hundreds. However, whatever one thinks the answer to that question is, he cannot deny that a good many of the earlier psychologists were actively trying to bring about a scientific psychology. The intention of this chapter is to mention briefly only those streams and developments of thought which have exerted an important influence on the scientific psychology of today. It will not be possible to be exhaustive in this respect. Our sole purpose for this chapter is to introduce and clarify historically the point of view which Husserl adopted in regard to psychology.

It is self-evident that we cannot correctly evaluate Husserl's contribution to psychology when we read and understand his work out of our own time-perspective. Reading Husserl's conception of phenomenological psychology we often fail to appreciate that at the time of the first formulation of his ideas no depth psychology existed, nor did behaviorism, or Gestalt psychology. Also structural and personalistic psychology had not yet come into being. It is for this reason that it is of some importance to describe briefly the historical development of psychology as it presented itself around 1900. Only such a description will provide us with the background needed to do justice to Husserl's thought.

However, there is still another reason why this book begins with a brief survey of psychology's history. As will become clear later, Husserl has tried many times to explain his position as it was related to the other psychologies of his day. But in these explanations he rapidly lost sight of everything except what was of some importance in regard to transcendental phenomenology and phenomenological psychology. In order to be able to evaluate Husserl's own ideas on the origin and development of psychology objectively, we are in need of a broader and more independent historical perspective.

The Genesis of Psychology from Philosophy

Naturalism and Psychology

The nineteenth century is characterized by the triumph of the methods used in the natural sciences. In the second half of that century many scientists were convinced that the era of idealism and speculative philosophy had come to an end. Brilliant discoveries in physics, chemistry, and biology prepared the way for the general conviction that truth could be revealed only by means of the research of natural science. Not surprisingly the "science of human consciousness" adopted the methods of physics. Psychology started to make use of experimental laboratories. The experimental data were subjected to mathematical analyses. A whole new world of possibilities had opened up. Those working in the field of psychology around the turn of the century must have felt conscious of being part of a new science with virtually unlimited possibilities. All that had been thought about man over a period of more than two thousand years was pushed aside as irrelevant, and finally forgotten. The psychologists wanted to build their science on the solid foundation of experimentally verified facts which they themselves uncovered in their laboratories. With the experimental and mathematical methods of physics they felt they were in possession of the key to all their problems.

Of course, there were differences of opinion among the psychologists of those days, but these differences were overshadowed by one major unifying theme. Psychology must move away from its previous association with philosophy and proceed to ever closer ties with the methodology of physics. The affinity with the natural sciences became so close at times that it was impossible to see where psychology ended and physiology started. Then around 1900 the unified front was threatened.

A great number of factors must be considered in order to appreciate the growing conflict within psychology. Most important of these is the controversy about the mathematico-experimental methods employed. Many were disillusioned when it became clear that these methods soon reached the limits of their usefulness when applied to the realm of the psychical. The methods had been fertile in the area of sensory psychology, but outside this limited area, in the realm of higher mental processes, the results had been disappointing. Sharp criticism arose from many sides and was directed to those basic assumptions in psychology which previously had been held inviolate. Within the confines of experimental psychology a new psychological stream gradually emerged. Whereas experimental psychology had directed itself toward the discovery of universally valid laws of human behavior, the new differential psychology was primarily interested in human differences.

The crisis caused by the growing inner division of psychology was intensified by pressures from allied disciplines. Philosophy had grown strong again after the initial onslaught of the natural sciences. A number of philosophical movements, some reinspired by Kant, others by Hegel, bombarded the psychology oriented toward natural science. The distance, however, between these philosophies and the objectifying psychologies was still too great for either one to take the other completely seriously. More profoundly threatening to the unity of psychology were the waves which were later caused by the so-called Philosophy of Life which became allied with the resurrected

vitalistic biology. This stream of thought created dissent within
the scientific disciplines themselves. Many a scientist declared
that the method employed by the natural sciences need not be
the only scientific method. Its success with the problems posed
by inorganic nature does not imply that this method can be
transferred to other problems. Rather than ascribing the excel-
lence of this method to its innate correctness or perfection,
these scientists realized its success was due to the fact that it
had been designed for a specific purpose. The lesson to be
drawn from such a conclusion is not the indiscriminate application of one successful method, but the purposeful devising of
new methods for particular problems. Rather than borrowing
the methods of physics, the psychologist, the sociologist, and
other scientists dealing with man should design methods suited
to the problems relevant to them. Husserl arrived via his own
philosophy to similar conclusions. His extensive, sharp conflict
with the dominant psychology of his day will be studied later in
greater detail. We must first focus attention on the main events
in the origin and development of psychology. For as I said
before, it is my opinion that a short exploration of the history
of the ideas briefly indicated above will prove helpful to understanding Husserl's view on psychology in general and its historical development in particular.

THE PHILOSOPHICAL ORIGIN OF PSYCHOLOGY

For centuries psychology was primarily a philosophical psychology. More than two thousand years had to pass before an
empirical psychology could sufficiently loosen its ties with
philosophy to become an independent science. When Plato
(427–347) and Aristotle (384–322) laid the foundations of psychology, they envisioned a purely philosophical study of the
human soul. Yet, particularly in Aristotle do we find traces of
what we now call the empirical sciences of man. He pointed,
for example, to the dangers of the overstimulation of the senses,
to the difference between the *feelings* of pleasure and pain, and
to several other aspects of our affective life. When Aristotle spoke
about memory he based his discussion on immediate experience

and arrived at a formulation of some laws of association. Yet he never suspected the possibilities of a truly empirical psychology. In this respect, the history of psychology runs parallel to that of physics.

According to Aristotle, psychology must study the life-manifestations of plants and animals as well as humans. These life-manifestations all emanate from the soul. Plants and animals have a soul, as do humans.

The first form of organic life is due to the vegetative soul. It forms the foundation of vegetative life and the last principle governing the purposive functions of assimilation and propagation in man and animal. The animal or sensitive soul constitutes the principle of animal existence. It governs and makes it possible for animal and man to perceive, to desire and to move. The thinking rational soul forms the immortal principle of thinking and striving in man. Man possesses only one life-principle, the rational soul, which is the principle of thinking and striving as well as the ulitmate source of man's other functions. On could say that in man the nutritive and sensitive principles are incorporated in the rational soul. If one considers this thinking soul as the principle of one determinate function, then it is called (precisely taken as the foundation of this particular function) the faculty in regard to this function. Therefore, because of the fact that the one and single thinking soul is the source and root of many possibilities of functioning, one can attribute to the soul many faculties, that is many possibilities which become actually functioning only through the influence of that which is external to it. Finally, the soul forms a substantial unity with the body so that not a single human possibility can become actual except through the cooperation of the body. In other words the soul is the animating *entelechy* of the body.[1]

1. E. Boring, *A History of Experimental Psychology*, New York, 1957, pp. 158–159; M. Langeveld, Ph. Kohnstamm, C. Van Parreren, J. Linschoten, B. Kouwer, D. Van Lennep, A. Oldendorff, B. Palland, *Inleiding in de Psychologie*, Groningen, 1957, pp. 319–322. See also: F. Nuyens, *Ontwikkelingsmomenten in de zielkunde van Aristoteles. Een historisch-philosophische studie*, Nijmegen-Utrecht, 1939, pp. 199–231 and 244–288; C.

Husserl referred rarely to Aristotle's psychology. We might note here that on one of these occasions he seems to do an injustice to this psychology when he describes it as one of the objective disciplines among the sciences of experience, trying to become the compeer of the mathematical sciences of nature.[2] Otherwise, however, Husserl's criticism of Aristotle's position regarding psychology is justified to a large extent. But one might ask oneself whether it makes any sense to find fault with Plato and Aristotle because they did not know all about the issues that were clarified by Descartes, Kant, and Hegel only recently. On the other hand, it is clear that in *First Philosophy* from which these remarks are borrowed, Husserl does not intend to give an objective discription of the history of philosophy and psychology.

Be this as it may, continuing our historical outline we note that psychology remained a philosophical discipline throughout the Middle Ages. The main ideas were still taken from Plato and Aristotle but they were interpreted from a completely new view on the world which to a great extent was determined by Christian faith and Christian theology. Thomas Aquinas (1224–1272) was one of the first to see philosophy as it had been viewed in antiquity, namely, as a completely autonomous science. Like Aristotle he saw psychology as a purely philosophical discipline studying all life-manifestations. This view led him to consider psychology as a discipline in its own right, separate and distinct from faith and theology. The thoughts of Aquinas, which essentially remained in harmony with Aristotle's view, governed psychological thinking up to the sixteenth century. At that time a new stream of thought broke through.[3]

THE NEW PSYCHOLOGY

According to Husserl, it is John Locke who fathered the new developments in psychology. Husserl saw Locke as building on Descartes, on the one hand, and on Thomas Hobbes on the

---

Van Peursen, *Ziel—Geest—Lichaam. De mens als oriëntatie vanuit zijn wereld*, Utrecht, 1956, pp. 96–109.
2. E. Husserl, *Erste Philosophie*, 2 vol., Den Haag, 1956, vol. I, pp. 52–54.
3. M. Langeveld, *op. cit.*, pp. 323–325.

other. Hobbes, in turn, chose Bacon for his point of departure.[4]
One could say in Husserl's view that Bacon created the methodology of the new psychology, while Descartes provided the
scientific, theoretical backbone. Husserl made only cursory
mention of Bacon and Hobbes. Most of the time he restricted
himself to mentioning their names only. However, to clarify
Locke's position it seems advisable to consider Bacon in some
more detail than Husserl did. Although neither Bacon nor
Descartes specifically designed an empirical psychology, we cannot fail to notice the tremendous influence their theories exerted
later on the beginning efforts at an empirical psychology. That
this influence on psychology was very unfortunate under other
respects cannot detract from the ultimate importance of these
thinkers' contributions to the development of empirical psychology in the 19th century.

BACON'S CONTRIBUTIONS

Francis Bacon (1561–1626) is without doubt the most important representative of the Renaissance in England.[5] One of his
many projects was to bring about a completely new organization
of the sciences. From science Bacon expected, among other
things, a revolutionizing of human ways of dealing with each
other and with nature. He expected that man would be able to
acquire unlimited power over his environment. Bacon was completely dominated by the thought that only science could achieve
greatness for man, and that the conquest of the world could be
achieved only by means of science. All that which earlier renaissance thought had intimated about a wonderful and somewhat
fantastic future, Bacon sought to realize by means of systematic,
methodically directed scientific effort.

True science, according to Bacon, starts with experience,

4. E. Husserl, *Phänomenologische Psychologie*, Den Haag, 1962, pp. 350,
520, 3, 52, 309; Edmund Husserl, *Erste Philosophie*, vol. I, p. 19; Edmund
Husserl, *Die Krisis der europäischen Wissenschaften und die transzendentale
Phänomenologie. Eine Einleitung in die phänomenologische Philosophie*, Den
Haag, 1954, pp. 207, 233–234.

5. Ueberweg-Moog, *Grundriss der Geschichte der Philosophie: Die
Philosophie der Neuzeit bis zum Ende des XVIII. Jahrhunderts*, Berlin, 1924,
pp. 193–206; E. Boring, *op. cit.*, pp. 13–14.

that is to say with careful observation and experimentation. Starting with hypotheses of limited generality, we work toward more generally valid hypotheses by means of the inductive method. Once these generally valid hypotheses are achieved, we go back to the concrete facts and events and try to interpret and understand them. Underlying this plan for action is the steady belief that a clear conceptualization of factual happenings will bring about man's ultimate conquest of nature.

To achieve this idea, Bacon worked out a grandiose plan in his *Instauratio Magna*.[6] Only a small part of this plan was ever realized, and Bacon could never reach a very high level in the concrete realization of it because despite his heroic efforts to the contrary, he remained somewhat of a victim of late scholasticism. He never quite succeeded in completely accounting for his *"inductio,"* while his attitude toward the deductive methods remained altogether too negative.

In the first part of his *Instauratio Magna*, entitled *De Dignitate et Augmentis Scientiarum*, Bacon attempted to give and justify a division, classification, and description of the different sciences. In the further determination of the 'intellectual globe' he also planned to indicate what was already achieved in every science and what was still to be done. He divided the sciences according to what he perceived to be the fundamental characteristics of the human soul, namely, the memory, the phantasy, and the intellect. Thus, he reached a division of the sciences as history, the arts, and philosophy. According to the subject matter discussed, philosophy is divided into natural theology, philosophy of nature, and anthropology. It becomes quite clear that this schema does not yet allow for an empirical psychology.

The second part of the *Instauratio Magna*, entitled the *Novum Organum*, contained Bacon's sharp attack on Aristotelian logic. He criticized especially its one-sided interest in deductive reasoning in general and in the syllogism in particular. According to Bacon, man can approach truth from two fundamentally different directions. With the data provided by the

6. R. Bacon, *Novum Organum Scientiarum* (Ed. G. W. Kitchin), Oxford, 1855, p. 19.

sensory apparatus, he can jump to the most general principles (axiomata) and then fill in the gap between the two by means of deductive reasoning. Another possibility is to go from the data of the senses to the axioms by means of a continuous and gradual ascension so that the most general axioms will be reached only in the final phase of the process of reasoning. The first method leads only to unproductive 'mental anticipations' while the other method leads to a 'true interpretation of nature'. The larger part of the *Novum Organum* is taken up by a very careful description of the ground rules of the inductive method. Despite his discovery of a number of important methodological principles, Bacon did not succeed in constructing a complete and radically founded theory of induction.

We might note here that Bacon did not want to limit the inductive method to the field of history or the arts. He considered the inductive method appropriate for the different philosophical disciplines as well. Yet, he never succeeded in his ambition, which was to reconstruct all of philosophy and to eliminate from it all methods except the inductive one. Hobbes, and later Locke, Berkeley, and Hume tried to realize Bacon's ideal. In doing so they became the founders of the empiricist philosophy. Bacon's ideal also took concrete form in the natural sciences which started to develop at that time. Bacon's intention, whether consciously or unconsciously pursued, was to renew the sterile philosophy of the late scholastic period with the aid of the natural sciences.

Not surprisingly, the dominant streams of philosophical thought were incapable of assessing the true worth of the positive, natural sciences. Thus, a tense situation was soon created between philosophy and the natural sciences. That is why the natural sciences allied themselves with empiricism which, in turn, itself was the fruit of a positive-scientific intention. Furthermore, we must not neglect in this context the very strikingly successful results of the new natural sciences; this success accounts, at least partly, for the fact that many philosophers turned away from classical philosophy and sought to ally themselves with empiricism. Finally, it is understandable that later

the other positive sciences which started to develop in the 18th
and 19th centuries, turned to the successful natural sciences to
learn about methodology. Ultimately this complete concentra-
tion on the positive and natural sciences resulted in philosophical positions called "positivism" and "scientism."

DESCARTES

With much the same intention as Bacon, although in an
entirely different manner, René Descartes (1596–1650) tried to
solve the philosophical problems created by the natural sciences
of the 17th century.[7] Descartes' philosophical training seems to
have been restricted to an inferior eclectic Thomism generally
taught in his day. In this philosophy he resented most of all the
fact that it could not progress beyond a recital of authors with
their conflicting opinions, making a mockery of man's quest for
certitude. Frequently the opinions of the various authors were
at exact opposites. Their irreconcilable differences led to stale-
mates which gave rise to the thought that the human mind is
incapable of real progress. Descartes never drew such a conclusion. On the contrary, he was deeply convinced of the great
possibilities of human thinking as in his view we can learn from
the lucidity, and the exquisite certitude of the mathematical
principles. The fact that the human mind did not have any
success in philosophy, cannot be blamed on the human mind
as such. It is, rather, the method of philosophizing which has
kept man from making progress in this realm of thought. Descartes' search was in the direction of a new method of philosophizing based on the methods of mathematics. With the aid of
this method he wanted to reconstruct all of philosophy from the
bottom up. It was his view, furthermore, that this philosophical
aim implied a radical break with the millenia of philosophizing
which preceded him.

7. Ueberweg-Moog, *op. cit.*, pp. 219–242; J. Maréchal, *Le point de départ
de la métaphysique.* 5 Cahiers, Bruxelles-Paris, 1944–1949, Cahier II, pp.
43–78; G. Gusdorf, *Introduction aux sciences humaines. Essai critique sur
leurs origins et leur développement,* Paris, 1960, pp. 88–93; E. Boring, *op. cit.*,
pp. 160–165.

Descartes was deeply convinced that science should be unique and unitary. It had to be built up from the very foundations to its ultimate completion by one single man, without presupposing any results reached in the past, by deducing all truths from a few fundamental principles and by presupposing nothing except that which is clear and distinct in itself and as such can be recognized by everybody. Much as mathematics starts from a very few clear axioms and proceeds from there on to prove all its further statements, so philosophy must start from a few evident and absolutely certain truths; all other truths must be derived from these basic ones by means of the strictly logical rules of the syllogism.

Of course the major question is how to bring to the fore the ἀξιώματα πάντων within the philosophical realm. Descartes declares that it can be found by means of a speculative, methodical, and universal doubt. It is well-known how he arrived at his *cogito* through this methodical doubt, and how, from the *cogito*, he thought to be able to deduce to the criterion of all fundamental truths which would serve him as the foundation for his strictly scientific philosophy. Thus, he wrote in his *Discourse on Method:* "and having remarked that there was nothing at all in the statement 'I think, therefore I am' which assures me of having thereby made a true assertion, excepting that I see very clearly that to think it is necessary to be, I came to the conclusion that I might assume, as a general rule, that the things which we conceive very clearly and distinctly are all true . . ." [8]

It is also a known fact that from his *cogito* Descartes drew certain very important conclusions concerning the nature of the thinking subject. In the *Discourse on the Method* he wrote how, after a careful reflection on the *cogito,* he arrived at the conclusion that he should, on the basis of the *cogito,* understand himself to be: "a substance the whole essence or nature of which is to think, and that for its existence there is no need of any place, nor does it depend on any material thing; so that this 'me', that is to say, the soul by which I am what I am, is

8. R. Descartes, *Discours de la méthode,* in *Oeuvres Complètes,* (Ed. Adam-Tannery), 12 vols., Paris, 1897–1910, vol. VI, pp. 31–32.

entirely distinct from the body, and is even more easy to know than the latter . . ." [9] Thus, the essential attribute or essence of the soul is that it is capable of thought.

In his philosophical physics he arrived at the conclusion that extension constitutes the essential attribute of the material world. Material substances are but spatial quantities devoid of any active attributes. All changes in the material world are but changes in space by means of local movements which follow fixed mechanical laws. All of the material world can, thus, be viewed as one gigantic mechanism which can be made completely intelligible once we know the laws governing its movements.

Descartes approached living bodies much the same way as he approached all of the material world. Plants and animals, even man's body, are considered to be mechanisms, distinct from inanimate bodies only in terms of complexity. All vital functions of organisms can be fully understood, once all the aspects of the movement of its particles are carefully considered.

This vision evidently leads to ruinous results for an anthropology. A dualistic concept of man is now inevitable. Without hesitation, Descartes continued on his way and proposed that the soul is a simple, immaterial, immortal substance with thinking as its essential attribute. The body possesses extension as its essential attribute and is, as such, not essentially different from other material substances. All the vital functions of the living human body can be explained by means of mechanical causes. There occurs, then, an unbridgeable gap between the body and the soul. A whole series of later philosophical additions and amplifications to these basic notions were not successful in restoring the unity of man for Descartes. What he had split asunder he could no more join together.

Descartes' views concerning the human body are, for the most part, contained in his *Traité de l'homme* and *Les Passions de l'âme*. Modern research has shown that Descartes' conception of the human body is not as original as once thought. Insights

9. *Ibid.,* pp. 32–33.

similar to his were current long before in the Arabian world
and can be found in such writers as Ibn an Nafis. These were
taken over in modified form and spread to the Western world
by Michel Servet and William Harvey. Nor is Descartes the only
one in the first half of the 17th century to propose and develop
the idea of a 'man machine' and a 'man automaton.' The names
of Hobbes and Mersenne must, without a doubt, be mentioned
in this connection also.

One can say, however, that in Descartes the myth of man as
machine reaches its most complete expression. The various
automatons, clocks, instruments, and machineries which had
been so copiously produced since the Renaissance functioned
as the original models for the understanding of the human
organism. The living body was thought of as a wonderful mechanism fashioned by the divine artist. "God has fabricated our
body as a machine, and He has wanted that it functions as a
universal instrument always operating in the same way according to its own laws." [10] This human mechanism can be subjected
to scientific investigations and be shown to obey mechanical
laws in all its life functions. The human body functions "in the
manner of watches, artificial fountains, windmills, and other
similar machines." [11]

Descartes maintained that the human organism functions in
a completely autonomous fashion without the assistance of our
thinking and willing. Every thought about the soul in terms of
an entelechy of the body becomes superfluous in this way. To
avoid any ambiguity, Descartes speaks no longer about the soul
of man but about his spirit; "and I consider the spirit not as a
part of the soul, but as that soul which thinks taken as a
whole." [12] That is why the *Traité de l'homme* tried to give an
account of such human functions as digestion, respiration, blood
circulation, movement, sleep, perception, memory, and desire
in terms of a mechanistic physics. "I want you in this machine

10. R. Descartes, *Entretien avec Burman,* quoted by Gusdorf, *op. cit.,* p. 89.
11. R. Descartes, *Traité de l'homme,* quoted by Gusdorf, *op. cit.,* p. 89.
12. R. Descartes, *Réponses aux Cinquièmes Objections aux Méditations,*
quoted by Gusdorf, *op. cit.,* p. 90.

to consider these functions as exclusively resulting from the disposition of its organs, no more and no less than this is the case with the movements of a watch or another automaton . . . ; in such a way that in regard to them one does not have to conceive in it of any other vegetative or sensitive soul, nor of any other principle of movement or life except its blood, agitated by the heat of the fire which . . . is of the same nature than all other fires which are found in inorganic bodies." [13]

This conception showed man as consisting of two separate and distinct substances, each of which must be studied by a different discipline. Man's spiritual substance forms the proper subject-matter for philosophy and man's body must be studied by the mechanistic physics. It becomes very clear that this vision leads away from a philosophical anthropology. Descartes failed to even pose the basic problem of an anthropology in an adequate way. For, the science of the human body is not a science of man, since in Descartes' view the body is not an essential part of man.

Descartes achieved the foundation of a positive science of the body but only at the expense of an existential separation between man and his body. Philosophy leaves the study of the human body to a positive science but must in this way pay the price of excluding the body from the human reality. To make it a fitting subject for scientific investigation, the body is to be estranged from man himself. After thus splitting the human world into these two independent parts, Descartes was at a loss to restore the unity which all of us experience in daily life. Attempts in this direction in *Les Passions de l'âme,* for example, fail miserably.

Closer analysis reveals thus that Descartes' vision of man becomes understandable only in the light of an implicitly adopted neo-Platonism. While remaining within this perspective, Descartes, on one hand, tried to account for man as spirit, man as a person, in terms of a spiritualistic metaphysics. On the other hand, he also wanted to account for the fact that man as

13. R. Descartes, *Traité de l'homme,* quoted by Gusdorf, *op. cit.,* p. 90.

far as his body is concerned can be brought within the realm of the positive sciences. In this way he indeed achieved a strict science of the body, but this science was no longer a science of man. "The mechanistic anthropology is perhaps a genuine mechanics, but it surely is not a genuine anthropology." [14]

Descartes' importance to psychology lies especially in the fact, that his research concerning the human body laid the foundation for the later physiological psychology and reflexology. His studies of consciousness on the other hand formed the basis for a future psychology of consciousness. Boring [15] mentions deservedly as concrete points in which Descartes contributed to the genesis and development of empirical psychology, the following topics: "the mechanistic approach, the dualism of mind and body, their interaction, the brain as the important locus for the mind, the localization of the mind nevertheless in the entire body, and yet the specific localizations within the brain, the innate ideas which led on into the doctrine of nativism."

At this point it is useful to return to a thought which we pursued earlier. Following Aristotle, philosophical psychology had directed its study to life in all forms. The study of plants, animals, and human beings all formed part of that approach. We could speak here of psychology as a philosophical study of vital functions and their manifestations. Descartes restricted his philosophical psychology to the domain of conscious phenomena because of his dualism. The post-Cartesian rationalistic movement represented by such thinkers as Leibnitz, Spinoza, and Wolff continued to regard the body and consciousness as wholly separate. A separate philosophy of conscious phenomena logically followed from that premise. Later, under the influence of the empiricism of Locke, Berkeley, and Hume, *a positive scientific psychology of consciousness* grew out of this movement. We mentioned how Descartes recognized a positive scientific study of the human body that existed side by side with the

14. G. Gusdorf, *op. cit.*, p. 93.
15. E. Boring, *op. cit.*, p. 165.

philosophical psychology of conscious phenomena. This positive science of the body came to bloom in the 17th and 18th centuries, ultimately forming the foundation for our present day biology and physiology. These two sciences gave rise to a *physiological psychology* in the 19th century, which came to exist side by side with the psychology of consciousness. Toward the end of the 19th century, we see a merging of these disciplines into the new empirical psychology.

Besides the two conceptions of psychology about which we spoke, there developed in the eighteenth century a third, namely that of a faculty psychology. For it soon dawned on many thinkers that the phenomena of consciousness could be classified according to a number of basic categories. First, there were proponents of a dichotomy which divided all phenomena of consciousness according to two basic categories, namely thinking and striving. Later others, under the influence of Kant, proposed a trichtomy which also included emotions or the domain of the affections. All these authors felt that the phenomena of feeling, of knowing, and of striving were possible only on the basis of a certain number of capacities or functions inherent in the human soul. The meaning of such expressions as "capacity" and "function" were subjected to considerable intellectual scrutiny. Some thought that a faculty ultimately referred to a certain reality in the human soul which should be understood as the cause, the immediate underlying principle, giving rise to the conscious phenomena in question.

Others understood function to mean a propensity for action which in no real way could be distinguished from the soul. Practically speaking, the philosophical consequences of both positions are similar. Both strive to analyze our conscious life into a number of functions each of which must have a determinate faculty as its 'cause.' These viewpoints, however, reduced psychology into a classification of psychical phenomena, the ultimate explanation of which consists in the fact that they are manifestations of the operations of accurately defined faculties of the soul, which as little 'homunculi' in the big 'homo' sometimes cooperate and sometimes fight with one another.

Soon a sharp reaction set in and faculty psychology was

bitterly attacked. Many psychologists felt that their curiosity could not be exhausted by means of a classification schema. They wanted to know what is really meant by a phenomenon of consciousness, what role it plays in the psychological life of man, and what laws can account for psychical phenomena. These questions compelled many thinkers to seek closer ties with the natural sciences.[16]

The Empiricism of Locke and Hume. The Psychology of Mill and Spencer

DURING THE 17th and 18th centuries the natural sciences gradually acquired momentum under the impact of Galileo, Newton, and others. The great success of the sciences was generally ascribed to the fact that these thinkers had boldly turned away from Aristotle's philosophy of nature and its deductive methods and had shifted their attention toward inductive and empirical methods.

Psychological thinkers thought, quite naturally, that they would also be entering a golden age of discoveries as soon as the example of the natural sciences could be followed. As we noted above, Descartes had already created a general epistemological climate in which this course of events could take place. Furthermore, Bacon had shown how a science could become empirical and make use of induction. Locke and Hume were the first to build psychology on these new foundations. Yet, we cannot call their psychology a truly empirical science, albeit only because of the fact that they still regarded their psychological work as properly philosophical.

Locke (1632–1704) agreed, on the whole, with the most important of Bacon's insights: true knowledge is acquired through perception and experience. He also agreed that knowledge becomes the purer the further away it stays from abstract and deductive thought; that true knowledge is never more than the complete reflection of reality and that this reflection can be

16. B. Kouwer en J. Linschoten, *Inleiding tot de psychologie*, Assen-Amsterdam, 1958, pp. 20–23.

acquired through immediate experience or by means of an appropriately applied induction.[17]

In his *An Essay Concerning Human Understanding,* Locke explained his view more fully. In this work he makes an explicit distinction between two forms of knowledge: particular knowledge which is acquired on the basis of sensation and reflection, and universal knowledge which issues from our ideas and their relationships. The particular knowledge provides us with a restricted amount of factual knowledge; general knowledge forms a basis for the sciences. However, *all* true knowledge of reality arises out of, and remains restricted to, experience.

The very essence and substance of things is not, by any means, directly accessible to our experience; that is why we are in principle unable to know them. The interrelationships between the different real aspects and real properties of things also escape us. They remain, too, in principle, inaccessible to us. True metaphysics, genuine philosophy of nature, and real anthropology, thus, remain impossible. Yet, the reality of things which are revealed to us through the senses, cannot be denied. The elementary representations or simple ideas are not simply products of the mind, nor are they innate. That is why they necessarily give us a genuine knowledge of things which in a natural way have a certain influence on our mind by means of the senses.

A closer look at simple ideas reveals the necessity of distinguishing the subjective secondary qualities which exist along with the objective primary qualities. The primary qualities are the real properties of real things; the secondary qualities, on the other hand, depend on our sensory organization.

Following Aristotelian tradition, Locke accepted as true the thought that the soul does not possess innate ideas. All representations and concepts arise necessarily out of our experience alone. At birth the human soul is like a blank tablet on which not yet anything is written. The soul is born, however, with the innate capacity to think. All that which accumulates in concepts and ideas over the span of a man's life arises out of experience.

17. Ueberweg-Moog, *op. cit.,* pp. 531–569; J. Maréchal, *op. cit.,* Cahier II, pp. 183–199; E. Boring, *op. cit.,* pp. 168–176.

As we said before, this esperience consists of the *sensations* or the impressions which reach us from the outside through the senses, and the *reflections* or impressions which the soul receives concerning its own state of being by means of inner experience. Experience, both of the external and the internal variety, gives man his simple ideas which then, in turn, become part of his higher mental constructs. A special operation of the mind which is thought to be partly passive and partly active, has to accomplish the transformation of the simple ideas into the complex ideas. In the construction of complex ideas out of simple ideas different functions cooperate with one another. It is especially association which plays an important part in this transformation.

Psychology must take its startingpoint in *reflection;* it is its task to investigate how the simple reflections give rise to the higher mental constructs. Its aim is to formulate the laws which govern these transformations. Locke strives, here, for an empirical associationistic psychology which as far as its methods are concerned must orient itself toward physics and chemistry. Yet this psychology still remains essentially a philosophical psychology since its main function is to delineate and establish the validity of man's knowledge. *An Essay Concerning Human Understanding* can, therefore, be considered the first well-rounded, systematic epistemology. The problems to which Locke directs himself were not originally conceived by him; for they had engaged the attention of Descartes and others. The novel aspect introduced by Locke is his insistence on solving the problem of knowledge without the aid of a metaphysical *a priori*. That is why the psychology we find in Locke from the very start is standing in an epistemological perspective. It will be evident that here the epistemological problems can be formulated and solved only in an empiricist sense.

HUME

Husserl most always mentions Berkeley and Hume in one breath.[18] He considered both of these thinkers of prime importance in the early development of psychology. In actuality he

18. See for instance: Edmund Husserl, *Phän. Psychol.,* pp. 287, 328; Edmund Husserl, *Krisis,* pp. 194, 198, 202, 212, 272, 447.

dealt only at length with Hume, and he restricted his considerations of Berkeley almost only to mentioning his name now and then. Without a doubt it is Hume who must be considered of the greater importance for psychology, although we do not deny that Berkeley's epistemology, his approach to perception in general, and to the perception of space in particular, are undeniably substantial contributions to the new psychology. Yet, we will restrict ourselves here to Hume's philosophy.

The phenomenalism of Hume (1711–1776) is historically of great importance because it represents the logical conclusion to the English empiricism of Bacon, Hobbes, Locke, and Berkeley.[19] In *A Treatise on Human Nature* and especially in *An Enquiry Concerning Human Understanding* Hume defended an extreme empiricism that gradually ended in phenomenalism. Hume takes his startingpoint in certain basic conceptions of Locke's philosophy and in a certain sense his work is an attempt to realize Locke's view in a more consistent way. Hume was especially fascinated by the success of physics since Galileo and Newton. He felt that physics and chemistry had finally hit upon the right methodology and that their success was due to the use of experimentation, induction, and mathematics. He dreamt of himself as the founder of a completely new science which would make use of essentially the same methodology.[20] The complete title of his earliest work sheds some light on this ambition: *A Treatise on Human Nature, Being an Attempt to Introduce the Experimental Method of Reasoning into Moral Subjects*.

The first part of this work showed a close kinship to Locke's ideas. Hume begins with an exposition on the origin, the composition, and the associative connections of ideas. This point of departure was in agreement with Locke as we can see when he wrote: "All the *perceptions* of the human mind resolve themselves into two distinct kinds, which I shall call *impressions* and *ideas*. The difference betwixt these consists in the degree of force and liveliness with which they strike upon the mind and

19. Ueberweg-Moog, *op. cit.*, pp. 399–413; J. Maréchal, *op. cit.*, Cahier II, pp. 207–242; E. Boring, *op. cit.*, pp. 186–193.
20. J. Maréchal, *Ibid.*, p. 208.

make their way into our thought or consciousness." [21] Thus Hume distinguished two kinds of basic psychological elements: the first type encompasses all that which makes itself known to us via the external senses; the second type includes all that which somehow reaches our awareness by means of the internal senses. A closer inspection shows that one has to distinguish between two different kinds of impressions; Hume calls them *simple* and *complex* impressions. A painstaking analysis of the *complex impressions* reveals the underlying indivisible simple ones. The same can be said of the ideas. Complex ideas are built up out of simple unitary ones. It is further assumed that the simple ideas always correspond to simple impressions. "After the most accurate examination . . . I venture to affirm, that the rule here holds without any exception, and that every simple idea has a simple impression which resembles it; and every simple impression a corresponding idea." [22] We can now go one step further and assume that all our simple ideas find their origin in simple *impressions*. "All our simple ideas proceed, either mediately or immediately, from their correspondent impressions." [23] Complex ideas can develop out of complex impressions, although this is not always the case; they can also be formed out of simple ideas.

Sensory impressions are, thus, considered the most fundamental data of consciousness. According to Hume, the cause of the origin of our impressions is in principle outside the sphere of possible human knowledge. All search for their manner of origin is *senseless* in the dual meaning of the word. "As to those impressions, which arise from the senses, their ultimate cause is, in my opinion, perfectly inexplicable by human reason, and it will always be impossible to decide with certainty, whether they arise immediately from the objects, or are produced by the creative powers of the mind, or are derived from the Author of being." [24] Sensory impressions create two types of ideas in us: *the ideas of the memory,* and *the ideas of the imagination.* The ideas of memory are more clear and distinct and are closely

21. David Hume, *A Treatise on Human Nature* (Ed. Selby-Bigge), London, 1896, p. 1.
22. *Ibid.,* p. 3.
23. *Ibid.,* p. 7.
24. *Ibid.,* p. 84.

allied to the impressions. The ideas of imagination appear as less clear to us and are formed in a more or less arbitrary way. It is even possible that complex ideas are formed in a completely free and arbitrary way; the imagination there, however, still respects the law that there must exist a perfect harmony between the simple impressions and the simple ideas. That is why the imagination is of extraordinary usefulness to man in analyzing complex ideas [25] because in it we have an instrument that enables us to eliminate one by one the simple ideas from the complex ideas.

As we have seen, complex ideas can be built up out of simple ones. Can the mind fashion complex ideas in an entirely arbitrary way? Without a doubt, there is a certain regularity to be observed in the way ideas are formed. This regularity is thought to come about as the result of a 'gentle force.' This force usually accomplishes its purpose, but it, nevertheless, is not absolute in its effectiveness. The force should not be regarded as some sort of occult phenomenon; what is meant by this 'gentle force' becomes clear when one considers the laws of association. These laws of association rest on the assumptions that either a certain similarity exists between two or more simple ideas, or that there exist certain spatio-temporal relationships, or that they are connected by means of the relation of cause and effect. Between the simple ideas a mutual 'attraction' gradually is formed on the basis of this force and this attraction manifests itself in a great number of divergent forms and modalities.[26] It is not necessary at this point to pursue in greater detail the strongly nominalistic and empiricist thought of Hume.

From what we have said up to now it is abundantly clear that Hume, too, designed his associationism with the intention of solving epistemological problems which were clearly formulated for the first time by Descartes and which Hume wanted to attack without recourse to any *a priori* metaphysical assumptions. It might be of interest to note briefly the conclusions ultimately reached by Hume. After demonstrating how scientific

25. *Ibid.*, pp. 8–10.
26. *Ibid.*, pp. 11–13.

judgments concerning matters of fact always imply a causal principle, Hume subjected this causal principle to a rigorously critical appraisal. He ended by rejecting all transempirical reality. "The only existences of which we are certain, are perceptions, which being immediately present to us by consciousness, command our strongest assent, and are the first foundation of all our conclusions. The only conclusion we can draw from the existence of one thing to that of another, is by means of the relation of cause and effect . . . The idea of this relation is derived from past experience, by which we find, that two beings are constantly conjoined together, and are always present at once to the mind. But as no beings are ever present to the mind but perceptions, it follows that we may observe a conjunction or a relation of cause and effect between different perceptions, but can never observe it between perceptions and objects." [27] In this way Hume's empiricism ended in a purely phenomenalistic position, skeptical of all forms of metaphysics.

In the course of the nineteenth century the philosophical ideas of Locke and Hume bore fruit and formed the basis of a first form of an empirical psychology. However, even here the new science initially enjoyed little independence; its methods and terminology had been taken bodily from the physical sciences and caused psychology itself to become a natural science completely imprisoned in the problematic characteristic of physiology. The first form of associationism tried to imitate Newtonian physics and Daltonian chemistry in its application of the analytical-synthetical methods. Soon attempts were made to analyze all psychological phenomena and to reduce them to basic elements, which are called elementary sensations. All that which takes place in our consciousness can ultimately be reduced to these sensations; thinking, feeling, striving, all are constructed from these elemental sensations. Once the complex psychological units have been reduced to their elements, the next step is to restore these elements to their place in the complex structures of which they naturally formed a part. The laws of association

27. *Ibid.*, p. 212.

were to guide this process: when the conscious awareness of sensations occurred in close temporal succession to each other, associations would automatically become established between them, so it was assumed. The force of the association would be determined by the number of times the elements appeared together in consciousness. All conscious phenomena were, thus, explained on the basis of the temporal proximity of the sensations in question: each compound psychological event is no more than the sum total of the constitutive independent elements. Associationism became a truly naturalistic and atomistic psychology.

These and similar thoughts can be found in Thomas Brown (1778–1820), James Mill (1773–1836), and Friedrich Beneke (1798–1854). In contrast to the others, Beneke emphasized strongly the active part played by consciousness during the formation of the higher mental phenomena.[28]

John Stuart Mill and Henry Spencer brought more refinement to associationism. But both these thinkers felt again attracted to psychology because of its epistemological significance. They resembled in this respect Hume whose psychological work, as we have seen, was permeated by a deep philosophical intention. Münsterberg, Ebbinghaus, and Ziehen belong to this same category of thinkers. We shall return to them when we later discuss the psychology of the 19th century more specifically. Herbart and Wundt were probably the first thinkers who succeeded in cutting themselves loose from this 'psychologism.' Up to a point, we may consider them to be the founders of a completely independent empirical psychology. Yet, their psychology still remained a form of associationism whose task it is to clarify the phenomena of consciousness in a causal way by making use of the methodology of physics and chemistry.[29]

JOHN STUART MILL

In order to follow the further developments of psychology, we must turn here to examine a few of the ideas of John Stuart

28. E. Boring, *op. cit.,* pp. 205–209, 219–226; J. Flugel, *A Hundred Years of Psychology:* 1833–1933, Edinburgh, 1945, pp. 23–35.
29. J. Flugel, *op. cit.,* pp. 76–87.

Mill and Henry Spencer. The principal ideas of Mill (1806–1873) can be found in his *Logic* and especially in his *Examination of Sir William Hamilton's Philosophy*.[30] As his father had done before him, John Stuart Mill maintained impressions and ideas as the basic elements out of which all higher mental phenomena arise. His interpretation of these basic elements, however, goes back to Hume's original explanation from which Mill's father had deviated. Besides the law of contiguity, he accepted again resemblance as a principle of association; later he also added the principle of frequency to the principle of contiguity. In 1843 Mill formulated the principle of intensity that he replaced in 1865 with the principle of inseparability.

It is not only in the number of laws of association adhered to that John Staurt Mill differed from his father; his interpretation of their meaning differed markedly, too. James Mill was of the opinion that the elementary units of our psychical life dissolve and mix into the higher, more complex phenomena. John Stuart Mill became convinced that this could not be the case; taking his startingpoint in his father's view that ideas sometimes grow together so quickly by means of association that one is even unable to notice them separately, John Stuart Mill came to the conclusion that the elementary units do not mix but that they time and again form new combinations and compounds. Here thus we find a psychology genuinely worthy of the name 'mental chemistry.' Since an idea can disappear in a larger whole, then this larger whole must be more than the sum of its elements. When we combine sodium and chloride the resultant salt is more than the sum of these two elements; something new has appeared. It follows that the laws which hold true for the wholes cannot be derived from the laws which govern the particles. "When many impressions or ideas are operating in the mind together, there sometimes takes place a process of a similar kind to chemical combination . . . These are cases of mental chemistry, in which it is possible to say that the simple ideas generate, rather than that they compose, the complex ones." [31]

30. E. Boring, *op. cit.*, pp. 227–233; J. Flugel, *op. cit.*, pp. 76–79.
31. J. Stuart Mill, *Logic*, quoted by E. Boring, *op. cit.*, p. 230.

In his *Examination of Sir William Hamilton's Philosophy,*
Mill opened another important problem area. In this book he
was, among other things, concerned with the reality of the material objects which we perceive. His solution of the problem
started with the assumption that the human mind has the capacity to anticipate. It, thus, is possible that "after having had
actual sensations, we are capable of forming the conception of
possible sensations"; we do not experience these sensations actually, but we at least could experience them. One of the most
characteristic differences between a perception and that which
furnishes the material basis for it lies in the fact that perception
appears as ephemeral, passing, and changeable, while matter
manifests itself as stable and enduring. This opposition leads to
great difficulties for the thinkers in the Lockean tradition. Mill
tried to solve these difficulties, while still remaining within the
empiricist perspective, by noting that the perception itself, indeed, is of a passing, ephemeral nature, but that the possibilities
of sensation can be permanent. The conviction which we share
that there exists solid, unchangeable matter to which our sensation directs itself is based on our perception of the permanent
possibilities of sensation. Matter appears in this light as a
permanent possibility of sensation; sensation itself in turn is
nothing but the 'belief' in these possibilities. "The conception
I form of the world existing at any moment, comprises, along
with the sensations I am feeling, a countless variety of possibilities
of sensation: namely, the whole of those which past observation
tells me that I could, under any supposable circumstances, experience at this moment, together with an indefinite and
illimitable multitude of others which I do not know that I could,
yet it is possible that I might, experience in circumstances not
known to me. These various possibilities are the important thing
to me in the world. My present sensations are generally of little
importance, and moreover are fugitive: the possibilities, on the
contrary, are permanent, which is the character that mainly distinguishes our idea of substance or matter from our notion of
sensation." [32] We notice here how John Stuart Mill reached back

32. J. Stuart Mill, *Examination of Sir William Hamilton's Philosophy,*
quoted by Boring, *op. cit.,* p. 232.

to the thoughts of Berkeley and James Mill, although he gave it his own characteristic turn. The problem, as he formulated and tried to solve it, continued to arouse interest for a long time; we encounter it in almost the same form in Ach and Titchener. And without any doubt Husserl's treatment of perspectivity retained fragments of this view, also.

Henry Spencer (1820–1903) added a few very important elements to classical associationism. Since his valuable contribution to psychology remains irrelevant to a correct understanding of Husserl's thought, we will mention him here only in passing.[33]

Psychology Becomes an Independent Science. Herbart and Wundt

IN THE psychological work of John F. Herbart (1776–1841) we see recurring some of the basic ideas of Locke.[34] Like Locke, Herbart searches beneath the complexity of psychical phenomena for stable and simple elements. In his system these basic elements or elementary representations are to be conceived of as qualitatively different active forces which mutually facilitate or hinder each other. The ensuing, constantly changing co-operation or battle between the elementary representations make up the whole of psychic life. The elementary representations are discrete, sharply distinguished entities which differ from one another in quality. The quality of such a representation is in itself invariable, but it can change in intensity. A representation which cannot be further analyzed is called a simple and elementary representation; all other representations are compound. Representations which in the battle did not succeed in coming to the fore in consciousness disappear in the realm of the unconscious while they maintain themselves as tendencies which will embrace every opportunity in order to enter again into consciousness.

Herbart distinguished a conscious and an unconscious realm.

33. E. Boring, *op. cit.*, pp. 240–244.
34. E. Boring, *op. cit.*, pp. 250–261; J. Flugel, *op. cit.*, pp. 15–22; B. Kouwer and J. Linschoten, *op. cit.*, pp. 27–28.

The two realms are separated from each other by means of a consciousness-threshold. Consciousness can contain only a limited number of representations at any given time. While a few representations hold the stage, all the others must disappear into the unconscious realm. These repressed representations possess a certain 'lifting-power' which propels them toward consciousness and can be measured. Very frequently there occur battles between different representations over the right to appear in consciousness. Cooperation, however, is not excluded and so-called fusion between different elements can take place; the representations, red and blue, can fuse to become the representation purple. Sometimes complication takes place whereby representations of the different sense modalities come together to form a higher unity.

According to Herbart the higher psychological units such as thinking, feeling, and striving are built up out of these elementary representations which unite according to the fixed laws of association, fusion, and complication. The whole of life is envisioned as one large functioning mechanism, devoid of freedom and spontaneity. Ultimately, Herbart sacrificed the human in man in order via measuring, calculation, experiment, and mathematical considerations to construct a 'psychology' which under methodological respect could be the peer of physics and chemistry.

WILHELM WUNDT

The basic thought of Herbart can be found in the works of Wilhelm Wundt (1832–1920) [35] although it appears there in a modified, less extreme form. Wundt started as a physiologist; he had become convinced in the course of his work in physiology that psychological phenomena cannot be adequately explained on the basis of physiological processes. He was convinced that physiology can be no more than a supportive science to psychology, and that psychology and physiology differ completely as to the intention of their research. From this we should not

---

35. E. Boring, *op. cit.*, pp. 316–344; B. Kouwer and J. Linschoten, *op. cit.*, pp. 23–31; J. Flugel, *op. cit.*, pp. 176–191.

draw the conclusion that the methods used in the two sciences should be equally different: psychology, as well as physiology, should model itself after the physical sciences as far as their methods are concerned. As far as the content is concerned, however, psychology differs completely from the other sciences.

In physics and chemistry, we, indeed, are concerned with immediate experience; the concern is not for the immediate experience as such, however, but for that which manifests itself by means of it or eventually conceals itself in it. The realm of the immediate experience is for the physical sciences but an instrument by means of which the proper data of the physical sciences come to light. Psychology, on the other hand, investigates experience for its own sake; it tries to investigate experience by means of experience. That is why the suitable method for psychology is introspection, by which Wundt meant the attentive and immediate witnessing of one's own experience.

Although Wundt saw man's psychic life as a totality, he, nevertheless, thought that this totality cannot be understood unless it is seen as a composite of elementary, psychical units. Analysis of human consciousness reveals that there are two elements to be distinguished: the elementary sensations and the elementary feelings. All higher conscious phenomena can be built up out of these fundamental elements. Although such phenomena as sensations and feelings come to the fore only by means of a process of abstraction, Wundt, nevertheless, undertook to determine carefully all the characteristics of these elements. All elements have this in common that in them one can distinguish a quality and an intensity. The gradations in intensity continuously follow a straight line from low to high; there is, however, more than one quality dimension. There are also a number of characteristics that distinguish feelings from sensations. Feelings characteristically form contrasting pairs. Furthermore, there exists a greater variety among the elementary feelings than among the elementary sensations, and the former are also more numerous. Yet, the origin of the feelings is a simple one inasfar as they proceed from the subject taken as a whole whereas the sensations because of their relationships to completely different objects, are founded in numerous different conditions which, partly at least, can be isolated from one another. Finally, Wundt placed feelings in a three-dimensional continuum along the axis of pleasure-displeasure, stimulation-sedation, and tension-relaxation.[36]

It is one of the tasks of psychology to explain how a number of combining elements can give rise to the composite higher phenomena of consciousness. These composite phenomena are divided into two main groups, namely, the representations which are parallel to the sensations, and the emotions which correspond to the elementary feelings. Within the realm of the representations Wundt distinguishes furthermore, between intensive spatial and temporal representations whereas the principal forms of the emotions are constituted by feeling-combinations, affections, and the processes of the will. In all these cases Wundt understands by a compound, conscious phenomenon one or another composite component of our *immediate* experience which by means of certain characteristics isolates itself from the content of this experience in such a way that it can be conceived of as a relative unity and indicated by a special name. The division of the composite conscious phenomena follows the elements out of which they supposedly are built up; when the sensations dominate, they are called representations, whereas they are called emotions in case the elementary feelings are predominant. The composite phenomena of consciousness often maintain mutual connections; under the influence of certain synthetic processes, they can appear as simultaneous complexes or they can form progressive chains.[37]

The higher psychical complexes of Wundt possess characteristics as a whole which the underlying elements, as such, do not possess. The higher mental complexes are thus no longer regarded as mere aggregates of elements. And like these higher complexes the whole of our psychical life as well forms a unity of a higher order; a whole that is more than the sum of its parts. The synthesis which comes into being in this way is creative in regard to a determinate group of characteristics. Wundt, there-

36. R. Müller-Freienfels, *op. cit.*, pp. 46–47.
37. *Ibid.*, p. 47.

fore, speaks of *creative synthesis,* a concept that foreshadows the later Gestalt psychology. For the same reason Wundt's psychology has been called a 'mental chemistry' by some of his contemporaries, since in his view the constitution of higher unities is governed by causal laws. However, one has to realize here that in Wundt's conception psychical elements are not static things but psychical processes whereas the expression 'causal laws' in this context only refers to a connection which is characteristic of man's psychical development.

Be this as it may, psychology's next task was to study the fundamental principle according to which the psychological elements combine with each other. Following the English tradition in this respect, Wundt spoke of *association* in cases of the combination of elements in which consciousness itself remains passive. Association can appear in the form of *fusion* when, for example, two colors or two tones make up a new color or tone in which the identity of each is lost; in the form of *assimilation* when two representations change each other without their complete loss of identity; Wundt speaks of *complication* when elements which belong to the domains of different senses are joined. When consciousness plays an active role in the combining of elements Wundt speaks of *apperception.*

The higher phenomena of consciousness such as thinking and willing certainly do not depend exclusively on association; apperception always plays a role in their constitution. Apperception is a process of the will that governs the course of our psychical processes by consciously putting certain phenomena in the focal point of consciousness and referring others to the perceptive horizon. Apperception, thus, is the teleological orientation of our attention toward certain psychical contents. Wundt's psychology in this way by-passes certain of the serious objections that are leveled at the orthodox, mechanistic associationism. His psychology is no longer an interplay of blind mechanical laws; but the higher psychical phenomena are governed and guided by apperception in such a way that these psychical processes develop not in a blind and mechanical, but in a teleological way.

Wundt's concept of apperception was further especially characterized by the fact that it includes a feeling content. Apperception is on that basis placed among the volitional processes. Physiologically seen Wundt also assigned a localization center to the apperception which he placed somewhere in the cortex of the forebrain.

Volition forms the ground in which all those psychical processes are rooted, the psychical elements of which are constituted by the elementary feelings. It is in the process of apperception that volition comes in immediate contact with the representational contents of consciousness. However, since the processes of the will manifest themselves as events which despite all their diversity nevertheless appear as mutually coherent and also as homogeneous, an immediate feeling of activity originates which accompanies each volition. This feeling of cohesiveness then spreads over the whole of our psychic life. It is this feeling of cohesiveness which Wundt calls the ego. This self, thus, is not a representation; it is a feeling which is essentially connected with the universally present experience and representation of the body.

Wundt's psychological work is not limited to considering how the phenomena of consciousness are put together nor how they develop and relate to each other. Psychology, according to him, must try to find the principles and laws underlying all psychical phenomena, to investigate the 'causality' operative in all psychical processes. Central in this investigation is the position occupied by the concept 'soul'. Wundt referred here to an explanatory concept which enables investigators to make causal interpretations. However, the conception that the soul is a substance was rejected by Wundt; on the contrary, it is Wundt's view that the soul is to be understood as a principle of activity, that is to say that the very essence of the soul consists in the immediate reality of the processes themselves.

This point of view opens a new perspective to the traditional body-soul problem. Instead of two irreconcilable substances, body and mind, we now have two different perspectives of one and the same experience. Psycho-physical parallelism is thus rejected, at least up to a point; this became especially evident in Wundt's treatment of the psychical elements and the higher phenomena of consciousness. As we saw, the processes by which the higher phenomena of consciousness are formed, is guided by values and teleological principles. Precisely such principles and values cannot be accounted for within a framework of strict psychophysical parallelism. It becomes necessary to accept a separate and independent psychical causality which, in turn, requires new and special principles.[38]

Still, Wundt remained a prisoner of Descartes' dualism. For he held still to the separation of body and consciousness. And although he buries consciousness itself in the sum, or better in the structure, of fundamental elements and contents of consciousness, yet his contributions to psychology have been many and varied. He established empirical psychology as an independent science and succeeded, to a large extent, in substituting teleologically oriented interpretations of psychical life for the mechanistic interpretations of his predecessors. In doing this he broke ground for the later holistic psychologies. It is regrettable that Wundt could not pursue his ideas to where they almost inexorably lead.[39]

Physiological Psychology.

EARLIER WE pointed out how a physiological psychology gradually came to take its place beside the psychology of consciousness. The interest of several of the great physiologists of the 19th century had been focused on the structure and function of the senses. Their studies had made it clear that the senses could not be studied adequately without psychological considerations because the functioning of the senses cannot be understood completely without taking into consideration the conscious contents which in this way come into being. The physiologist, thus, came into contact with psychology. The psychologist, from his side, felt equally a need to incorporate the physiological aspects of the

38. *Ibid.,* pp. 48–50.
39. *Ibid.,* pp. 50–51.

senses. The contact between the two disciplines resulted in a physiological psychology in which the psychological aspects came to be almost completely dominated by physiological considerations; psychology surrendered almost completely to physiology.

Phrenology contributed to this process when Gall (1758–1828) and Spurzheim (1776–1832) formulated a theory which assigned a determinate location center to each cognitive and drive function. This view led to the problem of what consciousness precisely is and in what way it might be tied to the functioning of certain organic factors. Furthermore, the research of Bell (1774–1842), Magendie (1783–1855), J. Müller (1801–1855), and Fechner (1801–1887) led to a completely new experimental science on the border between physiology and psychology. Fechner must be considered the real founder of this new science called psychophysics or psychophysiology. The results of the investigations of Fechner and Weber (1795–1878), much of which remain relevant today, reinforced the view that psychology is to be conceived of in function of physiology. Outstanding proponents of the new physiological psychology, besides Fechner and Weber, were H. Helmholz (1821–1894), the young Wundt, H. Ebbinghaus, G. Müller, and T. Ziehen. G. Müller is, without doubt, the most important representative of this movement. Yet we will restrict our consideration here to a short discussion of Ziehen and Ebbinghaus because Husserl seems to have been more closely acquainted with their work than with any other representative of this group.[40]

ZIEHEN AND EBBINGHAUS

Like Ziehen, Ebbinghaus (1850–1909) remained for the most part within the framework of associationism. He, too, saw elementary sense experiences as the fundamental elements of psychical life. These sense experiences are either caused by

40. E. Boring, *op. cit.*, pp. 27–45, 51–58, 61–77. 80–94, 96–114, 275–295; B. Kouwer and J. Linschoten, *op. cit.*, pp. 31–37.

external stimuli or they appear in consciousness as reproductions, in which case he spoke of representations.[41] These representations associate with each other, following simple associative laws. These associations ultimately give rise to all higher phenomena of consciousness. This scheme has difficulties in accounting for feelings. As we have seen before, the process of reducing feelings to elementary sensations is at least a very awkward feat. Such thinkers as Stumpf and others tried to escape the difficulties by considering feelings as a special group of experiences, which they called elementary feeling experiences. Ziehen preferred to see feelings as characteristic properties of the sensations, thereby denying their place as independent elements of consciousness. Ebbinghaus considered feelings as accompanying phenomena to certain sensations and representations. The bond, however, between the feelings and the sensations is relatively free, since the comings and goings of the organism exerts a great deal of influence upon the feelings which will accompany the sensations or representations. It looks as if, at this point, Ebbinghaus was breaking through the traditional associationistic schema since he conferred upon the body the task of co-influencing the process by which different elements come to be associated with each other.

Yet, the experiences of drive and volition are explained by both Ebbinghaus and Ziehen in a way that again remains true to the principles of associationism. Drive and volition are regarded as mere accompaniments to sensations and representations. The bodily movements which spring from these drives and volitions are consequently declared unsuitable for further psychological considerations. Ebbinghaus says, in so many words, that movements cannot be considered to be psychical phenomena. Only while they appear do they become conscious; and this consciousness comes about through sensations, namely through experiences of muscular tension and movement of limbs or certain other parts of the body, that is to say by kinesthetic experiences.

41. See for what follows: R. Müller-Freienfels, *op. cit.*, pp. 37–44; E. Boring, *op. cit.*, pp. 386–392, 371–379, 427; J. Flugel, *op. cit.*, pp. 198–205.

Ziehen is in agreement here. For him movements simply are not true psychical phenomena in the sense that sensations and representations are; they are merely the effects of psychical processes.

All higher psychical processes thus are thought to come about when the sensory elements of consciousness and their representations combine with each other according to the laws of association. Ebbinghaus, Müller (1850–1934), and Ziehen all follow this pattern in its large outlines, although their observations on certain psychological phenomena force them to introduce modifications from time to time. A few examples will make this clear. Attentiveness, for example, is not considered to be a special process of apperception as we saw in Wundt; it is explained, instead, as a by-product of the laws which govern our representations. Ziehen makes use here of his concept of "constellation." According to him there are four factors which will determine whether a particular stimulus will be "chosen" as the object of attention. He mentions, in this connection, the intensity of the stimulus, its degree of resemblance to a certain corresponding memory image, the strength of the accompanying feeling, and the constellation of the representations. Added to this are the muscular experiences which account for the consciousness of activity accompanying the state of attentiveness.

Perception itself is explained in much the same way as was attentiveness; it comes about as a result of the associative co-operation of the representations. But we see here another instance where the classical view on the laws of association is transcended. It is admitted that a perception is something more than the sum of a number of concurrent or subsequent sensations brought about by the perceived object. It is further conceded that a perception is on the one hand more and on the other hand less than the consciousness of the received stimuli which is supposed to be in perfect harmony with the object. But the enrichment as well as the impoverishment are explained in terms of our past experiences, that is to say in terms of accidental representations being called forth by means of association. It is, thus, not an inherent characteristic of our soul that makes certain objects or events appear to us as they do. The mere fact that there are certain groups of stimuli which have regularly become associated with each other time and again, accounts for the richness or poverty of the content of our perceptions.

Conceptual thinking is also explained on the basis of representations. The extremely vague concept of 'general representations' is used, in this connection, together with the questionable notion of 'word representation.' During the formation of the general representation, the mind forms a great number and variety of representations. These representations have not been chosen in an unpatterned, random fashion, nor do they entirely fit into a preconceived scheme; they occur in response to the soul's own intrinsic nature. While these representations do not answer any objective outside reality we, nevertheless, remain convinced of the existence of those things. Ziehen gives a very complicated explanation of how a concept could be constructed out of an innumerable amount of composite representations, even though these representations cannot be called forth in our experience. There is also an attempt to explain abstraction and the formation of concepts themselves through association. Even the self is but a representation, although the most important one. If in consciousness this representation comes to the fore in a very strong way it is called self-consciousness.

Finally, emotions and affections, too, must be explained with the help of representations. In Ebbinghaus' view affections are feelings, that is to say, accompanying phenomena of experiences and representations which are founded in the operation of representations which come to the fore by means of association; these feelings manifest themselves immediately with great force. Also such complex phenomena as man's concrete behavior, and especially his free activities must, likewise, be made the subject of an analogous explanation. Depending on the mutual relationships between the different representations, the different phases of deliberation, choice, being inclined, planning and decision making come into being. Outside stimuli set off this complicated chain of events and the play between the relevant representa-

tions which themselves had their origin in earlier impressions
but now belong to the permanent store of representations in the
soul.

Müller, especially, has tried to think this point of view
through in a more consistent way than this was done by his
eclectic contemporaries Ebbinghaus and Ziehen. Many of his
findings are of lasting value and especially is the clear, analytical
method of this group of physiological psychologists certainly of
lasting value.

Whatever else this movement may have produced in lasting
contributions, it is not surprising that a counter-movement was
formed which protested the one-sided over-simplified view of
man's psychical life. This protest has been partly met by the
assertion that psychology employs atomism only as a methodological means in order to establish some order in the complex
web of psychical data. One also has attempted to make the
atomistic themes themselves more acceptable by means of additional categories and theories and by granting that a one-sided
quantification in psychology is unacceptable. All this remained
patchwork, however, and the time became ripe for psychologists
to look for an entirely new foundation for their science.

Husserl's Teachers

WE HAVE thus far outlined our history up to the point where
Wundt, Brentano, and Stumpf introduced the young Husserl
to psychology. It is rather remarkable that Husserl mentions
Wundt and Stumpf very seldom whereas he seems to remember
Brentano's viewpoint on literally innumerable occasions. Probably we could find the reason for this in the fact that Husserl
was a philosopher and that he judged his professors on the basis
of their strength as philosophers. As we have spoken about
Wundt already, we shall restrict ourselves in this section to a
discussion of the psychological thought of Brentano and Stumpf.
We shall further limit ourselves to those aspects of their psy-

chological theories which have a direct bearing on Husserl's point of view.

Franz Brentano

Franz Brentano (1838–1917) was without doubt a professional philosopher, not a psychologist.[42] As a philosopher he undertook the immense task of liberating philosophy from all merely traditional convictions; of scraping from philosophy all the corrosive dead weight it had accumulated through the centuries. His aim was nothing short of restoring philosophy to its original splendor. Brentano was educated in the neo-scholastic philosophical tradition. After being ordained a priest in 1862, he initially concentrated on Aristotle and the great medieval thinkers. Later, he became convinced that Bacon, Descartes, Leibnitz, and Locke were philosophers of the greatest magnitude. He was fundamentally opposed to Kant, Fichte, and Hegel. Later it was especially in the thought of Lotze and John Stuart Mill that he found ideas which were compatible with the insights he had gained in his historical and critical investigations. Originally, Brentano was convinced that the only possible method for philosophy would be the one used by the sciences.

From 1886 until his death he spoke appreciatively of positivism. Already in 1869 he recognized in August Comte one of the important philosophers of his time. Brentano, however, was equally convinced of the possibilities inherent in metaphysics if only it could be developed and explored with the aid of the methods used in the empirical sciences. Brentano never developed a complete philosophical system; he limited himself to a few important, clearly defined issues, in whose treatment he remained within the large framework of positivism.

One of the first and most important problems to Brentano was providing a solid foundation for a truly scientific philosophy. This foundation could certainly not be found by merely re-

42. H. Spiegelberg, *The Phenomenological Movement. A Historical Introduction*, 2 vol., Den Haag, 1960, vol. I, pp. 28–50; E. Boring, *op. cit.*, pp. 356–361; J. Flugel, *op. cit.*, pp. 144–148.

turning to Aristotle. In connection with his studies on the immortality of the soul, a topic to which he devoted a great deal
of his teaching, Brentano came into profound contact with
psychology. Probably under the influence of John Stuart Mill,
he reached the conclusion that psychology ultimately could
provide the solid basis for philosophy. After this insight had occurred to him, Brentano still considered Comte a great philosopher, but rejected his views on the impossibility of metaphysics
and psychology.

Brentano saw clearly that the psychology of this day would
not be able to form the needed starting-point for a new philosophy. Neither the psychology of James, nor that of Mill, Fechner,
Wundt, or Lotze was capable of assuming such an important
task. Part of the difficulty was that these psychologists had not
been able to circumscribe the subject matter of their discipline
adequately, nor was there sufficient justification for the use of
its basic concepts. Brentano hoped to be able to fill the lacunae
in the existing psychology. He wanted to replace the existing,
mutually antagonistic psychologies and lay the foundation for a
truly scientific, genuine psychology that could eventually form
the basis for philosophy.

Brentano's work itself, however, was not of a psychological
nature. He was interested in psychology only to the extent that it
could further his philosophical quest. In his *Psychology From
the Empirical Point of View* Brentano emphatically supports
empiricism, although he makes it known form the start that a
certain 'ideal intuition' would not be incompatible with empiricism. He does not state precisely what he means by 'ideal intuition' but we can gather from the general context that he
referred to an immediate intuition of ideal entities; he most
certainly did not refer to an *a priori* knowledge in the sense of
Kant.

According to Brentano, empirical psychology should be
divided into a descriptive and a genetic psychology. The descriptive psychology is the more fundamental one of the two
since it makes no sense to investigate the causal connection
between psychical phenomena if we do not first know what

these psychical phenomena are. This division into descriptive and genetic parts was completely new to psychology although similar divisions had been established in such sciences as anatomy, physiology, and geology. There is, however, a great difference between the descriptive character of psychology as Brentano saw it and the descriptive character of a science such as anatomy. In descriptive anatomy one can take one's starting point in a rather accurate circumscription of the subject matter of this science and of the essential distinctions, divisions, and categories to be used in the further development of the science. Psychology, on the contrary, does not yet possess those circumscriptions. In Brentano's view it is precisely the first task of *descriptive* psychology to explain how one can accurately delineate the subject matter of psychology and, furthermore, to bring to light the fundamental distinctions and categories which are vital and absolutely indispensable for an accurate description of psychical phenomena. Brentano claimed that this task can be accomplished only through a careful, intuitive investigation into the immediately given psychic phenomena, their properties, and affinities.

Furthermore, Brentano considered descriptive psychology as having a logical priority over genetic psychology. Descriptive psychology is not only relatively independent from genetic psychology, but even forms the foundational science in its regard. In an analogous way descriptive psychology even possesses the same function in regard to all other sciences. It is in this way that Brentano intended to constitute a completely independent psychology which first founds itself and, then, is able to clarify the foundations of all other sciences. The important point here is that psychology can no longer orient itself towards physics, since physics must precisely be radically founded by psychology.

But how can such an autonomous psychology be made a reality? Did not Comte give conclusive proof that introspection lacks all scientific value? Brentano admits that in introspection the intentional and deliberate self-observation does not have any scientific value. Yet, every perception of objects in the world is always accompanied by a reflection and, thus, by immediate awareness of our own psychical phenomena which as immediately present possesses an apodictic evidence. Such an inner awareness, however, is only an accompanying phenomenon that is presented to us together with the external perception. Since our attention is focused on the external phenomena we easily fail to be completely aware of the internal phenomena and, thus, it is very difficult to describe the internal perception adequately. Brentano maintains that it is possible to focus our attention on this internal phenomenon at the moment when it is already passed in actuality and briefly lingers on as a memory. Brentano was not entirely happy with this view since it made this all-important evidence of the internal phenomena dependent upon memory. But as he saw no other way to get at these internal phenomena, except by means of the immediate memory, he felt that we should make peace with that fact.

The next task which Brentano posed for himself was to distinguish the realm of the psychical from the non-psychical. After making a careful comparison between psychical and physical phenomena he came to the conclusion that their essential difference could be described in terms of intentionality. All psychical phenomena are intentional; they are necessarily directed to an object which is separate and distinct from the psychical experience itself.

Brentano explicitly states that he came to his discovery after a study of intentionality as found in scholasticism; in his view this conception, however, was to be changed in many aspects. The principle behind Brentano's intentionality is that psychical phenomena imply a necessary reference to objects which are distinct from those phenomena as such. Later on he corrected this view somewhat to account for the fact that mood as well as feelings do not seem to point beyond themselves. That is why he later makes an explicit distinction between primary and secondary objects of reference. The primary object of reference is the object to which a psychical phenomenon directs itself. The secondary object of reference is the psychical phenomenon itself. Psychical phenomena, therefore, can direct themselves to something outside themselves, but they also can turn upon themselves. It is evident that psychical phenomena would fail to become conscious if they could direct themselves only to outside objects. Note here how the whole realm of unconscious phenomena is excluded from the realm of psychology. Brentano could not find satisfactory answers to the problems to which this omission gave rise. In addition, he made the mistake of excluding from the psychological realm the study of the objects to which the psychical phenomena must direct themselves.

The intentional relationship that a psychical phenomenon maintains with its object becomes of further importance when Brentano tries to classify the psychical phenomena. The quality of this intentional relationship changes from one group of psychical phenomena to the next. On the basis of the different qualities of their intentional relationships with objects, Brentano makes a distinction between acts of representation, of judgment, and acts of love and hatred. It seems strange to observe how he makes such a sharp distinction between representation and judgment and then see him lump all moods, affections, feelings, and strivings into one big category. This procedure is justified on the ground that in the phenomena discrete differences become noticeable when we move from the representations to judgment. Moving from love to hate, however, we never become aware of a definite point where one phenomenon stops and another begins. In this category the phenomena gradually flow into each other, making it unnecessary to establish fundamental differentiation within this area.

Brentano further saw the representations as the primary and most fundamental class of psychological phenomena; judgments, as well as the acts within the group of love, and hatred, all presuppose representations. The fact that all psychological phenomena either are themselves representations or depend upon one or more representations can be seen as the fundamental law of psychology. This law is not arrived at through induction but is immediately given in our first analysis of phenomena.

The problem of time occupies a central position in Brentano's philosophical and psychological considerations. He posed

the question of how time is experienced, and how the experience of the present differs from that of the past and the future.
The difference in temporal experience occurs when we approach
a phenomenon as a representation and not when we judge the
phenomenon. Representations are, therefore, especially marked
by the temporal modes. It is of further importance to notice that
the present time is the immediately given time, while the other
temporal modes present themselves only indirectly by means of
actual representations. Brentano concludes ultimately that the
non-present events which do not occur in the present time, are
devoid of reality unless they be given in some way or another in
the present. Because of his contribution to the problem of time,
and more especially in his manner of approach to temporal
problems, Brentano exercised a lasting influence directly on
Husserl and indirectly on Heidegger, Sartre, and Merleau-Ponty.

For a correct understanding of Husserl's phenomenology, it
is important to consider Brentano's emphasis on immediacy.
Brentano was so fearful of creating meaningless entities that he
declared everything fictitious when it does not refer directly to
the immediately given psychical and physical phenomena. Yet,
to escape the English nominalism of Ockham, Locke, and Hume,
he accepted the idea that every concept about reality must be
considered universal since experience teaches us only that which
is universal. This Aristotelian idea was not very compelling to
many of his pupils and it became a major impetus among his
followers to seek different philosophical paths.

In the first part of the *Logische Untersuchungen* in which
Husserl gives his critique on psychologism in logic, we do not
find Brentano's name mentioned. Many philosophers, including
Brentano himself, concluded that this omission implied that
Husserl must have felt that Brentano, too, was guilty of psychologism but that Husserl had not wanted to say this openly
out of respect for his former professor. Husserl took great pains
to convince Brentano, to the contrary. According to Spiegelberg
it would be indeed incorrect to consider Brentano guilty of
psychologism as it is defined by Husserl, since it was never his
intention to base logic in psychology. However, Brentano can be

considered guilty of psychologism in so far as he viewed all that which is not psychical as physical and that ultimately all the sciences, except the physical sciences, must be founded in psychology. Much as the physical sciences are rooted in mathematics, so are all the other sciences to be grounded in psychology. The psychology to which Brentano referred was, however, not the naturalistic psychology of his day, but rather a 'pure' psychology resting on entirely new foundations. These foundations can come to light only on the basis of a totally new experience.

CARL STUMPF

Carl Stumpf [43] (1848–1936) benefitted from an excellent and very extensive training. His initial plan was to become a philosopher, but his studies also included theology, mathematics, physics, physiology, and psychology. He was among others a pupil of Brentano and Lotze. His first works *Über den psychologischen Ursprung der Raumvorstellung* (1873) and *Tonpsychologie* (1883) betray profound psychological interest although they are written from a philosophical point of view.

Stumpf considered himself an empiricist. He esteemed both Locke and Leibnitz highly, but he was critical of Hume whose phenomenalism he considered unacceptable. Stumpf felt that a theory of knowledge should stress *a priori* insights, but these insights should be based on actual experience and arise out of an analysis of empirical data. In his analysis of empirical data, Stumpf tries to highlight the structural ties that exist between empirically elementary data. He thought that strict experimental procedures could be valuable, although he considered thought-experiments performed in 'free fancy' to be of greater importance. Stumpf maintained that such a procedure had nothing in common with John Stuart Mill's induction. On the contrary, it was his view that man has a capacity to grasp intuitively the universal in the particular and the necessary in the contingent. The ability to intuit does not function spontaneously

43. H. Spiegelberg, *Ibid.*, pp. 53–69; R. Müller-Freienfels, *op. cit.*, pp. 110–111; E. Boring, *op. cit.*, pp. 362–371.

and intuition has nothing in common with passive contemplation; the intuitive grasp is readied for functioning with a series of preparatory activities.

As we indicated above, it is difficult to consider Stumpf's work purely psychological, especially since he himself considered the distinction between philosophy and psychology of little importance. Yet, he was strongly opposed to psychologism. He found it impossible to reduce all philosophical problems to psychology, especially when he considered the area of epistemology. On the other hand, he also militated against the neo-Kantian school which rejected psychologism and wanted to clear philosophy of all possible psychological foundations. Stumpf felt that it was impossible to make a clear distinction between psychology and philosophy.

Probably under the influence of Mach, Hering, and Husserl, Stumpf introduced the term phenomenology in his *Erscheinungen und psychische Funktionen* (1906). In this book he interpreted his earlier psychological work as a phenomenological preparation for psychology. Stumpf here makes a sharp distinction between phenomena which are understood as the contents of the various functions and the 'psychical functions' themselves. These psychic functions include the perception of phenomena and their mutual relationships, the grouping of phenomena into complexes, the formation of concepts, judgments and the acts of understanding, feelings, moods and the acts of desiring and willing.

Stumpf's investigations clearly show that these two major groups of phenomena and functions can be *logically* separated. This follows from the fact that on the one hand psychical functions can be modified with the phenomenon remaining itself unchanged, while on the other hand the phenomenon may change without a subsequent modification in the psychical functions. Psychology is to study the psychological functions while the study of the phenomena should be taken up by certain preparatory sciences and the positive sciences. Stumpf divides the domain of the phenomena into those of the primary and those of the secondary phenomena. The primary phenomena are the contents of our immediate experience, which as *Sin-*

neserscheinungen or sensory appearances present themselves directly through the senses; the secondary phenomena consist in the contents of the derived functions. Out of these phenomena the mind forms the higher contents of consciousness such as concepts and values which Stumpf calls *Gebilde* or constructs. Among the phenomena themselves and among the phenomena and the constructs certain *relations* are entertained. *Phenomenology* is the preparatory science of the phenomena; *eidology* is the preparatory science of the constructs, while the *science of relationships* is concerned with the study of the relations between phenomena and between the phenomena and the constructs. Stumpf speaks of preparatory sciences since these disciplines have as their task the elucidation of the foundations of all other sciences, the natural and human sciences in the usual sense of these terms. Although these preparatory sciences are descriptive sciences, it is nevertheless not necessary for them to limit themselves to description; other methods can be used if they help advance the envisioned goal of that science.

It would be useless to introduce greater detail here concerning Stumpf's philosophy in that a deeper penetration would not advance substantially our insight into Husserl.

The Psychology of William James

ACCORDING TO Linschoten there exists an unmistakable relationship between the psychology of James and the phenomenological psychology of Husserl. It is quite certain that Husserl was acquainted with James' work and that he was influenced by him. It is equally certain that Husserl admired James and always spoke appreciatively concerning James' psychology. There is enough similarity between the two thinkers on a number of smaller issues that we might gain a deeper understanding of Husserl by means of an examination of James' thought.[44]

The sensory-motor actionism of William James (1842–1910)

44. J. Linschoten, *Op weg naar een fenomenologische psychologie. De psychologie van William James,* Utrecht, 1959, pp. 12–13, 27–44; E. Boring, *op. cit.,* pp. 508–517; J. Flugel, *op. cit.,* pp. 154–159.

is characterized by its rejection of the position that sensations, or sensations together with feelings and judgments constitute the fundamental elements of psychical life. Instead, James speaks of the sensory-motor reflex as the fundamental element; by this he understands the unity of sensation and motor reaction. However, the relationship with the older sensualism is still seen in the role ascribed to the kinesthetic muscular sensations.

Analogous ideas were proposed earlier by Alexander Bain (1818–1903) who had energetically pointed to the role of muscular sensations in all aspects of man's life.[45] Bain considered movement the most elementary factor in psychic life; it at once preceded and formed an essential part of the sensations. These movements are originally without direct purpose; only gradually do they become purposive under the influence of experience. These movements play a decisive role in the establishment of our consciousness of the reality outside ourselves. It is through these movements that an initially subjective consciousness can come into contact with its surrounding reality. This world outside consciousness even carries the meaning of exclusively being the sum total of all possibilities for activity. Our belief in the reality of the world outside ourselves rests on the connections that the sensory impressions maintain with certain movements. Striving and willing find their origin in pleasurable feeling that is associated with certain muscular contractions.

Besides the influence of Bain, we find in the psychology of James, traces of the thoughts of Lotze, Brentano, and Wundt. The work of Renouvier and Bergson exercized some influence on the later writing of James. Still, his psychology remains an original and very personal piece of work. A most adequate account of his psychological work can be found in *Principles of Psychology* (1890). In this work he protests the mind-stuff theory as it had been proclaimed by Spencer and Clifford. This thought required a psychological atomism in which feelings could exist independently without forming part of consciousness as such.

James reveals himself also as an opponent of the older

45. E. Boring, *op. cit.*, pp. 233–240; R. Müller-Freienfels, *op. cit.*, pp. 58–59.

associationism which had attempted to construct consciousness out of distinct and separable elements. He opposed these theories with his well-known concept of the stream of consciousness in which he tries to get hold of the gliding, flowing character of consciousness and by means of which he hoped to illuminate the fact that all the contents of consciousness point to the subject who experiences.

Despite continually changing circumstances which prevent a single state of consciousness from ever repeating itself, we, nevertheless, are impressed with a feeling of continuity underlying our consciousness. Whenever we try to isolate a particular state of consciousness we find it surrounded by fringes which assure this particular state a place in the larger integrated whole of consciousness. Important, also, is the distinction between substantial and transitory states in our psychical life. James' position is here again against the older associationism and he calls our attention to the transitional states which are maintained in between the substantial representations.

James does not start his main work with a description of the sensations. Instead, he focused his attention on the reflexes, the half-reflexes, habits, etc. This order is characteristic of his work as a whole. As criteria for the essential aspects of psychical factors, he uses purposiveness and choice of means. All external stimuli are translated into reactions. Man is an organism which reacts to impressions; his psychical faculties enable him to modify his reactions. Not a single impression remains ultimately without expression.

From the biological point of view adopted by James, all sensations serve the function of attracting or repelling us. All memories serve to either warn or encourage us, our feelings to spur us into action, our thoughts to give direction to our actions. Our reactions are partly innate, partly acquired. To the group of innate reactions belong those of fear, curiosity, etc.; the acquired reactions usually are modifications of innate reactions which manifest themselves, for example, in habits or in acts of will. It is strange that James gave little or no attention to the feelings of pleasure and displeasure.

This reaction-psychology sheds a completely new light on the

affections. We react to certain impressions with movements on
the basis of our innate mechanisms. These expressive movements
were considered the results of certain moods. James points out
that these movements are not the consequence but rather the
cause of the moods in question. James does not consider this a
materialistic view since the original depth and meaning of the
affects is not denied nor diminished by his theory. The same
basic thought that underlies James' treatment of the affects can
be found in his discussions on the will. James saw every representation as possessing a hidden force indirectly accounting for
the body's movements. Conscious willing is preceded by movements, and the will can function only with the help of the
memories of these movements. A very complicated play of internal forces and restraints decides ultimately which movement
will be executed. Freely realized acts are, thus, seen as the out-
come of interactions between certain opposing forces. When
we speak of the will we are referring to the complex whole of
these restraining and facilitating forces which determines our
actions. James tried to combine this mechanistic view with the
idea of freedom by stressing the attentiveness which as far as
duration and intensity are concerned, is not determined.

Of great importance, also, is James' analysis of man's self-
consciousness. He makes a clear distinction here between the
'self' as object of consciousness, the 'Me,' and the 'self' as subject
of consciousness, the 'I.' Within the realm of the 'Me' James
further distinguishes the bodily, social, and spiritual 'Me.' In
all these cases the 'self' is that which is being thought, not that
which does the thinking. It is very difficult for the psychologist
to grasp the pure 'I,' the thinking and conscious 'I.'

This thinking 'I' which is able to think the different modalities of the 'Me' as objects, cannot be a time-less unity; it is
equally impossible that it is a mere aggregate. In James' view
the fleeting stream of consciousness even lacks every substantial
identity; there is only a functional unity. This functional unity
between the different states of consciousness of past and present
consists in this that they all contain the same things and that
they in regard to the 'Me' all react in the same way. All of them

acknowledge it as such and encounter it as 'mine' and posit it opposite to all other things. This functional identity is the only kind of identity in James' view to which the psychical facts force the psychologist.

In this context we need not deal with James' philosophical theories, which, on the other hand, give to his psychological investigations their ultimate foundations, as they do not seem to be important for a correct understanding of Husserl's point of view.

Dilthey and the 'Naturalistic Psychology'

BEFORE TURNING to a short survey of Dilthey's thought on empirical psychology we will focus once more on naturalistic psychology and try to summarize the essential aspects of this trend. It is important for us to keep these essential aspects in mind if we want to come to a full understanding of Husserl's criticism of the psychology of his day.[46]

It is far from our intention to maintain that the authors of the 19th century which we have discussed would all fully underwrite what we feel to be characteristic of naturalistic psychology. We feel, however, that the characterization which follows applies to a greater or lesser degree to the explicitly or implicitly adopted points of view of the naturalistic psychologists. Naturalistic psychology or rather objectifying psychology sees as its task the investigation of that which lies within the realm of internal experience. It thus complements the other sciences which direct their efforts towards the realm of external experience. Strictly speaking, this division into external and internal experience is not a fundamental distinction since both the external experiences and the internal experiences depend upon phenomena of consciousness. External experience directs itself to a reality existing outside consciousness and seeks to discover the laws which are operative not in the contents of consciousness them-

46. R. Müller-Freienfels, *op. cit.*, pp. 17–26; M. Langeveld, *op. cit.*, pp. 349–357.

selves, but in the external objects in which they are founded. Internal experience focuses on the processes of our consciousness itself and seeks to establish there the intrinsic laws as they differ from the laws to which the objects of the outside world respond. The difference between our internal and external experiences is, thus, not determined as much by the type of object viewed as by the manner in which the object is viewed.

No matter whether the object is approached under the aspect of the external or the aspect of the internal, the natural scientist amplifies the given experience with a number of constructs that serve the purpose of further intelligibility. In the case of external perception the intelligibility is enhanced with such constructs as 'things,' 'substance,' 'energy,' etc., and in the case of internal perception with unconscious representations, instincts, dispositions, and finally with processes in the nervous system or in other parts of the body.

We do not need to ask ourselves the question here of whether such a separation between inner and outer experience can be considered tenable. Our purpose is to characterize that which has been chosen as an area of study by the objectivistic psychologists. Objectivistic psychology seeks to study the internal experience, the immediate contents of consciousness, and consciousness as such. This science seeks to grasp and order these immediate experiences by means of a number of constructs. Although the subjective experience forms the point of departure, the method is one of objectification, in the sense that the scientific attack on the subjective experience is effected with the same means which proved so effective in our dealing with external experience. This approach turns away from a basic, intrinsic principle that governs the experiences of internal life and according to which the inner experiences which appear isolated and separate in thought, exist, nevertheless, embedded in the totality of the I-experience. The separation of the internal experience can occur only on the level of thought, and then only under certain conditions. In opposition to this principle of unifying embeddedness, the 'natural-scientific' approach forcefully isolates experiences and then classifies these isolated facts according to a lawfulness borrowed from the outside world of things.

The ideal of naturalistic or objectivistic psychology is that of chemistry. The proponents of the older associationism speak frankly and admiringly of a mental chemistry. Physics is similarly held up as an inspiring ideal for the older psychology to follow. It is assumed that the same lawfulness operates in both the inner and the outer world; this lawfulness rests in both cases on causality. Even though the objectifying psychologists did not always draw the complete consequences of this thought, even though a few among them partially rejected these consequences, we, nevertheless, cannot judge their opponents to be in error when they charge that objectivistic psychology seeks ideally to reduce consciousness to mental elements, and that it then tries to join these elements again by means of a mechanistic causality.

The results of experience are given to one subject only, but the science of intersubjectively valid facts requires the reporting of these experiences in as completely objective a manner as possible. To meet this demand, and also to evade the difficulties involved in dealing with the subjective states, the objectifying psychologists tried to connect the inner experiences to external observable facts. For the natural sciences had shown how these external facts might be presented in an objective manner. The connection between an internal state and an external objective fact was most easily made between the sensation of a stimulus, and the stimulus itself. Most objectifying psychologies chose, therefore, sensory perceptions as their point of departure; the ease with which the stimulus situation could be dealt with in terms of the desired methodology made them an excellent choice as the first and most basic psychological facts. Representation can then be seen as a reproduction of elementary sensations which in turn can be tied to particular stimuli of the outside objective world. Concepts can be seen as modifications of representations and can, thus, be thought of as mediately maintaining connections with the outside world. The vague group of the affects and the impulses of the will present greater difficulties. It proved possible to connect this group with certain external stimuli once it was observed that feelings always *accompany* sensations and representations, and that these affects, instincts, and impulses actually grow out of these sensations and respresentations. Psychical life is more and more considered as a mirroring of the external world. The soul is no longer thought of as a substance, and is turned instead into a mere collection of elements of consciousness which are themselves passive reactions to an active external world.

In the area of sensory perceptions the naturalistic psychologist further proposes the existence of a close relationship between consciousness and excitations in the organs and their further neural ramifications. This proposition leads us to the conclusion that it might be possible to coordinate certain conscious experiences with bodily states. Attempts were made, subsequently, to connect the workings of certain parts of the brain with imagination and concepts. We might speak here of an attempt at localization and spatialization. If the processes of consciousness and the physiological processes cannot be considered as one, it might at least seem plausible to consider them as strictly parallel processes. However, by considering the phenomena of consciousness strictly as phenomena which accompany bodily processes one objectifies them at the same time. This view, indeed, gave rise to two major advantages: it now became possible to subject psychological phenomena to a process of measurement and quantification, and it became clear further that the unity of consciousness could be based in the unity of the organism. In fact, however, this view made psychology a branch of physiology. It is, therefore, not surprising to hear the objectifying psychologists speak so frequently about a physiological psychology.

After a relationship has been established between the elements of consciousness, the bodily processes, and the external stimuli, the naturalistic psychologist has to create order among the psychological events. To accomplish this task he again turns for inspiration to the physical sciences and then seeks for the lawfulness which governs the course of conscious psychological events. The lawfulness of psychological events rests in part on the connections between the psychological event and the external stimuli or the physiological processes; for the larger part it rests, however, on an inherent regularity of the psychical itself. Careful inquiry into this inherent regularity of the psychical yielded the well-known laws of association together with the laws of attention, of memory, etc. These laws were considered universally valid for all human beings and, as such, analogous to the natural laws.

Closely associated with this approach is the view that our activities are purposeful in appearance only. When the will proposes itself a purpose, this singleness of purpose is the cause of the process which in this way it has started. All psychological life must run a mechanistic, causally interconnected course; the human organism must be thought of as a very complicated machine. One of the major tasks of psychology is to replace man's apparent purposefulness with causality. It, therefore, becomes important to investigate the myriad interlocking factors which form part of the causal chain. Sooner or later, however, the fact must be faced that the successive psychological states do not readily lend themselves to causal explanations. It, thus, becomes necessary to invent an unconscious that can link the broken chain of causality together. The unconscious forces which are used for this purpose usually are more or less identified with physiological processes.

The actual causality remains operative on the level of the unconscious: the causality which we find operative in consciousness must be explained by an unconscious, underlying, physiological pattern. Although many accept the necessity of a hypothetical, unconscious foundation in order to save the causal explanation of conscious phenomena, they nevertheless deny a need for a distinctly psychological substratum. What is sought is a *psycho-logy* without the *psyche;* a study of man without a soul. Psychology is but the science of the phenomena of consciousness, and consciousness is nothing but a succession of separate states of consciousness. A substantial mind empowered with special capacities is rejected as an unnecessary hypothesis. If essential structures can be found in consciousness, they must necessarily

rest on patterns and structures of the brain and the rest of the
nervous system. When the subject of the 'I' is brought up it
always refers to a content, a representation, or a concept.

In matters of methodology this objectifying psychology turns,
of course, to the natural sciences for its inspiration with the
result that the experimental and mathematical methods become
of enormous importance. Factually this psychology never passed
beyond physiology since the qualitative aspects of psychological
life refuse to be permanently reduced to quantitative aspects.
When Weber and Fechner succeeded in finding a stable correlation between the quantitative aspect of a stimulus and the qualitative aspect of the resulting sensation they no doubt did very
useful work, although it is doubtful whether such work can be
called psychological. This is essentially the insight that started
to break through around the turn of the century, and it is with
the advent of this view that the naturalistic ideal started to
loosen its grip on psychology.

Although it is certainly true that Husserl came in contact
with psychology through Brentano, Wundt, and Stumpf, and
even though Husserl, discouraged by Ebbinghaus' strong criticism of Dilthey's publications, failed to read Dilthey directly,
it appears, nevertheless, that Husserl saw in Dilthey a congenial
spirit which he especially valued for his battle against positivism
and psychologism, and also for his attempt to found psychology
as a 'science of mind.' Particularly in the later works of Husserl
does the name Dilthey appear regularly in connection with
empirical and phenomenological psychology. Our discussion of
Dilthey's work, however, must remain rather short, and so we
shall restrict ourselves to briefly noting only those aspects of his
thought that are really relevant to Husserl's view on psychology.[47]

Dilthey's philosophical investigations originate in the historical sciences; he was particularly familiar with the history of the
'sciences of mind.' His main concern as a philosopher was the

---

47. See for the following: H.-G. Gadamer, *Wahrheit und Methode.
Grundzüge einer philosophischen Hermeneutik*, Tübingen, 1960, pp. 205–228,
229–240; W. Biemel, in E. Husserl, *Phän. Psychol.*, *Einleitung des
Herausgebers*, pp. *xvi-xxi*.

establishment of the independence of these sciences *vis a vis* the natural sciences in regard to both the object and the method of their study. With this goal in mind he developed a completely new epistemology for the 'sciences of mind.'

He felt that the classical historians had devised a methodology for the historical sciences that could be considered on a par with that of natural science. A complete and appropriate epistemology had failed to arise, however. Dilthey sought to construct such an epistemology. In his *Einleitung in die Geisteswissenschaften* Dilthey starts to work in that direction. Since he never completed the projected second part of this work we must turn to *Der Aufbau der geschichtlichen Welt in den Geisteswissenschaften* for a fuller understanding of his vision. According to Dilthey we should not seek to base the moral sciences of mind on any particular metaphysics since all forms of metaphysics are but historical, perishable phenomena. The humanities can only be truly based on the empirically proceeding self-revelation of those who study and form part of the 'sciences of mind.' The epistemology on which the natural sciences are founded makes nature appear as a mere shadow projected by some hidden reality. In contrast to this, man is also capable of approaching reality directly as it is given in his internal experience. This fundamental distinction in the object of study for the natural sciences and the humanities shows also in the methodology of the two sciences. The occurrences characteristic of the mind's history are to be understood from the inside and can psychologically be relived in phantasy; natural phenomena remain in principle foreign to us and can only be apprehended by reason in an 'external' way. The moral sciences always study man as a whole since all that man does issues from the whole of his mind. The elements of the historical world consist of human individuals. The scientific study of these individuals, therefore, forms the basis of the 'sciences of mind.' The psychology of Dilthey's time was not capable of studying people in a way that would be beneficial to the humanities. It remained too much entangled in abstractions and moved too far afield from the concrete reality of the life of the individuals to be able to form a solid foundation for the humanities. More specifically this psychology refused to remain true to the phenomena to be considered. Instead of faithfully considering the phenomena of man's life, this psychology turned to building hypothesis upon hypothesis in order to reduce the complex phenomena to the more simple ones. Such a *fabricating,* explanation-oriented psychology remains forever an unempirical weave of hypotheses. Only as an analytical and descriptive discipline can psychology turn into a science. As such it could be the most elementary and the first among the 'sciences of mind.' Dilthey sought, thus, a new descriptive and analytic psychology that would be capable of dealing with the real, living whole of factual psychological life. Such a psychology would give teleological rather than causal explanations in analyzing the structural pattern of the human *psyche.* This general, descriptive psychology would eventually need to be supplemented with a comparative psychology which has as its task the investigation of human differences. Its practical task consists also in filling up the void that exists between general psychology and the different concrete 'sciences of mind.'

Dilthey later came to the conclusion that psychology would not only form a foundation for the humanities, it would also be the only possible starting point for philosophical epistemology. Starting from psychological descriptions and analyses, Dilthey himself even proceeded to deal with the problem concerning the reality of the outside world. He disagreed with the view which stated that the outside world must exist on the grounds that our experiences require a transcendent cause. The reality of the world can be demonstrated in every experience in which the will encounters external opposition.

Thus it is Dilthey's view that descriptive and analytic psychology has as its task to focus attention on the uniformly recuring psychological phenomena just as they relate to a larger whole. This larger whole to which the smaller, separately considered aspects tend, is not a fabricated, hypothesized whole, but is actually lived and experienced as such. Psychology is the description and analysis of a pattern that is as old and original as life itself. It is with that purpose in mind that the psychologist should focus on the regularities of that pattern of psychical life. He observes, analyzes, experiments, and compares, and does not shun anything that will help him accomplish his task. The importance of psychology among the other sciences rests upon the fact that its discovered patterns can be immediately verified in inner perception. These patterns form, in turn, part of a more encompassing whole which again is not hypothesized, but instead appears as a primary, and immediately given fact. Dilthey, thus, puts great stress on the intellectuality of perception, the capital importance of the immediate experience, and on the fact that all happenings appear to us internally as united through their meaning for the whole of our life; that which is important, therefore, appears in sharp relief against the unimportant.

Of special importance to the psychology of Dilthey are the concepts of *structural coherence* and *development*. Structural coherence refers to the ultimate pointing of the part to the whole. It refers to the fact that all parts and experiences of life bear an inner relation to each other. Each single experience refers to a whole of which it is a part; it is united structurally with other parts in a coherence. Since coherence is found everywhere in our conscious life, it is a category which issues from life itself. It is this presence of structural coherence in the different manifestations of our lives, in our passions, joys, sufferings, that enables us to grasp the meaning of human life and history.

Structural coherence tends toward fulfillment and happiness, and, therefore, is teleological in nature. It is important to understand that this structure presents itself as an original inviolate whole, as inner coherence *sui generis,* as an interaction between the individual and the environment which cannot be understood on the basis of mechanical causality. Development and structure are closely connected. It is impossible to understand the development of a human being without having insight about his structure; we can understand a man only when we know what he has become. The descriptive psychology does not need to fall back upon a physical or metaphysical conception of development; psychology must describe this development faithfully in terms of the laws that become manifest immediately in the very process itself.[48]

Dilthey's major importance lies, no doubt, in the general area of the historical sciences and in the fact that he sought to establish the autonomy of the 'sciences of mind' *vis a vis* the natural sciences. His importance for the development of psychology is minor although his ideas, especially as they were further developed by Spranger, are important to us today.

Towards the end of his life Dilthey became concerned with philosophy's ability to provide man with a 'world view' *(Weltanschauung)*. He answered this question negatively. Philosophy can do no more than describe the different types of world views. All these world and life views are but of relative importance; it is impossible to point to the one true point of view. This aspect of Dilthey is not critical to our understanding of Husserl and we will, therefore, not expand these views further.

It is important to note that Dilthey saw Husserl as a spiritual kinsman. Husserl in turn appreciated Dilthey's stand against positivism and his attempt to incorporate psychology into the 'sciences of mind' and to make it the foundation for all the other humanities. When Husserl opens a sharp attack on naturalistic psychology in his *Logos*-article he is no doubt indebted to Dilthey. Without him Husserl could not have spoken in quite the same way; without him Husserl could not have been understood either. In the second part of this article, however, Husserl protests Dilthey's historicism and his 'World-view-philosophy' because it leads ultimately to scepticism. In his *Phenomenological Psychology* Husserl deals at length with Dilthey's importance for psychology; he tries to delineate their respective points of view carefully, and to elucidate at the same time a number of problems that had arisen between the two authors in an earlier correspondence. We shall return at length to these matters.[49]

48. R. Müller-Freienfels, *op. cit.,* pp. 168–169.
49. W. Biemel, *Ibid.,* p. *xxi.*

II TOWARD A PHENOMENOLOGICAL PSYCHOLOGY

Phenomenology as a Descriptive Psychology

If we wish to understand Husserl's philosophical development and the birth of his phenomenology, we would do well to follow Walter Biemel's advice and turn to the year 1887 when Husserl was working on his *Philosophie der Arithmetik*.[1] In this study it was not his intention to present a complete philosophy of mathematics, but, rather to prepare the ground for it. Husserl's immediate aim was to provide us with logical and psychological analyses concerning the concept of numbers.[2] He saw the philosophical study of the number-concept as primarily an investigation into the psychological origin of numbers; but this must be understood as Husserl really intended it.

Husserl felt that we cannot penetrate into the essential aspects of a number by directing our attention to things that can be counted. Instead, we must turn to the one who is doing the counting, to the psychological acts that give rise to these concepts. Yet, the emphasis in this study is not on the successive psychological acts which constitute the foundation of our counting, but, rather, on the numbers themselves and the modes in

1. W. Biemel, "Les phases décisives dans la développement de la philosophie de Husserl," in *Husserl* (Cahiers de Royaumont, Philosophie, no. III), Paris, 1959, 32–71, p. 35.
2. M. Farber, *The Foundation of Phenomenology. Edmund Husserl and the Quest for a Rigorous Science of Philosophy*, Cambridge Ma., 1943, pp. 25–26; H. Spiegelberg, *The Phenomenological Movement. A Historical Introduction*, 2 vol., Den Haag, 1960, vol. I, pp. 92–93.

which they arise in consciousness when we are present to objects that can be counted. While counting objects our consciousness *imposes*, as it were, a number upon these objects. This number finds its origin in our consciousness and is formed on the basis of the data of an original perception.[3]

In his *Philosophie der Arithmetik* Husserl tried to unify all the discoveries and important insights he had gathered during his academic training. It is therefore not surprising that he attempts to base his philosophical investigations concerning the number-concept on the dominant logical and psychological views of his day. We find in this work the clear traces of Husserl's former teachers, Weierstrass, Kronecker, Wundt, Stumpf, and Brentano; we also find indirect traces of Bolzano, Locke, Hume, Mill, and Spencer. It soon occurred to Husserl that the task of combining logic and psychology in the area of mathematics was proving to be extremely difficult. The difficulty in combining so many heterogeneous elements accounts at least in part for the change in point of view which can be indicated as having occurred in Husserl's philosophical development around 1894.

Although in this work Husserl is still far away from his later phenomenological philosophy, we nevertheless already find in it quite a number of elements which were to occupy a central place in his later phenomenology. In *Philosophie der Arithmetik* there are already the first indications of Husserl's later conception concerning constitution, reduction, eidetic intuition, and intentional analysis. The form in which these fundamental concepts are described, however, reveals Husserl's early, and as yet unsuccessful, attempts to escape psychologistic tendencies. But already in 1894 it had occurred to Husserl that the position of psychologism against which Stumpf had already raised his voice, must be considered unacceptable and that particularly mathematics and logic cannot be adequately based on psychology. This does not mean, however, that psychology must remain entirely irrelevant to these sciences; Husserl only points to the impossibility of *basing* logic and mathematics on psychology.

---

3. M. Farber, *op. cit.,* pp. 58–60; see also: *Ibid.,* pp. 25–60 (passim).

Under the influence of Frege's criticisms concerning the *Philosophie der Arithmetik* and also of Natorp's objections to Lipps' psychologism, Husserl began around 1895 to include in his lectures a vigorous but objective criticism of psychologism. As a result of his further investigations, especially in the area of logic, in 1900 Husserl published the first part of his *Logische Untersuchungen* which he entitled *Prolegomena zur reinen Logik.*[4] In this study he built a strong case against psychologism as it relates to logic.

First, he shows the absurd consequences to which a psychologistic position would lead if applied coherently to logic; secondly, he examines critically the prejudices which form the basis of psychologism. Among other things, Husserl asks himself the question: how much can a psychological law help to determine the validity of the axioms and statements of logic. He shows in a convincing manner that Mill and Spencer were wrong when they believed that the *principium non-contradictionis* could be interpreted as a psychological law derived from our actual and factual thinking. Another necessary result of psychologism is that it inevitably leads to sceptical relativism. If we proceed to make logical laws dependent upon the psychological characteristics of the various logicians, we make the validity of all our principles and laws relative. We make man in all his instability the measure of all things. Husserl perceives a contradiction in such relativism since it denies the possibility of true and certain knowledge while at the same time underwriting the apodictic truth of this contention.

Psychologism is based on a number of prejudices, the most notable being that logic is ultimately concerned with psychological phenomena. Husserl breaks through this prejudice by pointing out that logic is not concerned with the intellectual processes which go into a logical statement or judgment, but that it is concerned with what results from these processes. Logic is concerned with 'ideal' entities such as terms, propositions and conclusions. The refutation of psychologistic prejudices leads

4. W. Biemel, *Ibid.*, pp. 41–44; H. Spiegelberg, *op. cit.*, vol. I, p. 93; M. Farber, *op. cit.*, pp. 4–7, 37–38, 57–58.

Husserl to an analysis and description of the essential structures
of the realm of the logical. After removing the psychologistic
prejudices from logic, he proceeds to construct a foundation for
the study of pure logic which will remain free of all psychological
impurities.[5]

After the first part of the *Logische Untersuchungen* appeared, many philosophers felt that between 1894 and 1900
Husserl had been converted from psychologism to a form of
realistic objectivism or possibly even to classical Platonism. They
were quite surprised when in 1901 the second part of the
Logische Untersuchungen appeared in which two of the six
essays seemed clearly to betray a reverting to the position of
psychologism. But in fact, nothing of the sort had taken place.
Husserl maintained in this second part the fundamental insights
which he had uncovered in the first part, namely, that mathematical and logical entities must be seen as 'ideal beings.' Although an ideal being acquires form and unity in consciousness,
it, nevertheless, retains an independent being or a being-in-
itself. Psychological considerations can never totally account radically for these ideal beings.

In the second part he tries to show that much work remains
to be done, even if it has been shown conclusively that the
logical and mathematical entities have a being of their own as
ideal beings. One would still have to explain the typical correlation which exists between the ideal objects of pure logic and the
subjective experiences in which they are constituted.[6] The first
part of the *Logische Untersuchungen* had shown that we must
accept a world of mathematical entities which remains independent of the psychological activities through which they become part of our knowledge. The second part has as its task the
explanation of how we can become conscious of these ideal
entities. This is, without a doubt, the task of a psychology of
human knowledge. The psychology of Husserl's day was not
capable of fulfilling such a task. Husserl, therefore, started his

5. H. Spiegelberg, *op. cit.*, vol. I, pp. 94–95.
6. *Ibid.*, p. 101; Q. Lauer, *The Triumph of Subjectivity. An Introduction
to Transcendental Phenomenology*, New York, 1958, pp. 26–27.

own search for a descriptive science of the psychological activities which constitute the entities of pure logic. It is to this descriptive psychology that the term 'phenomenology' is applied in the introduction to the second part of the *Logische Untersuchungen.*[7]

The idea of a pure logic is often interpreted as an attempt to separate logic completely from any psychology whatsoever. The impossibility of this position is precisely the main point brought home by the second part of the *Logische Untersuchungen.* In *Phänomenologische Psychologie* Husserl says that the most fundamental problem of the *Logische Untersuchungen* consisted in the question of how the hidden psychic experiences which are in mutual relationships with the ideal entities of formal logic manifest themselves; and, in particular, how these experiences can come about as corresponding and completely determined 'achievements' in such a way that the knowing subject is able consciously to grasp these ideal entities in a knowledge which, at least in principle, is genuinely evident.[8] For even the ideal entities of formal logic are known to us only in and through experience, although evidently it is true that the experience of which we are speaking in this case, is of a special type. No philosophy can, therefore, afford to deny or to misapprehend these experiences which form the ground of the ideal logical entities. This seems to imply that a philosophy which concerns itself with the foundation of logic needs to avail itself of some type of psychology of knowledge. The psychology of around the turn of the century was simply not capable of elucidating the foundations of logic. Husserl needed, above all, a descriptive study of those processes which make it possible for us to speak of such things as pure logical entities, of the processes thus which constitute these entities and enable us to represent them to ourselves. We shall return to some of these implied problems later in this chapter.[9]

7. H. Spiegelberg, *op. cit.,* vol. I, pp. 102–103; W. Biemel, *op. cit.,* pp. 44–45; Edmund Husserl, *Phänom. Psychol.,* pp. 27–28.
8. Edmund Husserl, *op. cit.,* pp. 24–28; W. Biemel, *op. cit.,* p. 47.
9. W. Biemel, *Ibid.,* pp. 45–46.

We mentioned that in the introduction to the second part of the *Logische Untersuchungen,* Husserl made use of the term 'phenomenology' referring to the study of those fundamental processes. Following Brentano in this respect, he also indicated this study with the term 'descriptive psychology.' Husserl speaks in this context about epistemological investigations which are closely connected with a pure phenomenology of all our cognitive experiences.[10] This whole sphere must be studied in order to arrive at an epistemological explanation and foundation of pure logic. Somewhere else he specified this point by saying that it is not his intention to make the whole of psychology the basis for logic. Only certain chapters of psychology can be relevant to the preparatory phase for the theoretical investigations concerning logic. Psychology needs only to investigate the genetic relationships between the experiences of those empirical objects which form the basis for the fundamental abstractions which enable the logician to grasp the very essence of the ideal entities in an evident way.

Epistemologically speaking, it is very important to distinguish between those purely descriptive investigations concerning cognitive experiences which do *not* touch on the theoretical-psychological implications, and those genuine psychological studies which seek purely empirical explanations. To avoid all confusion in this aspect Husserl found it preferable to speak of phenomenology rather than descriptive psychology.[11] Yet, as early as 1903 he noted a number of mistakes in his first characterization of phenomenology. For, as any other positive descriptive science, descriptive psychology is interested only in factual empirical data. What Husserl really intended was a description of ideal types of logical experience which answered ideal logical laws.

He was interested especially in descriptive analyses of the different forms of thought, of the different shades and forms of our intuitive consciousness, of the modes of immediate or sym-

10. Edmund Husserl, *Logische Untersuchungen,* 2 vol., Halle a.d.S., 1900–1901, vol. I, p. 2.
11. *Ibid.,* p. 18.

bolic representation, all this being of the utmost importance for the radical uncovering of the laws of pure logic. The study of the pure essence of these experiences must, from beginning to end, remain neutral before the question of what happens in concrete and real instances. All that must remain the domain of empirical psychology which includes descriptive psychology.

The new phenomenology has as its task the study of essential relationships as these can be understood even separately from either empirically or experimentally conceived actual cases. Once this has been realized, philosophy will be in a position to account in an epistemologically adequate manner for our knowledge of the logical entities. Also, philosophy can then come to terms with its pretentions concerning the foundations of logic, by genuinely proving the adequacy of its view on the fundamental types of experience.

In the second edition of the *Logische Untersuchungen,* which appeared after the publication of *Ideen* in 1913, Husserl characterized his 'pure descriptive psychology' as follows. The purely descriptive phenomenology of our knowing and thinking, or, for that matter, of *all* experiences that were dealt with in the *Ideen,* is exclusively concerned with our experiences inasfar as they in regard to their essential universality can be grasped and analyzed in intuition, and not with our empirically apperceived experiences taken as factual facts, that is as experiences of concrete human beings occurring in and belonging to the phenomenal world of facts. Pure phenomenology must bring the very essences of and the essential relationships between our experiences to light in a genuinely descriptive way. That is why all of its statements are *a priori* statements in the strict sense of the term.[12]

In the formulation of this view on the relationship between pure logic and phenomenology Husserl incorporates an insight which recurs throughout his writings and which can be found as far back as his *Philosophie der Arithmetik.* This is the notion

12. Edmund Husserl, *Logische Untersuchungen* (Zweite Auflage), 3 vol., Halle a.d.S., 1913, vol. II, 1, p. 2. See also: H. Spiegelberg, *op. cit.,* vol. I, pp. 101–103; M. Farber, *op. cit.,* pp. 198–199.

that a parallel must exist between the structures of our subjective acts and their objective correlates. This parallelism forms the basis for further investigations into the correlative nature of these two aspects in all phenomena. Wanting to study one aspect without regard for the other leads to artificial abstractions which can have value only when replaced within the true context of the concrete phenomenon from which it had been isolated. Later Husserl spoke about this in terms of a parallelism between the noetic and the noematic content of each intentional phenomenon.[13]

This last remark brings us beyond our immediate concern which is with Husserl's development between 1887 and 1903. We therefore must return to a point that will prove to be of the utmost importance in understanding the relationship between his later phenomenological philosophy and phenomenological psychology. To what exactly was Husserl referring when he spoke in the *Logische Untersuchungen* of phenomenology as a descriptive psychology, and what is the relationship between this discipline and empirical psychology?

As we mentioned, Husserl tried in the second part of the *Logische Untersuchungen* to arrive at an epistemological explanation and foundation of pure logic. In the first part of this work he explained clearly that the traditional empirical and experimental psychologies were absolutely inadequate as tools with which to forge such a foundation of pure logic. Originally, Husserl had thought that a descriptive psychology as indicated by Brentano might be such a tool, but immediately after the publication of the second part of the *Logische Untersuchungen* he realized that this could not be so. It became clear to him that, although such a descriptive psychology might be an important aid to psychology in general, it, nevertheless, would be unable to guide us to the *radical* foundation of the epistemological aspects of our knowledge.

For such a foundation can be achieved only when we exclude all transcendent interpretations of immanent data, which not

13. H. Spiegelberg, *Ibid.*, p. 103.

only include our view on the psychological activities and their conditions inasfar as they refer to real ego's, but also the physical things which have an existence outside ourselves.[14] Considering the fact that it was never Husserl's intention to condemn empirical psychology as such, and that his criticism was directed only to the so-called naturalistic and objectivistic schools in psychology, in time he saw the necessity of distinguishing between empirical psychology and descriptive or phenomenological psychology.[15]

In 1903, however, Husserl had not as yet developed a clear distinction between phenomenological psychology and phenomenological philosophy. Nor was it quite clear how these two disciplines related to empirical psychology. Later [16] he expanded and clarified his formulation of 1903 and defined phenomenological psychology as an aprioric science which alone is capable of providing us with a sure foundation for a strict empirical psychology. This phenomenological psychology had as its task the systematic explanation of the different types and forms of intentional experience. It was to reduce these intentional experiences to their first intentions and, thus, to elucidate the essence of the psychical and the very essence and characteristics of the soul. Phenomenological psychology directs its attention exclusively to *intentional* experiences which must be described as phenomena. A phenomenological description refers here to a description of facts and events exactly as they manifest themselves to human consciousness. A certain reduction must be performed for the event to emerge as pure phenomenon. Reducing natural phenomena to pure phenomena involves two separate steps: 1) A systematic and radical bracketing of any objectifying point of view in regard to every experience, and 2) a careful analysis and description of the very essence of that which now no longer appears as a thing but only as a 'unity of meaning.' This description, in turn, implies two distinguishable

14. M. Farber, *op. cit.*, p. 199.
15. H. Spiegelberg, *op. cit.*, pp. 149–150.
16. Edmund Husserl, "Phenomenology," in *Encyclopaedia Britannica* (14th Ed.), London, 1927, vol. 17, col. 699–702.

tasks, namely, the description of the noetic aspects, and a description of the noematic aspects of the phenomena. Phenomenological psychology can, thus, be purified and freed of all empirical psycho-physical elements. We must note, however, that it will not be possible to speak about 'facts' in such a purified psychology.

Psychology taken as a whole, which comprises both empirical and phenomenological psychology, must be characterized as a positive science within the domain of the natural attitude. This natural attitude is precisely that which separates psychology from philosophy. For philosophy realizes itself in the transcendental attitude. Yet, it is rather easy to move from phenomenological psychology to transcendental phenomenology by radicalizing the psychological reduction to a transcendental reduction. In that sense, we can see phenomenological psychology as a good preparation for transcendental phenomenology, although this latter can also be developed independently of phenomenological psychology.

The main difference between the psychological and the phenomenological reductions lies in the fact that in the transcendental reduction not only do we place the world between brackets but also we exclude from our consideration the soul of the scientist and the community of souls, taken as the souls of human beings in the world. Psychology reduces the world of the natural attitude to a subjectivity which as soul remains part of the world it inhabits. Transcendental phenomenology goes beyond this psychologically purified ego into the realm of transcendental subjectivity.

Again we find ourselves ahead of Husserl's stage of development between the years 1887 and 1903. Later we will have to take up anew some of the topics we have discussed above. We shall then see that the descriptive psychology of the *Logische Untersuchungen* is actually only a forerunner of what Husserl later on clearly defines as phenomenological psychology.[17] This phenomenological psychology is not capable of leading to the true

17. Edmund Husserl, *L. U.*, vol. II, 1, pp. 347–348; Edmund Husserl, *Phän. Psych.*, 348, note 1.

foundation of logic and the other sciences because it itself remains a natural and positive science. Only transcendental phenomenological philosophy can provide such a foundation. This we must try to explain more fully.

Phenomenology as 'Critique of Reason'

IN HIS *Logische Untersuchungen* Husserl mentions a 'phenomenology' which he characterizes as a descriptive psychology. Around 1903 it became clear to him that he needed a transcendental phenomenology instead of a descriptive psychology. An intense study of the first two meditations of Descartes' *Meditationes de prima philosophia* and of Kant's *Kritik der reinen Vernunft* brought him to this insight. We can find the first systematic treatment of Husserl's new insights into phenomenology in a series of five lectures given at the University of Göttingen in 1907. As far as the main lines are concerned it can be seen now that Husserl remained true to those insights throughout his career. These lectures were entitled *Die Idee der Phänomenologie* and were intended as an introduction to a series of lectures called *Hauptstücke aus der Phänomenologie und Kritik der Vernunft*. Husserl started this lecture-series in 1904 with the famous *Vorlesungen zur Phänomenologie des inneren Zeitbewusstseins*. The well known *Dingvorlesung* also formed a part of this series. The birth of *Die Idee der Phänomenologie* is of great importance for a proper insight into Husserl's later development; therefore it seems advisable to show here how it came into being.[18]

Five years after the publication of *Logische Untersuchungen* Husserl found himself in a serious crisis. He saw clearly that his philosophical search for the foundations of pure logic had brought him to the brink of a new philosophical science that might lead to radically new insights concerning philosophy as a

18. W. Biemel, in E. Husserl, *Die Idee der Phänomenologie. Fünf Vorlesungen,* Den Haag, 1950: *Einleitung des Herausgebers,* p. vii; W. Biemel, *Les phases décisives,* pp. 46–52.

whole. He saw equally clearly that he had not yet hit upon the right way of representing his ideas in a convincing manner. Under the added weight of the misjudgment of his fellow-professors, Husserl started to doubt his own abilities as a philosopher and in the summer of 1906 he asked himself repeatedly and in full earnestness, whether it would not be better for him to give up his philosophical career.

On September 25, 1906, he noted the following in his diary. "In the first place I want to mention the general task which must be materialized if I want to call myself a philosopher. What is to be constructed first of all is a critique of reason, a critique of our logical, practical, and valuing reason. Without getting a clear insight into the meaning, essence, methods, and main points of view concerning a critique of reason, and without contriving and founding a general project in this direction, it will be impossible for me to live as philosopher." [19]

Already in 1906 Husserl felt that he had found his way towards a transcendental philosophy, following his re-examination of Descartes and Kant. Phenomenology understood as descriptive psychology must be superseded towards a transcendental phenomenology. Only an entirely new method can open the door to this transcendental phenomenology. Once this door is found, philosophy will rest upon an absolute foundation. *Die Idee der Phänomenologie* (1907) contains the first systematic treatment of this new concept of phenomenology. Its task is no longer limited to providing a foundation for logic and mathematics but comes to include the foundation of all other sciences as well.[20]

In these lectures Husserl pointed to what he considered a far-reaching difference between the 'natural' and the 'philosophical' sciences. The natural sciences come to light in a natural attitude while the philosophical sciences take their starting point in a philosophical attitude. The natural attitude does not concern itself with the epistemological problems of knowledge with

19. Edmund Husserl, *Ms. X x 5*, pp. 17–18, quoted by W. Biemel, in *Die Idee, Einleitung*, pp. *vii–viii*.
20. W. Biemel, *Ibid.*, pp. *viii–ix*.

which philosophy has struggled since Descartes. In this attitude man is in his perception and thinking turned upon objects which might appear in many different ways dependent upon various factors in regard to source and degree of knowledge. Objects originally appear to us in perception as objects among other objects in the world. These other objects in the world appear to us as the horizon out of which the object in question as figure, arises. Ultimately all knowledge and all science of man refers to the world. In that attitude all this is taken to be self-evident.

That which is offered to us in the act of perceiving is expressed in judgments. These judgments appear first as singular and later acquire universality by means of generalization and abstraction. These judgments can give rise to new judgments by means of induction and deduction. It sometimes happens that two judgments, which have been arrived at in this manner, fail to agree; in that case we must have erred in our reasoning or in some other manner. We resolve the threatening ambiguity by retracing part of our earlier incorrect pronouncements. It is in this way that natural knowledge makes strides. It progressively takes possession of reality which at first is taken to exist as a matter of course and to be investigated further and further in regard to its extent, content, its elements, relations, and laws.[21] It is, thus, that the different sciences within the natural attitude, both the ones that direct themselves to the real world as well as the ones that direct themselves to ideal entities, come into being.[22]

In the natural attitude the *possibility* of human knowledge is a self-evident fact. Also, the success of the sciences remaining within the domain of the natural scientific attitude, contributed to the general feeling that it is unnecessary to pose the question concerning the possibility of knowledge. It is, of course, possible to make both human knowledge and scientific research in themselves an object of study within the natural perspective, since within that perspective one can make all that is into an object

21. Edmund Husserl, *Die Idee*, p. 18.
22. *Ibid.*, pp. 17–18.

for study. Also, human knowledge itself is a 'natural fact,' a psychological fact that can be studied, as such, by psychology. This science reveals our knowledge essentially as a knowledge-of-an-object; this is so because of knowledge's own immanent nature which makes it necessarily concern itself with objects. This relationship, too, can be studied in the sciences of the natural attitude; this is done, for instance, by psychology which, thus, is a science of the natural attitude. It is even not impossible to construct ontologies upon such a basis. It is possible, for example, to distinguish different 'regions' of objects in the world whose essences can be carefully described; this could lead to an ontology of nature, of living things, of the social, and of art. But even in these cases we never leave the domain of the natural attitude.[23]

It is possible, however, to assume an entirely different attitude towards objects and the knowledge we have concerning them. We can say, for example, that our knowledge represents the psychological experience of a certain subject; in knowing, the subject is confronted by the known objects. The question now arises, how can the subject be sure that his knowledge corresponds really with those objects? At this point, the self-evident givenness of the objects within the natural attitude becomes problematic. How can I, as the knower, know that there is something outside my subjective experiences? This question can, of course, be answered by pointing to the fact that I have truly nothing else but phenomena with which to work. Only I myself am real and all else is mere phenomenon. We could join Hume in declaring that all transcendental objectivity is a mere human fiction which, as such, must be explained by psychology. If we take this position and think it through carefully, sooner or later we will meet insoluble contradictions which will force us to abandon such a point of view. Yet, even though I see clearly that such a point of view is untenable, I still have not found a convincing positive answer to the questions posed above. Furthermore, what help is it to us to speak here about contradictions

23. *Ibid.*, pp. 19, 79–80.

when logic itself must face the same problems insofar as it is itself a natural science. Whatever way we look at it, within the realm of the natural attitude we remain incapable of solving the problem concerning the possibility of human knowledge. Despite the tremendous success of the natural sciences, it seems that our knowledge must eventually end in scepticism, that is, in nonsense, as long as we cannot give an adequate answer to the problems concerning the possibility of knowledge.[24]

The crossroads where all these questions, which throughout the centuries have been asked concerning the possibility of knowledge, converge is formed by epistemology (*Erkenntnistheorie*) and metaphysics, which, as far as its content is concerned, is closely connected with epistemology. Epistemology has a twofold task: 1) The natural reflection concerning the relationships between knowledge, knowledge-meaning, and the known object must almost certainly fall into error; epistemology's task is to bring these errors to light and to show clearly the impossibility of any sceptical theory concerning the essence of knowledge. 2) Next, it must embark on a careful study concerning the nature of knowledge which must result in a positive solution to the problems dealing with the relationships between knowledge, the meaning of knowledge, and the object of knowledge. While turning to the solution of these questions, epistemology automatically becomes a critique of the natural knowledge in all natural sciences to the extent that it will provide a correct interpretation of the results of the natural sciences. This might end, once and for all, the arbitrary interpretations of the sciences in terms of materialistic, spiritualistic, dualistic, psychomonistic, or positivistic preconceptions.

The epistemology which will clarify the distinctions between philosophy and science will also have to point to the fact that the natural sciences cannot make definitive statements concerning Being. A metaphysics is needed to concern itself with the question of Being, but such a metaphysics can only come about as a result of the critical evaluation of the natural sciences.[25]

24. *Ibid.,* pp. 19–21, 81–82.
25. *Ibid.,* pp. 21–23.

If we hold temporarily to the fact that epistemology has as its task the explanation of the very essence of knowledge and of its objects, then it seems that we could say that epistemology and phenomenology of knowledge are one and the same discipline. It seems, also, that epistemology, in the sense in which we understand it here, should form the basis of phenomenology as a whole. Thus the phenomenology which we want to describe more completely is itself a complex of philosophical disciplines. Yet, it is above all a method. "The term 'phenomenology' denotes a science, a system of scientific disciplines. But it also and above all denotes a method and a way of thinking, namely the specifically philosophical attitude and the specifically philosophical method." [26]

Many are of the opinion that philosophy can only make a claim to being a genuine science insofar as it takes over the method of the natural sciences. Some believe in a harmonious unity of all sciences, even insofar as their method is concerned. This point of view is in perfect harmony with the philosophical ideals of the 17th century when it was thought that the fate of philosophy was intimately connected with the extent to which it would be able to imitate the exact sciences in their methodology. The most exemplary of the exact sciences in this respect were thought to be mathematics and mathematical physics.

This equating of the different disciplines under methodological aspect is closely connected with the equating of philosophy with the other sciences as far as its content is concerned. Even today we find a number of people who not only believe that philosophy should be necessarily related to the other sciences, but that it even should be founded in the results of the natural sciences. As we shall see later, such a positivistic scientism is completely unacceptable since it is based on arbitrary prejudices. Although the natural sciences may presuppose each other within certain limits at least, which are determined by their respective subject matters, we cannot say this about philosophy. For, "philosophy lies in a wholly new dimension. It needs an entirely new starting point, and an entirely new method

26. *Ibid.*, p. 23.

which in principle distinguishes it from any natural science." [27] Implied herein is the thought that the logical and methodological procedures of the natural sciences are radically different from the method of philosophy and that philosophy cannot simply take up the data of the natural sciences and proceed from there. For, it is impossible to see how the natural sciences and their results would be of much help in solving the critical problem of knowledge. When viewing this knowledge as problematic we see, also, its methodological procedures and foundations as problematic. These procedures and foundations become, therefore, irrelevant as a starting point or as a methodical ideal for epistemology and the metaphysics which grows out of it. The rigorous and exact mathematical sciences are, in this respect, in the same position with the natural sciences. "It is then clear that one cannot say that philosophy (which takes its starting point in epistemology and which, whatever else it may be, is founded in epistemology) has to model itself after the exact sciences as far as method is concerned (or even in regard to its subject matter!), or that it should have to adopt their method as a standard, or that it is philosophy's task to develop and complete the work done in the exact sciences with the help of a method which allegedly is the same for all sciences." [28] Philosophy works within the realm of a completely new dimension and it employs radically new methods. As long as we fail to understand that point we will fail to understand philosophy.

Building on these basic principles, Husserl tried to describe this new transcendental phenomenology in *Die Idee der Phänomenologie*. His primary concern is, first, to find his way to the realm of 'absolute data.' In this he follows the spirit of Descartes' method of the methodical and universal doubt. However it soon occurred to Husserl that the method of the methodical and universal doubt itself cannot suffice to lead to what is absolutely given because of the problem of transcendence innate to our natural knowledge.

That is why we need a transcendental reduction of our nat-

27. *Ibid.*, p. 24.
28. *Ibid.*, p. 25.

ural knowledge in which we leave out of consideration all that is transcendent in our knowledge. Thus, a field of *pure* phenomena is uncovered. Then it becomes clear that we must add to the transcendental reduction a so-called eidetic reduction since the philosopher ultimately is not concerned with facts but rather with the aprioric knowledge of the essences which correspond to these facts. It is, further, important to note that the pure experiences which we find after the reductions are essentially intentional. The *eidos* of the transcendental phenomena can, therefore, be brought to light only by means of an intentional analysis. This analysis, when executed within the sphere of transcendental reduction, shows how the different modes in which objects can appear are constituted by transcendental subjectivity. The constitution of our time-consciousness is in Husserl's view an excellent example of what really is at stake here.[29]

Die Idee der Phänomenologie is of special importance to us because it contains a clear description of this new view on phenomenology. We have seen how Husserl spoke in his *Logische Untersuchungen* (1901) about a phenomenology which he describes there as a descriptive psychology in the sense of Brentano. Around 1903 he began to see that a descriptive psychology still is a natural and positive science. As such, it cannot form the radical basis for logic and mathematics. Although descriptive psychology will doubtlessly contribute to the long established empirical psychology, we will have to look elsewhere, towards a *philosophical* science of consciousness, if we hope to find a radical basis for logic, mathematics and all other sciences. In 1907 he identified this philosophical science of consciousness with transcendental phenomenology. *Die Idee* contains a short but adequate description of this new science.

Philosophy as Strict Science

In 1911, Husserl published his well known article *Philosophie als strenge Wissenschaft* in the journal *Logos*. Walter Biemel sees this article as the fruition of the long development

29. *Ibid.,* pp. 27–76 (passim).

of Husserl's thought between 1887 and 1911. He calls it "the
rock on which Husserl's thought as a whole rests." [30] Although
it is not our intention to follow Husserl through all the phases
of his development, we feel, nevertheless, that is is very important to consider carefully this article in which we find such a
clear expression of Husserl's plan for his phenomenology and
of the relationship between phenomenology and empirical
psychology.

Husserl touches upon this problem in *Die Idee der Phänomenologie,* but in this article he approaches the problem from
a completely new angle. Let us not forget that Husserl started
out as a mathematician and physicist and that he decided only
relatively late to become a philosopher. While under the philosophical influence of Wundt and Brentano he noticed the following: 1) The great difference in the scientific results of mathematics and physics since Descartes, Galileo, and Newton on the
one hand, and of philosophy on the other. 2) The almost
constant lack of a clear theory of the sciences which prevented
the emergence of philosophy as a true and genuine science.
This is especially astonishing when we realize that the ideal of
philosophy, since Plato's era, has been to become a real science.
All of his life Husserl remained a somewhat deficient student of
the history of philosophy. If he had taken his historical studies
more seriously, it is likely that his thought would have taken a
very different turn. Husserl had little interest in, and probably
little talent for, history. He had the mind of a mathematician
who is more interested in ideal structures than in their concrete
realizations. Only much later does he arrive at the insight that
the ideal structures of philosophy are in need of a history if they
are to develop. He himself, at first, contrived a philosophical
ideal without much reference to the history of philosophy in
order, then, to evaluate history from the viewpoint of this ideal.
Husserl himself wanted a philosophy which would be as scientific as mathematics.[31] Luckily he bypassed the mistake that
Descartes and many others since him have made; he did not

30. W. Biemel, "Les phases décisives", p. 54.
31. Q. Lauer, *Phénoménologie de Husserl. Essai sur le genèse de
l'intentionnalité,* Paris, 1955, pp. 4–7.

envision a scientific philosophy modeled after mathematics. He searched for a philosophy that, albeit in a completely different way, would lead to an analogous, indubitable certitude in a different order of things from the one with which mathematics deals. Descartes' ideal was an impossibility for Husserl since he felt that an essential difference between philosophy and science existed. Furthermore, Husserl claims, the natural sciences themselves are not yet founded in a sufficiently radical manner as we can see from the crisis in the investigations concerning their foundations. At first, Husserl tried to come to a radical foundation by means of a rejuvenated psychology. When this turned out to be impossible he returned to philosophy. Since philosophy still lacked scientific character Husserl tried to develop a philosophy which would be able to found itself in a radical way. Philosophy could then in turn provide the sciences with the sure foundation which they lacked so desperately.

One of Husserl's fundamental intuitions thus is that philosophy needs an absolute certitude that is *essentially* different from the certitude of mathematics and the other natural sciences. It is only much later that the developing phenomenology itself was to clarify this intuition in a convincing way.[32]

Throughout his life Husserl was never to abandon this insight, although he continually adapts his explanation of that ideal to the rapidly moving scientific climate of the Germany of his time.[33] When he writes in 1935 at the age of 76 that the ideal of philosophy as a strict science is a dream that has passed by,[34] he does not mean that this ideal is passed for him. It becomes clear in the context of the rest of the paper that he is pointing with some bitterness to the fact that his own life will come to an end soon and that there is no successor who will carry on his ideals.[35]

It is clear that Husserl envisioned a philosophy as a strict science. According to him philosophy has, since its first dawn in

32. H. Spiegelberg, *op. cit.*, vol. I, pp. 76–82.
33. Edmund Husserl, *Cartesianische Meditationen und Pariser Vorträge*, Den Haag, 1950, p. 28.
34. Edmund Husserl, *Krisis*, p. 508.
35. H. Spiegelberg, *op. cit.*, vol. I, p. 77, note 1.

Greece, aspired to provide an all embracing rationally justified knowledge of all that is. This has been philosophy's aspiration even at times when philosophy was least in the position to make that aspiration come true. Despite this centuries old pretension, philosophy has not succeeded in realizing it fully. This remark also takes into account the time since the Renaissance during which a conscious attempt has been made time and again to constitute a philosophy as a strict science by means of a critical reflection and ever more penetrating considerations of the philosophical method (Descartes, Kant, Fichte, Hegel, Comte). The result of this endeavor was that mathematics and physics and later also the 'sciences of mind' evolved into completely independent sciences. Yet, the question as to the relationship between philosophy and science remained unanswered, as did the important problems concerning philosophy's intrinsic dimension, and its own instrinsic methods and aims. Kant liked to say: "One cannot learn philosophy, but only to philosophize." Husserl sees such a statement as unacceptable since it tries to make peace with the unscientific nature of philosophy. Contrary to this Kantian notion he feels that philosophers should seek the means to raise philosophy to a truly scientific level.[36]

If we look at things honestly, Husserl continues, we can easily see that the philosophy around the turn of the century could scarcely be called an imperfect science since, in fact, it was no science at all. Every science is imperfect, physics and mathematics not excluded, but this does not prevent us from having full confidence in what they say. The sciences fulfill at least the basic requirements which consist of a clearly defined method, a generally accepted content, and a refusal to deal in mere opinions, notions, and points of view which have nothing to substantiate them but subjective impressions. The imperfection of philosophy however, is of a very different nature. There is not yet a generally accepted, doctrinal content and every philosophical position still is a question of personal conviction only. Standing before these facts, we are immediately confronted

36. Edmund Husserl, "Philosophie als strenge Wissenschaft" in *Logos*, 1 (1910–1911) pp. 289–290.

by the question of whether philosophy actually can become a strict science and of how we must proceed to provide it with a truly scientific character.[37] Husserl tried in this article to give a satisfactory answer to both problems.

The history of philosophy shows, according to Husserl, that the periods which are of the greatest moment for philosophy are always those in which later philosophers critically destroy the pretentions of earlier philosophers who thought that they had already founded philosophy as a strict science. For, during this critical period the new generation of philosophers makes serious attempts to realize the philosophical ideal in a new way. True, naturalism, positivism, scientism, historicism, and the other movements of the 19th and 20th centuries also felt that they in fact had already realized philosophy's great ideal. Yet, their opinions contradicted each other, a situation that ultimately must lead to the destruction of philosophy. Following up the course of history, Husserl says, it seems advisable to prepare the ground for a true solution to the problem under discussion by giving both a positive and negative critique of these varied positions.[38]

The basic mistake of the 19th and 20th century convictions as Husserl saw it is that they see only experiential facts and, therefore, they can: "look upon positive science as the only rigorous science and recognize as scientific philosophy only one that is based on such a positive science."[39] Scientific does not mean the same thing, however, as physical, for example. It is, therefore, possible to have a philosophy as a strict science even though its scientific nature is entirely different from that of the physical sciences. It is equally futile to try to turn empirical psychology into a strictly scientific philosophy, and then ask it to furnish a scientific foundation for logic, epistemology, aesthetics, ethics, pedagogy, humanistic sciences, and even metaphysics.[40]

37. *Ibid.*, pp. 290–291.
38. *Ibid.*, pp. 292–293.
39. *Ibid.*, p. 296.
40. *Ibid.*, pp. 296–298.

It is true, of course, that a psychology which is oriented towards the physical sciences remains critical up to a point. Yet, even such a psychology is based on a group of presuppositions which cannot be critically accounted for by means of psychology's own methods. A philosopher may not presuppose anything.[41] When epistemology tries to investigate the problems involved in the relationship between consciousness and reality, then it can only arrive at Being as the correlate of our consciousness, that is to say Being just inasfar as it is intended by consciousness in perception, memory, expectations, etc. But it is also clear that its investigation should be focussed first on a scientific knowledge of the very essence of consciousness, on that which consciousness *is itself* in its many appearances. At the same time there must be an insight into what consciousness 'means,' and into the different ways in which it intends objects and the way in which it makes these objects appear as valid or real.[42] "What it means, that objectivity is, and manifests itself cognitively as so being, must precisely become evident purely from consciousness itself, and thereby it must become completely understandable. And for that is necessary a study of consciousness in its entirety . . . To the extent, however, that consciousness essentially is consciousness-of, the study of the essence of consciousness implies that which is meant by consciousness, and also its object as such." [43]

It is not difficult to see that empirical psychology has no methods to deal with this matter while, on the other hand, it cannot function without presupposing it. Empirical psychology, therefore, cannot pose a true solution to our problem.[44] The task of carefully working through such analyses without presuppositions falls to the 'phenomenology of consciousness.' Without a phenomenological analysis psychology remains without a complete foundation for its method as well as for its technical concepts and language. Without "the systematic real-

41. *Ibid.*, pp. 298–300.
42. *Ibid.*, pp. 300–301.
43. *Ibid.*, p. 301.
44. *Ibid.*, pp. 301–302.

ization of 'analysis' and 'description' of the data that manifest
themselves in the different possible directions of immanent intuition" [45] we remain incapable of elucidating the meaning of
words in a really original way.[46] We hear it said from time to time
that we should rid ourselves of the futile analysis of words, that
we should question the 'things themselves' and return to the
experiences which provide our words with meaning in the first
place. That sounds impressive but what are we to understand
here by the expression 'things' and the term 'experience'? We
cannot possibly refer here to fashionable interpretations by the
psychologists. On the contrary, we should understand by 'experience' and 'thing' that which emerges within a particular experience; it is this experience, in which the 'object' and the
'experience of the object' emerge, that phenomenology tries to
describe.[47]

For the rest, psychology itself is proceeding in the wrong
direction. Since its inception it has falsely assumed that it should
model its methodology on physics. But, if psychology objectifies
its object of study in the same manner as does physics, it must
end up reifying consciousness and, thus, missing its essential
meaning. It is not difficult to see that the realm of the psychological is a realm in its own right and that psychology is in need
of its own psychological experience and of its own methods.[48]
It is also clear that we can make a *radical* study of consciousness,
and consciousness' objectivity only on the basis of a phenomenology in which a central place is accorded to a reduction, an
ideation, and an apodictic evidence based on this particular
intuition. With the help of such a phenomenology it becomes
possible to construct an epistemology and a truly scientific philosophy.[49]

We can make use of this same critique to counter the current
form of scepticism which is put forth by historicism. Scepticism

45. *Ibid.*, p. 303.
46. *Ibid.*, pp. 302–305.
47. *Ibid.*, pp. 305–309.
48. *Ibid.*, pp. 309–314.
49. *Ibid.*, pp. 314–322.

destroys itself because it necessarily includes a number of contradictions. The ideal of the so-called *Weltanschauung* philosophy must be rejected on the same grounds. For it is simply impossible to construct a coherent world-view with the findings of the natural sciences as long as these sciences themselves lack a radical foundation.[50] In any case, such a philosophy cannot replace or reduce the need for a philosophy as a strict science.

Philosophy, as Husserl sees it, needs to follow its innermost prompting and develop into a strict science. What we remarked above we must repeat here with emphasis, namely, that in view of the fundamental distinction between philosophy and science, the scientific character of philosophy must not be equated with the scientific character of the natural sciences. As far as the natural sciences are concerned we have at our disposal any number of refined methods. Philosophy simply has not developed such methods to a great extent. This lack of refined methods creates the impression that philosophy is and remains unscientific, and this still will be the case when philosophy emerges with the aid of phenomenology. Once phenomenology succeeds in creating a philosophy that truly is a strict science we still have a philosophy that is scientific in a different sense from the natural sciences. This would, however, never be a ground for calling philosophy less scientific.

If we look carefully, we can find that all sciences proceed from a number of presuppositions which never are radically clarified by those sciences themselves. Quite contrary to this, philosophy aims to leave nothing unsolved; it seeks to reduce everything to *first* 'presuppositions' which are in no need of further explanations because of the immediate evidence with which they manifest themselves. Only in that sense can philosophy be a 'science emerging from an ultimate foundation'; only thus can philosophy be made into a genuine science.

Thus, philosophy must, by means of its own method, seek to penetrate into the first 'presuppositions' of all our knowledge. Only then will it be in a position to give a *radical* account of

50. *Ibid.*, pp. 323–328.

our knowledge. We must return to the ἐιζώματα πάντων. "The science of the 'radical' must from every point of view be radical itself in all its procedures." [51] This radical attitude will bring us into contact with an 'ultimate self-justification' only when we forget all that we possess in convictions and all that we have learned before. We, thus, must try to reach the point of origin of all knowledge and Being. Although these ideals remind us greatly of Descartes' position, we, nevertheless, note a number of differences. We should, for example, not think about this point of origin of all knowledge and Being in terms of one single basic proposition such as the *cogito ergo sum,* but rather in terms of a whole source of experiences, as a field of immediately given data which because of their apodicticity can constitute the starting point of a radical philosophy.[52] It is precisely for this reason that we can apply the term 'phenomenology' to this view of philosophy because it chooses as its point of departure a field of original 'phenomena' which appear immediately to our consciousness. This field of original phenomena genuinely is a field of *original experiences* because the phenomena are *immediately* present to consciousness. Husserl, therefore, rejects the methods of induction and deduction or any other method of the natural sciences. He accepts for this purpose only an immediate and original way of seeing. For every *cogitatum,* of whatever class or order, there is a *cogitatio* to which we can point and in which we can perceive it originally as an 'it itself.' This original intuition is possible according to Husserl, only when the subject and the perceived object are immediately present to each other. The question is now: How do we get to "den Sachen selbst"? Husserl answers that it is there that precisely the task of phenomenological reduction lies.

We mentioned previously that Husserl never opposed empirical psychology as such; he only registered protest against certain trends in psychology which often go under the names of 'naturalistic' or 'objectivistic' psychologies. He understood these movements in psychology as exaggerated imitations of the nat-

51. *Ibid.,* p. 340.
52. *Ibid.,* p. 341; Edmund Husserl, *Krisis,* p. 176.

ural sciences which, thus, overlook the most fundamental characteristics of psychical phenomena.

Husserl was too closely associated with Brentano and Stumpf
not to fall victim here to exaggeration and over-generalization.
He would slowly come to realize that there is need for a phenomenological psychology that can bridge the gap between
philosophy and the best psychology of his time. Such a phenomenological psychology would need to be built after the
model of descriptive psychology as suggested by Brentano, although it would need to be worked out in a more consistent
fashion. After certain corrections of Brentano's thought this
psychology would further have to be enriched with a number of
the ideas of Dilthey.[53] As we have already seen, however, the
Husserl of 1911 was not yet ready for this.

To understand Husserl's attitude towards psychology we
must remember anew that psychology around 1910 consisted, for
the most part, in psychophysical and physiological investigations
which most predominantly acted in the service of the experimental and quantitative determination of the relationships between so-called objective stimuli and subjective reactions.

Brentano, James, and others brought a substantial amount of
rejuvenation to psychology for which they deserve our unre-
served praise. They were not able, however, to bring about
fundamental changes in the classical attitudes toward man. Husserl envisioned a new area of study which was not primarily
concerned with the psychical as a real part of a real organism,
but which, on the contrary, would concern itself with the psychical phenomena as they 'appear' immediately. This new study,
which, at first, was supposed to be of a philosophical nature,
would also provide a radical foundation for philosophy. Husserl points to Dilthey as the first to discover the radical mistakes
of naturalism and objectivism in the psychologies of his time.

Husserl's own criticism of this point appears for the first time
in his *Philosophie als strenge Wissenschaft*. Since this criticism
is of great importance for the rest of our considerations we
would do well to focus on it here.

53. H. Spiegelberg, *op. cit.*, vol. I, pp. 149–150.

In the first part of the *Logos*-article Husserl tried to show the necessity for a phenomenological philosophy. He described this new philosophical phenomenology as a transcendental science of pure consciousness which is distinct from psychology as the natural science of consciousness. He ultimately came to the conclusion that a close relationship exists between psychology and philosophical phenomenology insofar as both sciences are concerned with consciousness, even though there is great divergence in orientation between the two disciplines. Psychology should concern itself with empirical consciousness as it is found in nature, while phenomenology has as its task the study of pure consciousness or consciousness as seen from the perspective of phenomenology. Because of this close relationship between psychology and philosophy it becomes understandable that every psychological theory of knowledge can pretend to be a philosophical theory. Such confusion evidently leads to a position in which consciousness becomes reduced to a 'natural' phenomenon.[54]

We do not have to worry too much about the close relationship between psychology and philosophy, Husserl says, because the modern 'exact' psychology is utterly foreign to philosophy. Yet, this psychology is considered an ideal example of a 'scientific philosophy' because of its experimental methods. All this would not concern us except for the fact that it would be a serious mistake, indeed, to believe that this modern 'exact' psychology would be the only possible psychology. Let us not forget that the ground rule of this psychology sets aside all direct analysis and description of that which presents itself in an immediate intuition to consciousness. Instead it focuses on the indirect, psychologically relevant factors, although it will be clear that these factors acquire true comprehensibility only on the basis of a phenomenological analysis and description. Thus, psychology is turned into a discipline that furnishes *hypothetically* valid psychophysical facts and norms instead of trying to become a systematic science of consciousness which investigates the

54. Edmund Husserl, *Phil. str. W.*, pp. 319–322, 298–302.

psychical in an immanent way. But such a psychology cuts off all avenues toward a deeper understanding and toward definitive scientific verification.[55]

Contemporary 'exact' psychology is not conscious of any serious flaw in its methodology. It rejects each and every form of introspection and it looks to its experimental method itself to correct possible imperfections in its own experimental methods. For a psychology which aims at a radical analysis of its problems, a pure and systematic phenomenology is a prime requisite. For only such a phenomenology puts us into a position from which we can judge which research methods will be applicable. Only a phenomenological analysis can reveal the rich variety of fine distinctions between the different modalities of consciousness which remain hidden to the methodologically naïve experimenter. Present-day psychology remains unscientific, precisely because it considers itself to be methodologically perfect and scientifically pure. This presumption and this shortcoming shows itself time and again when an attempt is made to really penetrate a psychological problem.

Psychology is equally unscientific in all these instances where an insufficiently differentiated notion of the psychical leads to vague, to falsely clear, or to completely erroneous statements of a problem which, in turn, leads to pseudo-solutions. On the other hand, however, it is also clear that psychology cannot do without the experimental method, especially in cases where we must arrive at a determination of intersubjectively valid connections between facts. Yet, it remains true also, that the experimental method presupposes what no experiment by itself can achieve, namely, a careful analysis and description of consciousness itself.[56]

A few psychologists, such as Stumpf, Lipps, and others, recognized this flaw in experimental psychology and appreciated the renewal brought about by Brentano's thought. Acting accordingly they did their very best to continue to deepen the analytic and descriptive investigations of the intentional experi-

55. *Ibid.*, pp. 302–303.
56. *Ibid.*, pp. 303–304.

ences which Brentano had started. Their work, however, has not yet been recognized, let alone appreciated, by the dyed-in-the-wool experimentalists, Husserl claims. Time and again we hear the charge of scholasticism leveled at Brentano and his psychologist followers. The only basis for such a depreciating charge lies in the fact that these psychologists choose ordinary language concerning psychical phenomena as the point of departure for their analytic investigations. But how justified is such a charge of 'scholasticism' if applied to a phenomenologist who does not base his judgments on word-analyses, but who, instead, starts from a certain idiomatic expression and then bases these judgments on an analysis of the intuitively grasped phenomenon? [57]

A point of exceptional importance is the realization that when we take a psychological phenomenon in its full concreteness, that is in the way in which it should be apprehended in our phenomenological and psychological work, that this phenomenon acquires the quality of a more or less complex 'consciousness-of.' Now, as long as we fail in a careful, differentiated description of this consciousness-of in all its different modalities, and as long as we substitute for this task a number of vague and ambiguous expressions, we shall not even have started on the way toward a scientific psychology. A definitive scientific language necessarily presupposes a complete analysis of the phenomena with which it deals. As long as we fail to realize such an analysis, we will have psychological research that will continue to unearth ambiguities. A phenomenological analysis and description, therefore, is a primary requirement for the advance of psychology.[58]

During a time when scholastic philosophy was under heavy attack, we often heard the admonition to put away all empty word-analyses and to return to a questioning of the things themselves. We were to return to an investigation of experience itself which, in turn, would elucidate the meaning and justification of words. But what are we to understand by these 'facts' and what kind of 'experience' is it that we ask psychology

57. *Ibid.*, pp. 304–305.
58. *Ibid.*, p. 305.

to return to? Are these the answers that experimental subjects give in response to physchological tests? Is it the interpretation of these answers arrived at by a psychologist? The experimentalists place the original experience in the experimental subject and in the self-experience of the psychologist. Yet, they remain hostile to an expressly intended introspection since this would modify the conscious experience. It is contended that only the unintended experience of the self which takes place accidentally, as it were, could be of real significance. Without a doubt, there is something to be said for such a formulation. Contemporary experimental psychology makes a fundamental mistake, however, when it places its own analysis of psychological events on the same line with the analysis of experiences which form the basis of the physical sciences. For the analyses of psychology cannot be placed on the same line with physical analyses without destroying the specific character of consciousness and other psychological factors.[59]

The psychologist presupposes that his psychological knowledge is based on experience. He seeks to forge a basis for his empirical conclusions with the naïve, spontaneous memories of his past, strengthened by means of the methodical art of experimentation. In the description of these naive, empirical data, as well as, in the accompanying immanent analyses and their conceptual elaboration, a series of concepts is used whose scientific value determines the value of all the succeeding methodological steps. Yet, these important concepts never become the object of research within the field of psychology. These concepts appear as the ultimate result of the psychological investigation without ever having been themselves subjected to scientific investigation and verification. When we remain within the realm of experimental psychology, we will never arrive at truly scientific conclusions because each conclusion contains concepts which themselves lack scientific value. Even if we approach the problem logically we can see that no empirical approach can possibly yield such a value by itself. What is needed here is a phenomenological

59. *Ibid.,* pp. 305–306.

analysis of the essential characteristics of psychical phenomena. However disturbing this may sound to naturalistic psychologists, such a revealing of the essential characteristics cannot be done on the basis of empirical analyses.[60]

The basic mistake of empirical psychology since its inception in the 18th century has been the desire to model its methodology after the successful physical and chemical sciences. This desire was strengthened by the conviction that all empirical sciences should make use of the same methods since in their ultimate foundations they form really only one science. In much the same way as philosophy was led into blind alleys for several centuries after it took up Descartes' suggestion and tried to adopt methods which were developed by geometry and physics, so also has psychology been on the wrong track since Locke and Hume. A true method is not wedded to such *a priori* decisions but instead follows the nature of the things which it investigates.[61]

To illustrate this point further let us compare the realm of the psychical with that of the physical phenomena. A first preliminary investigation shows that we are dealing here with two entirely different domains. In contrast to the physical, the Being of the psychical, that is Being as a 'phenomenon' does not appear to be a unity which can be experienced as numerically identical in different and separate perceptions. In the realm of the psychical there is no distinction between Being and appearance. In the natural sciences the object of study is always a thing that manifests itself in and through its appearances. The appearances, however, which constitute the subject matter of psychology do not form a realm of Being which manifests itself by means of other appearances; a simple reflection makes this immediately clear. If we formulate it carefully we must say that all the phenomena which we call psychical are merely phenomena which as such do not belong to nature to which physics directs itself.

A phenomenon does not possess a substantial unity. It lacks 'real properties'; it does not undergo changes; it, therefore, be-

60. *Ibid.*, pp. 306–307.
61. *Ibid.*, pp. 308–310.

comes irrelevant here to speak of causality, at least in the sense in which it is used in physics. To ascribe a certain nature to a phenomenon, to inquire into its characteristic properties and its causal connections is simply nonsense. "It is the absurdity of naturalizing something whose essence excludes the kind of being that is characteristic of nature." [62] A thing is what it is and always remains what it is: nature is eternal. That is why the real qualities and characteristics of a natural thing can be studied by the physical sciences in a completely objective and repeatable way. A psychological phenomenon, however, comes and goes; it lacks a persistent and unchanging Being that, as such, could be objectively determined and analyzed in the way this is done in the natural sciences.[63]

Psychical phenomena cannot be approached with the type of experience which serves us to get acquainted with the things of the physical realm. A psychical phenomenon is not experienced as something that appears, but it is experienced in our reflection as that which passes by and sinks deeper and deeper into the past. Only in recall can it be re-experienced in modified form and then identified. A psychological experience also forms part of a more encompassing whole, the 'monadic' unity of consciousness that by itself is completely different from the physical nature in which things appear. To convince ourselves of this we need only think about such aspects as time and space, substantiality and causality. The whole, of which the phenomenon forms part, is a stream of phenomena unbounded on two sides, with a continuing line of intentionality which, at the same time, testifies to the all-penetrating unity, namely, that of the immanent time without beginning and without end, which cannot be registered by the clock of the physicist. In immanent 'seeing' in which we look after the stream of phenomena we move from phenomenon to phenomenon and never encounter anything but phenomena. Only when a synthesis is achieved between this immanent 'seeing' and the perception of transcendental things does there originate an intentional rela-

62. *Ibid.*, p. 312.
63. *Ibid.*, pp. 310–312.

tionship between the phenomenon and the experienced thing.

How can we make possible a reasonably justified scientific approach into this sphere? It seems obvious that such research must adapt itself completely to those experiences which manifest themselves precisely as experiences of the psychical. And the psychical is to be understood in the very manner in which it presents itself in these phenomena. But this means that our research will be meaningful only when "one admits no absurd naturalizing." [64] The history of psychology teaches that it is difficult to follow this advice, especially since it is quite hard to maintain the 'phenomenological attitude' without deviating.[65]

The immanent psychical is not nature; it cannot be determined as a substantial unity with real characteristics which can be verified by repeated experience, nor can it be taken out of the eternal stream of consciousness. How can we make such phenomena the subject of an inter-subjective science? Even though phenomena, as such, have no nature they still have an essence which can be grasped adequately by intuition. This last fundament of all psychological methodology must be correctly understood. "The spell of the naturalistic attitude, to which all of us at the very beginning are subject, and which makes us incapable of looking away from nature and, hence, of making the psychical an object of intuitive investigation from a pure rather than from a psychophysical point of view, has here blocked the road to a great science . . . , which is on the one hand the fundamental condition for a completely scientific psychology and on the other hand the field for a genuine epistemology." [66]

Husserl follows this with a short description of this new science. It becomes clear that he has a philosophical phenomenology in mind in the description of which he accentuates the possibility and function of ideation (*Wesensschauung*). He touches here only implicitly on the phenomenological reduction

64. *Ibid.,* p. 313.
65. *Ibid.,* pp. 312–314.
66. *Ibid.,* p. 315.

and the intentional analysis.[67] In a note [68] he promises to publish soon a more complete work devoted to phenomenological philosophy. Doubtlessly he refers here to the publication of his *Ideen* the first volume of which appeared in 1913.

It is quite clear that Husserl at this time does not yet expressly distinguish between phenomenological psychology and phenomenological philosophy.[69] Doubtlessly, he refers in the above mentioned passage to a philosophical phenomenology. This shows not only in the note [70] but becomes clear when we consider the whole context of the article. Although the distinction between the two disciplines mentioned above seemed not to have matured at this time, we could consider another note [71] and deduce from it that the phenomenological philosophy which is being defined here needs to be distinguished from the descriptive psychology which is described in the second volume of the *Logische Untersuchungen*. If we maintain this descriptive psychology as phenomenology side by side with the philosophical phenomenology, then we can consider it as the first indication of a phenomenological psychology. However, this view does not seem entirely satisfactory because the subject matter of psychology comes up at length, and it would seem only logical that Husserl would bring up such a distinction if he had realized its importance.[72]

Be this as it may, Husserl continues his *Logos*-article by pointing out that psychological knowledge ultimately must rest on an insight into the very essence of the psychical and that the essence of the psychical cannot be revealed by means of the physical or experimental methods. From this we are forced to conclude that only phenomenological analyses can lead empirical psychology out of its sterile entanglement with naturalism and objectivism. The fact that contemporary, empirical psychol-

67. *Ibid.*, pp. 315–319.
68. *Ibid.*, p. 319, note 1.
69. *Ibid.*, pp. 314–319.
70. *Ibid.*, p. 318, note 1.
71. *Ibid.*, pp. 319–322.
72. *Ibid.*, p. 321.

ogy has failed to develop a phenomenological method adapted
to its needs must be considered a fundamental error of that
discipline. For, as a consequence empirical psychology failed to
become a truly scientific discipline. Only an empirical psychology based on the solid foundation of such a phenomenology
and also using its own experimental procedures can give rise to
truly scientific observations. This reasoning points to the de-
sirability of having future generations of psychologists take up
closer contact with the philosophy which is being built on the
same phenomenological foundations.[73]

Phenomenological Psychology as It Appears in the 'Ideen'

AFTER 1907 Husserl was in the habit of drawing frequent paral-
lels and contrasts between psychology and phenomenological
philosophy. Before 1913 the psychology which he used to contrast
and clarify his philosophy was almost always empirical psychology. After 1913 he used phenomenological psychology for
this purpose because he had by then achieved a distinction
between the classical experimental psychology and an eidetic
psychology. Eidetic psychology was to provide a foundation on
which a true experimental psychology could be based; it would
also bridge the gap between experimental psychology and philosophy. In the *Ideen* Husserl mentions such an eidetic psychology; sometimes, he also uses the terms *rational psychology*
or *phenomenological psychology* to indicate this new eidetic
psychology. In the *Logos*-article the point of view toward
phenomenological psychology was still somewhat ill-defined and
unclear, but we see his point of view clearly and extensively
discussed in *Ideen* (1913). Already in the *Introduction* Husserl
complains that his treatment of psychology in the *Logos*-article
had given rise to misunderstanding and confusion. Many psychologists seemed to have felt indignant, others did not grasp

73. *Ibid.,* p. 321 and pp. 319–322.

that an essential distinction exists between eidetic psychology and phenomenological philosophy. He states in his *Ideen,* "that the pure phenomenology . . . , the same which emerged for the first time in 'Logische Untersuchungen,' and has revealed an ever richer and deeper meaning to me in my work during the last ten years, is not psychology . . ." [74] Psychology is a science of experience, it is a science of facts or of matters of fact in Hume's sense. It is also a science of realities. The phenomena of which we speak in psychological 'phenomenology' are real occurrences which, together with the real subjects to which they belong, take their place in the spatio-temporal world as the *omnitudo realitatis.* In contrast to this, pure transcendental phenomenology is not a science of facts but a science of essences, an eidetic science. We must further characterize the phenomena of transcendental phenomenology as irreal phenomena. Eidetic reduction brings us out of the realm of the factual into the domain of pure essences. A transcendental reduction, therefore, becomes necessary to cut the phenomena loose from the real, spatio-temporal world. Philosophical phenomenology is not a study of the essence of real phenomena but of transcendentally reduced phenomena.[75]

When we consider this description of transcendental phenomenology more carefully, it will become clear that (in the event Husserl already accepted a phenomenological psychology distinct from transcendental phenomenology and empirical psychology) the characteristic of phenomenological psychology is that it, unlike empirical psychology, employs an *eidetic* reduction, whereas it, unlike transcendental phenomenology, does not use a transcendental reduction. That this, indeed, is Husserl's intention becomes manifest in the following passages in which he discusses the general structures of consciousness. These structures can be studied by psychology, as well as by means of phenomenological philosophy. Consciousness, as it is given in

74. Edmund Husserl, *Ideen zu einer reinen Phänomenologie und phänomenologischen Philosophie,* 3 vol., Den Haag, 1950–1952, vol. I: *Allgemeine Einführung in die reine Phänomenologie,* p. 4.
75. *Ibid.,* p. 6.

psychological experience that is, as human and animal consciousness, is the proper subject-matter for psychology; "empirical psychology studies consciousness with empirical, and eidetic
psychology with eidetic methods." On the other hand, however,
the whole world just as correlate of transcendental consciousness
falls in modified form also within the realm of transcendental
phenomenology; and so, too, do the psychic individuals and
their psychic experiences. In other words, within phenomenology
itself, consciousness appears under different forms of apprehen-
sion and in different connections in different ways; first as absolute consciousness in transcendental phenomenology and, then,
as psychological consciousness in eidetic psychology. That is why
every transcendental phenomenological consideration of absolute consciousness can be re-interpreted in terms of eidetic
psychology which, strictly speaking, is itself not phenomenological at all, if we understand the term 'phenomenology' to refer
to a transcendental discipline. Be this as it may, one of the most
important tasks in this context consists in an adequate explanation of the essential relations between pure or transcendental
phenomenology, eidetic psychology, and empirical psychology.[76]

In his book *Ideen* Husserl, then, is of the opinion that eidetic
psychology must occupy a position midway between classical
empirical psychology and transcendental phenomenology. The
difference between eidetic and empirical psychology lies in the
use of the eidetic reduction; eidetic psychology and transcendental phenomenology differ in that only phenomenology makes
use of the transcendental-phenomenological reduction. Husserl
makes, in this book, occasional use of eidetic-psychological
descriptions. When he does this he always makes clear that he
is about to start on a number of expositions in which the
transcendental-phenomenological reduction does not matter.
"We start with a series of explanations within which we do not
have to concern ourselves with any phenomenological *epoché*.
We are oriented toward the 'real' world and, without giving
up our natural attitude, we reflect psychologically on our ego

76. *Ibid.*, pp. 175–176.

and its experiences. We indulge, precisely as if we had never heard of the transcendental attitude, in the very essence of 'consciousness of something,' in which we, for instance, are conscious of material things . . ." [77] In this study we must maintain the general principle that each individual occurrence has its own essence "that can be grasped in its eidetic purity, and in this purity must belong to a field of possible eidetic inquiry." The result of the research acquires transcendental-philosophical meaning only when it is reinterpreted from an entirely new point of view. This point of view is the result of the transcendental reduction.[78]

From this it will be clear that eidetic psychology is an *eidetic* science concerned with the essence of consciousness. It is based on an original *intuition,* but moves completely within the realm of the natural attitude. A comparison between this eidetic psychology of the *Ideen* and the phenomenological psychology of which Husserl speaks in his later works reveals to us that both doubtlessly refer to the same discipline. It is curious that in the *Ideen* Husserl does not yet mention a psychologico-phenomenological reduction as distinguished from a transcendental reduction. Such a reduction is essential for the definition of phenomenological psychology as we shall see.[79] We will return to this matter in more detail.

We mentioned that in the *Introduction* to the *Ideen* Husserl complains about the fact that his explanation of psychology in *Philosophie als strenge Wissenschaft* had given rise to such widespread misunderstanding. Many of his readers seemed not to have understood that in that article Husserl accepted an essential difference between eidetic psychology and transcendental phenomenology. From the above, however, it will be clear that Husserl's self-pity does not have much ground. True, one cannot deny that one will come upon the distinction between transcendental phenomenology and eidetic psychology, if one reads the *Logos*-article from the viewpoint explained in *Ideen*. How-

77. *Ibid.,* p. 74 and pp. 118–119.
78. *Ibid.,* p. 74.
79. However, see also: *Ibid.,* pp. 221–222.

ever, if one interprets *Philosophie als strenge Wissenschaft* from
the first edition of *Logische Untersuchungen* it becomes immediately clear why most of the readers did not notice this distinction. Be this as it may, these reflections may suffice to explain
and motivate our 'ambiguous' interpretation of the *Logos*-article
as given above.

Husserl's Later Vision of his Own Develop-
ment Between the Years 1887 and 1913

As WE NOTED, Husserl came into contact with empirical psychology around the year 1876 in Leipzig. Only later did he
become acquainted with philosophy. Influenced by his professors and especially by the works he studied, Husserl soon became
entangled in psychologism. We find clear traces of this fact in
his first work, *Philosophie der Arithmetik* (1891). After 1893 it
became clear to Husserl that psychologism is completely unacceptable. In his *Logische Untersuchungen* (1900–1901) he subjected this particular form of positivism to a rigorous but
objective criticism. He showed clearly that psychology cannot
possibly furnish a radical explanation of the foundations of logic
and mathematics. This clearly is the task of philosophy which
is to be distinguished from psychology. On the other hand, it
cannot be denied that such a radical explanation cannot take
place without study of the subjective acts that make possible
our awareness of the objects with which these sciences deal.
Combining these two ideas he came to the conclusion that a
philosophical phenomenology, viewed as a completely new
descriptive psychology, could provide the radical basis and explanation for these sciences.

Then around 1903 [80] Husserl started to reject this position, at
least to the extent that he felt that his *Logische Untersuchungen*
failed to clearly express his ideas. After reading the works of
Descartes and Kant, Husserl came to the conclusion in 1906 that

80. See: *Arch. f. syst. Philos.*, 9 (1903) 397–400.

a completely new philosophical science would have to be developed to furnish the radical solutions to epistemological
problems. This science would have to be completely and essentially different from psychology. These thoughts were first expressed in *Die Idee der Phänomenologie* (1907). The insights
seen in the writing of this work were taken up again and published in the *Logos*-article (1911). We find here a first, although
still hesitant, description of the genuine meaning of the eidetic
descriptive psychology of the *Logische Untersuchungen*.

Husserl himself has commented repeatedly on the confusion
occasioned by his continually changing points of view. That he
did change his views has already become clear in the preceding
pages. To convince ourselves further, all we have to do is to
compare the introductions to the second edition of the *Logische
Untersuchungen* (1913) and the first edition of the same work.
The most interesting and also the most complete description of
Husserl's own development between 1887 and 1913 is found in
his *Phänomenologische Psychologie* (1925).[81]

The introduction to this work gives an account of Dilthey's
influence on modern psychology and on the humanistic sciences
in general. Husserl praised Dilthey for his many insightful contributions but he also objected to many of his conclusions.

Then Husserl continues by noting that around 1900 the appearance of his own *Logische Untersuchungen* brought about a
drastic change in the philosophical situation which was created
by Dilthey. The second volume was of special significance in this
respect since it is in this work that Husserl tries to explain the
bestowal of meaning which comes about in the context of the
experiences which are characteristic of our logical thinking.[82]
There is question here of a special reflection of our intuition
upon the logical experiences which come about during the
thinking-process, but which nevertheless are not consciously experienced. Husserl now wanted to show how in the achievements of the inner logical experiences the constitution of all

81. E. Husserl, *Phil. str. W.*, p. 318, note 1; *Phän Psych.*, pp. 20–46 and 348,
note 1.
82. Edmund Husserl, *Phän. Psych.*, p. 20.

logical entities is enacted, entities which manifest themselves in our predicative thinking as concepts, judgments, conclusions, etc, and receive their universally and intersubjectively valid character from the fundamental concepts and laws of formal logic.

In the first volume of the *Logische Untersuchungen* Husserl had already explained how these 'meaning structures' can be purely grasped in a special intuition and why the explanations which in this regard are given by empiricism and psychologism, are completely inadequate. Against psychologism in particular Husserl brought to the fore 1) that objects such as concepts, statements, conclusions, truths and proofs are 'irreal' entities which because of their ideal identity nevertheless possess objectivity. In other words, in Husserl's view these objects are 'unities of meaning' in whose meaning-content one does not meet with any psychical act or subjective experience; for these are precisely *real* entities. Husserl pointed out 2) that there correspond to the named ideal objects certain ideal truths which do not refer to the world as the realm of the real entities.

From these considerations Husserl drew the conclusion that there must exist 'irreal' objects with their corresponding "irreal' truths with an ideal extension, which make that these 'irreal' entities can have bearing on ideal and also on possibly real things, the factual existence of which thus is not necessarily presupposed or pre-understood. There must, therefore, also exist sciences of irreal entities, aprioric sciences the idea of which theoretically governs a certain domain of ideal objects.[83]

The most important theme of the *Logische Untersuchungen,* however, consists in the descriptive investigations concerning the psychological experiences which are inseparably connected with the ideal objects of logic and mathematics. These ideal objects not only have bearing on ideal or possibly real individuals but also on possible psychological acts of each subject. We again arrive at the central problem posed by psychologism.

A closer consideration of the ideal objects of logic and mathematics reveals them as having their own characteristic being-for-

83. *Ibid.,* pp. 21–24.

itself and being-in-itself to which their pure truths refer in an *a priori* way, and which makes them be what they are, regardless of their being counted or thought of. On the other hand, we must realize that these objects arise only out of our subjective psychical activities and experiences. How can we explain this strange correlation between these ideal objects of pure logic and the subjective psychic experiences which allegedly constitute them? And what are we to think of these hidden psychical experiences which correlate with the ideal objects and must come about as special corresponding achievements if the subject is to get an evident knowledge of these idealities as its objects.

These questions form the main theme of the second volume of the *Logische Untersuchungen* as well as the main themes of phenomenology in general. The *mathesis universalis* (logic and mathematics) is concerned with mathematical idealities taken in themselves and also with their mutual ideal relationships. The second volume of the *Logische Untersuchungen* directed the theoretical interest toward the manifold achievements of the subject by means of which the mathematical is brought out *by* and therefore *in* the mathematician. It, thus, provides a theory concerning logico-mathematical knowing acts as they relate to the logico-mathematically known objects.[84]

It now becomes understandable how such research would acquire the title of descriptive psychology. The intent of this discipline was to shed a reflexive intuition into those thought-experiences of the thinking person which up to then had remained hidden, and to work out an eidetic description of these experiences. There was also a question of 'phenomenology' during this period; the term there pointed to the attempt to work radically and consistently back from the relevant categories of objects to the corresponding modes of consciousness in which these objects become conscious. It soon became apparent that a similar research was also needed for other than mathematical categories. Husserl felt that all the objects of our thought, including the real objects, should be similarly investigated.[85]

84. *Ibid.*, pp. 26–27.
85. *Ibid.*, pp. 24–28.

At the beginning, it was not quite clear yet how to accomplish this questioning from the objects back to the subjective experiences in which they emerge as conscious. It was clear from the beginning that the hypothetical constructs of the naturalistic psychology could be of no help. What was needed was a pure intuition followed by an accurate analysis and description which would reveal faithfully the intentional relationship of the act and its corresponding object. This problem had been posed previously by many philosophers but it never had been formulated correctly. It is especially noteworthy that these analyses revealed a number of dimensions of the problem which never had been seen before.[86]

The need for a thorough analysis and description of psychical experiences on the basis of an immediate intuition had been felt for a long time by logicians and scholars in the field of ethics and aesthetics. Brentano contributed greatly to this particular area. Of special importance in this connection is Brentano's emphasis on intentionality as the basic characteristic of all psychological experiences. The phenomena of knowledge had been explained by experimental psychology and physiology in terms of cause and effect. These explanations may not be devoid of use in themselves, but it is important to note that they bypassed the most fundamental fact in this area, namely, that each and every act of knowledge and each and every conscious act possess the aspect of being consciousness-of, regardless of the fact that the object of consciousness exists as a real object capable of influencing the subject. Scholasticism recognized the difference between a true and real object that exists in itself, and a purely intentional object precisely taken as that which is experienced as such. Brentano's merit is not so much that he rediscovered intentionality, but rather that he recognized that this thought should form the basis of psychology.

Descriptively speaking, we see intentionality as the basic characteristic of the realm of the psychical: it is with this in mind that we must approach psychological phenomena. Inten-

86. *Ibid.,* pp. 28–30.

tional analysis is a procedure to make this approach feasible. Dilthey arrived, independently of Brentano, at the conclusion that a purely descriptive analysis should replace causal explanations as far as the humanistic sciences were concerned. Yet, Husserl concludes, these thoughts remained mere trial-balloons.

The *Logische Untersuchungen* tries to materialize these ideas carefully and consistently although it does not succeed in an essential transformation of Brentano's and Dilthey's initial idea of a pure descriptive psychology. Brentano failed to see the true significance of the *Logische Untersuchungen*. Dilthey recognized the importance of Husserl's view, but Husserl did not originally know about Dilthey's approval since he had decided not to read Dilthey after reading Ebbinghaus' criticism of Dilthey's work. Later when Husserl started reading Dilthey's work he came to the conclusion that Dilthey doubtlessly prepared the way for phenomenology.[87]

It is unnecessary to give a detailed account of the methodological significance of the *Logische Untersuchungen*. A few remarks will suffice. Brentano had originally restricted himself to an external and merely classifying, descriptive consideration of intentional experiences. He did not, as yet, realize the great task of going from the different classes of objects back to the manifold modes of consciousness in and through which we become conscious of these objects. From that position we can turn back further and inquire into the teleological function of the conscious modalities in regard to the synthetic, verificational achievements of reason. All this is only partially realized in the *Logische Untersuchungen,* but the book shows that consciousness is not something which merely becomes conscious of its objects in a passive way, but an achievement which comes about in many different forms of syntheses and is everywhere intentionally and teleologically oriented toward the ideas of truth.

This new perspective on intentionality also makes possible a new view on empirical psychology. The old psychology was a naturalistic, causal, explanatory, elemental psychology. It now

87. *Ibid.,* pp. 30–35; W. Biemel, in Edmund Husserl, *Phän. Psych. Einleitung,* p. *xvi.*

became clear that consciousness is different from an external combination of 'natural' elements. Instead of a spatial interrelatedness we must pose here an intentional and motivational involvement. But even Brentano was still a protagonist of naturalistic psychology; he did not yet envision the possibility of an intentional analysis.[88]

However, in these considerations the essential aspects of this new psychologico-phenomenological method is still not yet mentioned. The form in which this method was presented in the *Logische Untersuchungen* made it clear that there is a great difference between the methods of phenomenology and empirical psychology. For more than 2000 years psychology had tried to become a science of experience. But when we turn from the ideal objects to the consciousness that gives rise to them, it becomes clear that the inner activities and passivities in which these objects come to light cannot be of an empirical and accidental nature. The experiences out of which the objects arise as conscious entities must possess their own essential and always identical structures. There is, thus, an *a priori* in psychology which corresponds to the *a priori* of pure logic. Something analogous to this is true for the objects of all categories.

Out of all this a completely new concept arose regarding the nature of psychology. This new psychology wants to study an entirely new theme, namely intentionality. More importantly, however, this psychology strives to become a non-empirical, *a priori* science. Instead of speaking about factual human subjects living in this world, phenomenological psychology deals with the ideal essence of a knowing subjectivity as such. Taking its starting point in a concrete case as an example this science tries to bring to light phenomenologically its essential characteristics and, then, its ideal possibilities in unconditioned universality. Neither Lotze nor Brentano had envisioned such a science.[89]

Already in the 17th and 18th century we see attempts to find an aprioric psychology. Kant's criticism brought these attempts

88. *Ibid.,* pp. 35–37.
89. *Ibid.,* pp. 37–39.

to an end. The psychologies of Leibniz and Wolff are ontological-metaphysical disciplines and although they are not purely intuitive and descriptive, they certainly are aprioric; the sensible, concrete facts are distilled until they yield intuitively grasped necessities and generalities. These psychologies failed because an aprioric, eidetic-intuitive psychology became possible only after the true meaning and the nature of the intentional analysis had been more fully understood.[90]

The second volume of the *Logische Untersuchungen* was not primarily concerned with a new psychology. This book concentrated on epistemological problems related to logic and mathematics. The problems arising out of these epistemological questions could not be solved without the help of an entirely new psychology. What was needed was a purely aprioric and yet descriptive science capable of showing how psychic life, especially in its knowing aspects, realized intentional activities. This investigation had to be of a special character because in it one had to explain how our cognitive life in itself and in virtue of its aprioric essence realizes achievements which can lay claim on ideal validity and thus, on truth.[91]

We notice here a curious shift in the historical relationship between psychology and the theory of knowledge. On the one hand, we have seen the century-long development of an empirical psychology which was thought to encompass epistemology, or at least was expected to provide the essential foundation for a theory of knowledge (Locke and Hume). Kant thought that it was the task of philosophy to build a transcendental theory of knowledge without any help from psychology. But when Kant speaks of psychology he refers to the psychophysical psychology of his time; he did not foresee the possibility of an aprioric psychology. Phenomenology puts the problem in an entirely different light and tries to solve it in a different way. Brentano and Dilthey saw already that epistemology must ultimately be rooted in an intuitive analysis of the act of knowing; but, they

90. *Ibid.,* p. 39.
91. *Ibid.,* pp. 39–41.

still lacked the tool for such an analysis, so that even they were not yet able to materialize a genuinely aprioric, intuitive, and descriptive psychology.[92]

Later, it became clear that in addition to this new psychology there was room and need for a transcendental phenomenology. For, the aprioric psychology which arose within the limited sphere of the *mathesis universalis* was not able to give a *radical* explanation of the foundational problems.[93] In this way it became manifest that even an aprioric psychology is not capable by itself of positing and answering all epistemological problems in a fundamental way. Only in the first volume of the *Ideen* do we find for the first time a methodically developed foundation for a universal science of transcendental subjectivity (which, thus, is to be distinguished from a psychological subjectivity).[94] This foundation is to be developed with the help of the phenomenological method based on a transcendental reduction, i.e., a pure description which remains within the transcendental sphere and which issues from a pure intuition of essences and intentional analyses.[95]

The distinction between aprioric psychology and transcendental phenomenology, which had been stressed by Husserl since 1913, nevertheless, failed to be understood and appreciated except by a very few philosophers. The fact that both disciplines make use of the phenomenological method and that a mere change in attitude brings us from one discipline into the realm of the other, induced many philosophers to think about the two disciplines as really one.[96]

On the basis of this short historical account we can characterize this new psychology, about which we spoke, as an aprioric, eidetic, intuitive or purely descriptive and intentional discipline which remains, moreover, entirely within the realm of the natural attitude. The expression 'aprioric' refers to the fact that

92. *Ibid.*, pp. 41–42.
93. *Ibid.*, pp. 42–43.
94. *Ibid.*, p. 44.
95. *Ibid.*, pp. 42–44.
96. *Ibid.*, pp. 45–46.

this psychology is focussed primarily on that, without which, the psychical as such cannot be thought. Only in the second place does it strive to understand psychological facticity, to formulate theories, and to find explanations, although scientists normally are primarily interested in these latter aspects.

Intuition and *description* point to the source of the *a priori*. The inner intuition reveals insights which by means of analyses that themselves again are guided by intuition, are transformed into general necessities of the intuited essences.

This method reveals that *intentionality* is the most general and fundamental characteristic of the realm of the psychical. Psychic life is conscious life and consciousness is essentially intentional. We must consider the double polarity involved in every psychic phenomenon which can be expressed as *ego-cogito-cogitata*. Consciousness not only implies an object, it also implies an ego, the person. Psychological investigations, thus, acquire a typical two-fold, teleological orientation. Out of this arises the necessity to investigate descriptively in two directions the systematically interwoven multiplicities of conscious acts which essentially belong to the conscious revelation of different realms of objects. In the transcendental attitude these investigations necessarily become foundational studies which, as such, lead to a radically founded philosophy. A psychologist does not want to remain within the philosophical attitude; he wants to remain in the realm of the *natural and dogmatic attitude*. Yet, this psychology can form a point of departure that ultimately will lead to philosophy although it can never assume the character of a necessary and founding science. Sciences of the natural and dogmatic attitude are sciences of the world and, therefore, are sciences which presuppose the world. The eidetic sciences remain also sciences of the world insofar as they, too, still seek knowledge of the world.

The pure science of the essence of the psychical life of man and community is essentially a science of the world. However, in the domain of the factical it seeks the apodictically necessary structures and laws of the psychical. It is only by means of, and together with such an eidetic science that any empirical science can become a rigorously scientific discipline. Besides the eidetic psychology an empirical psychology must thus be maintained which will concern itself with the determination of the factual as such. The *a priori* only provides a formal framework within which empirical facts, insofar as they are at least comprehensible, can find a place. How eidetic psychology will go about leading empirical psychology is a problem in and by itself. Here we must focus attention first on the fundamental principles of eidetic psychology, a task which constitutes the main theme of these investigations.

Husserl sometimes compares the function of eidetic psychology in regard to empirical psychology with the function which mathematics fulfils in regard to physics. However, it is nowhere his intention to reduce eidetic psychology to a 'mathematics of the spirit.' Each domain of investigation has its own *a priori;* and the *a priori* of the 'spirit' is radically distinguished from the *a priori* of nature as will become clear later. This is why eidetic psychology is totally different from mathematics even though it, from a purely formal point of view, shows a certain superficial resemblance to it.[97]

If we reflect upon what Husserl has written here about his own development between the years 1887 and 1913, we cannot fail to notice that he has given a *benigna interpretatio* of the relevant facts. Yet, we cannot call this interpretation essentially incorrect when we focus exclusively upon what Husserl intended to say in the first place in the *Logische Untersuchungen.* Another fact we note is the generous interpretation of Brentano's work which becomes especially impressive when we compare it to the total neglect of Wundt and Stumpf who, nevertheless, must have exerted quite some influence on their student Husserl, too. Finally we must mention the fact that Husserl unjustifiably characterizes all psychology between 400 B.C. and 1600 A.D. as inadequate forms of empirical psychology. This clarifies some-

97. *Ibid.,* pp. 46–51.

what the fact that he claims that Leibniz and Wolff were the founders of an 'ontological' psychology.[98] There are other aspects which should be mentioned in this context but we shall return to those in one of the later chapters.

98. *Ibid.*, p. 39.

III EPISTEMOLOGICAL CONSIDERATIONS. PHENOMENOLOGICAL PSYCHOLOGY AS 'REGIONAL ONTOLOGY.'

Dilthey's Importance for Psychology

The relationship between psychology and phenomenology was one of primary importance and of lasting interest to Husserl. The idea occupied him as early as 1887 when he was preparing his *Philosophie der Arithmetik* and we still find it in his last book *Krisis*. The previous chapter presented the main lines in Husserl's development between the years 1887–1913. We are now concerned with the insights to which Husserl came in this regard in his phenomenological investigations of 1925. It was during this year that Husserl presented a course on phenomenological psychology at the University of Freiburg. During the academic year 1926–1927 he gave a new series of lectures entitled *Die Frage der Möglichkeit einer intentionalen Psychologie,* followed in 1928 by a lecture-series called *Intentionale Psychologie.*

Since the content of the lectures was not substantially modified in the following two years, this chapter will deal mainly with the insights contained in the lecture series of 1925. This course was published as the main text by Walter Biemel in 1962 under the title *Phänomenologische Psychologie* together with a great number of other papers, lectures and manuscripts dealing with the same subject. In the pages to follow we shall refer to these other texts only when it seems to be of help in understanding the original lectures.[1]

Be this as it may, in this lecture-series Husserl is concerned first and foremost with the question concerning the relationship between phenomenology and psychology. More precisely expressed, the question concerns the description and definition of a psychology which is fully rooted in phenomenology. How far does such a psychology extend? What distinguishes a psychology rooted in phenomenology from the naturalistic psychologies? Husserl is convinced that psychology should be developed with the help of phenomenology. What new perspective would be opened up by such a psychology? What is the extent of the task assigned to phenomenology in respect to psychology? Husserl had already touched on these problems in *Ideen II* and they occupied much of his attention in his last work *Krisis*. Also in regard to the main goal intended, the lectures with which we propose to deal in this chapter remain within the perspective of *Ideen II* and *Krisis* inasfar as they, too, finally return to the question of what phenomenology precisely is. How can phenomenology be realized? Where and how does it find its radical foundation? What are its possibilities; what are its limitations? [2]
In preparing his answers to these questions Husserl uses psychology only as a point of departure.

In *Phänomenologische Psychologie* Husserl starts by defining his position in regard to Dilthey. Even though he failed to read Dilthey at first he, nevertheless, defends him as a great renewer in psychology. His objection to Dilthey concerns the fact that the latter tried to solve the fundamental problems of the humanistic sciences from a position that failed to reach the level of the truly transcendental. Husserl had mentioned Dilthey's *Weltanschauungs*-philosophy in his *Logos* article and hereupon an interesting correspondence had developed between Husserl and

1. W. Biemel, in Edmund Husserl, *Phänomenologische Psychologie: Einleitung des Herausgebers*, pp. *xiv–xv*.
2. *Ibid.*, pp. *xiii–xiv*.

Dilthey. The problems discussed there, however, are outside the scope of this chapter.[3] The lecture-series with which we are to deal mentions Dilthey only in connection with his importance to psychology.

Husserl starts the series with an historical introduction in which he mentions that psychology has a long history reaching back to Plato, the founder, and Aristotle, the systematic elaborator. We notice again how Husserl fails to point to the fact that this Greek psychology was a philosophical psychology, both in the way it was intended and in the way it was realized. Husserl felt that this early Greek vision of psychology persisted up to the 17th century. In that century Kepler, Galileo, Descartes and Newton laid the basis for the natural sciences. The success of these sciences, especially physics, was so great that many investigators tried to remake psychology in the image of physics. Immediately an impassioned endeavor was made to carry an analogous methodical reform through in psychology, too, and to renew it as a science which explains its statements in an exact way by taking its starting point in elementary laws.[4] Originally this attempt remained fruitless. Descartes' attempt to found a psychology on the basis of his dualistic view on man remained without success. The same can be said for the materialism of Hobbes, the monism of Spinoza, or even for the empirical psychology of Locke and Hume both of which started from a new 'internal experience.' These new psychologies began to faintly resemble the natural sciences only in the 19th century.[5]

In Husserl's view the reason for the initial failure to shape psychology after the image of physics must be sought in naturalism. Psychology tried to *imitate* physics while at the same time being concerned with phenomena of consciousness. It is true that the research of J. v. Müller, Weber, Volkmann, Helmholz, Hering, Fechner, and Wundt led to a naturalistic empirical psychology which achieved impressive results in its collaboration with physiology. But it is quite another question whether their

3. *Ibid.*, pp. *xvi-xxi.*
4. Edmund Husserl, *Phän. Psych.*, p. 3.
5. *Ibid.*, pp. 3–4.

psychology can be truly distinguished from psychophysics and physiology. That is why, despite the apparent success of this psychology, we find in the literature of around 1900 a great deal of criticism directed toward it. Dilthey and Husserl originated an important part of the criticism. Central in most criticism is the thought that the physical methods are incapable of revealing the specifically psychical aspect of man.[6]

In 1894 Dilthey's *Ideen über eine beschreibende und zergliedernde Psychologie*[7] appeared and proved immediately to be a work of prime importance within this context. Husserl first gives a description of the nature and the meaning of Dilthey's work as a whole and then tries to apply this to psychology.[8] Husserl maintains that Dilthey was one of the first to realize clearly that psychology was in danger of orienting itself in too drastic a way toward the physical sciences. Instead of a 'constructive' psychology which is oriented toward a causal explanation of our psychic life, he proposed a descriptive and analytic psychology. He saw the empirical psychology of his day as trying to materialize the ideal of the exact sciences, and in particular that of atomic physics. Progress in such a science proceeds by means of hypotheses and with the help of artificial constructs and leads to conclusions which transcend experience. In Dilthey's view such a procedure is completely inadequate for the study of the very essence of our psychic life because it implies a completely unacceptable extrapolation of physical concepts to the realm of the soul and the domain of history.[9] The methods briefly indicated above make sense for the natural sciences; they are even necessary there since these sciences are based on our external experience of the spatially extended things which, indeed, are to be causally explained. Dilthey saw that psychology must start with an internal experience of the interconnected unity of our conscious life; there is no question of elements or atoms here.

6. *Ibid.*, pp. 4–6.
7. *Sitz. Ber. d. Berl. Akad.*, 1894; also in W. Dilthey, *Gesammelte Schriften*, Berlin-Leipzig, 1913–1924, vol. 5.
8. Edmund Husserl, *op. cit.*, pp. 6–7.
9. *Ibid.*, pp. 7–8. See also: W. Dilthey, *Gesammelte Schriften*, vol. 5, p. 195.

The psychological realm has its own characteristics which differ from those of the physical realm and which must be studied within the framework of a *'verstehende'* or comprehending method. The concept of physical causality has no place in such a new method since 'the causality in the realm of the spirit' turns out to be a 'causality of motivation.' [10] Psychology needs above all a scientific analysis founded in a purely intuitive basis together with an equally scientific conceptualization and systematic description.[11]

Dilthey's great contribution lies in the fact that he clearly saw that there is a fundamental difference between a scientific description which takes its starting point in external experience and a scientific description which is grounded in the internal experience of purely spiritual entities. Especially must the unity of our psychical life be carefully brought to light and for this we definitely need an intuitive, creative, descriptive psychology. Despite the fact that it would restrict itself to pure description, such a science would nevertheless be able, ultimately, to provide an understanding of the realm of the psychical.[12]

Dilthey's notions fell largely on deaf ears. Most psychologists of his day failed to grasp the importance of his ideas. As we saw before, Dilthey's most fundamental idea concerned the radical discontinuity between the physical and the humanistic sciences. He was successful in applying this fundamental insight to the realm of the historical sciences; he was less of a success with psychology. His conception of naturalistic psychology was not entirely radical although he came to some fundamental observations. When he came to a positive defining of whay psychology should be like, he was less than convincing, partly because he did not state his case with sufficient illustrative material. In addition there are still more basic objections to his conception of psychology. He saw that psychology ultimately must arrive at laws which will transcend the analysis and description of individual cases. Yet, he did not see in a clear way that a universal description of essences which is founded in an immediate intui-

10. *Ibid.*, pp. 8–9.
11. *Ibid.*, pp. 9–10.
12. *Ibid.*, pp. 10–11.

tion of essences is possible, and that the laws of which Dilthey speaks can be based only upon such an intuition. He did not note either that intentionality constitutes the very essence of our psychic life and that, therefore, intentionality forms the proper and endless theme of psychology's methodical analyses, provided these analyses evidently are understood as the analyses of the essences of the intentional relations.[13]

Dilthey's method is adequate for the description and comprehension of that which is concrete and individual; it fails to understand the universal and the essential in that which is individual and concrete. He sees only natural historical generalities and natural historical typologies, that is, only *empirical* generalities. The area of essential typologies, of universal essences, and essential laws remained closed to him. Finally we note that Dilthey wanted to make comprehensive psychology the basis for epistemology. Husserl could be at peace with that idea only to the degree that this *verstehende* psychology would be understood as a phenomenological psychology, itself to be founded in phenomenological philosophy. Dilthey's conception of psychology suffers from a lack of precision; it never becomes quite clear what we are to understand by empirical psychology nor what is the object of its study. It is equally difficult to get a clear idea of which methods are to be used in psychology and what it is that provides the ultimate basis for its theories. It is precisely to these questions that phenomenological psychology directs itself.[14]

The Necessity of a Reduction Which Leads From the Scientific World to the World of Original Experience

THE FIRST, and in many aspects also the foremost problem, with which a systematic development of phenomenological psychology is faced concerns the epistemological background of psychology in general. Science as such has to materialize the ideal

13. *Ibid.,* pp. 11–13.
14. *Ibid.,* pp. 13–20. See also: H.-G. Gadamer, *Wahrheit und Methode,* pp. 229–237.

of a systematic knowledge in a definitive form. It justifies clearly described insights concerning a precisely delineated field of entities. The mathematical and physical sciences have been able to approximate this ideal most closely. Psychological movements and schools which can be traced as far back as 400 B.C. have shown themselves to be unable to realize this ideal. Dilthey and the phenomenologists did not consider the modern forms of empirical psychology an exception to that rule. Dilthey felt that modern empirical psychology not only failed to realize the above mentioned scientific ideal, but that it even had fallen short of genuinely approaching it.[15] Only a careful reflection upon the ultimate purposes and foundations of the sciences can bring some solution here.

The questions which must be asked in this connection are the following: What is it that provides a particular science with its unity as a science? How is this science distinguished from other sciences? What is the subject matter of psychology and from what perspective does it deal with it? We could say that psychology is not concerned with 'nature,' but rather deals instead with man and animal conceived as conscious beings and as centers of 'spiritual' and 'psychical' life. Yet, this conception seems to encroach upon the area of the humanistic sciences, and in particular on the field of history and the cultural sciences. We can assume the position that all the humanistic sciences are in fact psychologico-anthropological sciences and that empirical psychology is in reality a science concerned with the universal forms and laws of conscious facts, regardless of the individual actualizations of these forms and laws within an historical reality.[16]

It is easy to see that we encounter many problems with such a description of psychology. How would we get a clear idea of what we are to understand by 'nature' and 'spirit'? The natural sciences are born out of a one-sided interest, orientation and method. The 'nature' to which these sciences direct themselves is not a precisely delineated realm clearly distinguished from

15. Edmund Husserl, *Phän. Psychol.*, pp. 52–53.
16. *Ibid.*, pp. 53–54.

everything else which manifests itself in immediate experience. This 'nature' is rather an *idea*, which is to be realized by means of the theory which is connected with it. The merely 'subjective' characteristics of nature which find their origin in a subjective way of looking at things are suspect and are banned from this theory. However, it is not quite clear what is to be precisely understood by this 'subjective' or 'spiritual.' The humanistic sciences and even psychology have also been very confused on this point. The natural sciences which chose to speak about 'nature' never came to a *real* understanding of the meaning of 'nature' either. We, therefore, are still faced with the problem of an original and thoroughgoing description of 'nature' and 'spirit.' [17]

We note, first of all, that the concepts 'nature' and 'spirit' as we find them today as themes for scientific explorations, are not at all data of immediate experience. 'Nature' and 'spirit' are the fruits of a certain theoretical labor which has its origin in a determinate theoretical interest and is based on our natural, pre-theoretical experience. It is there, in the pre-theoretical experience, that these concepts appear in their original and concrete context. This concrete and intuitively given whole of the world of our pre-scientific experience forms the point of departure for our exploration of the ways in which the different forms of theoretical interest and the various directions of thought arise. It is from the perspective of that world that we must seek to find how 'nature' and 'spirit' could develop into two different, indivisible, universal themes of investigation which remain, nevertheless, related to each other.[18]

Such a delving into this all-embracing, concrete, and radical world, as it is immediately and continuously experienced in naive originality, can keep us from repeating forever the mistakes of naturalistic psychology and the objectivistic humanistic sciences which issue from the misconception of the spirit as a purely causally determined appendage of material bodies. Such

17. *Ibid.,* pp. 54–55.
18. *Ibid.,* p. 55.

a mistaken, arbitrary view leads straight to the conception of man and animals as psychophysical machines.[19]

It will be clear, therefore, that a radical investigation of the problematic concepts 'nature' and 'spirit,' taken inasfar as they point to the subject matter of the natural and humanistic sciences, must lead us away from these sciences themselves and back toward our pre-scientific world. Before every possible science whatsoever, this world is given in an immediate, pre-scientific experience as the world of our actual life, in which world-experience and world-theorizing still constitute an indivisible and inseparable unity. Let us not forget that all the facts with which the factual sciences deal are facts of the world. If this world were not given first in an original experience there would not have been any basis on which any science could form itself. This world of pre-theoretical, original experience remains constantly present to us, supported as it is by the steady, harmonizing stream of experiences.[20]

Although other perspectives are possible, as we shall show later, we will concentrate at the moment on the natural perspective. In the natural attitude we take that which announces itself in our experience, just as it immediately manifests itself. We take it as concretely being, and our natural life as a whole continually refers back to this self-evidently being and self-evidently real world. It is this world which is inextricably tied up with all our efforts. It is to this world that we direct our theoretical and practical questions; it is on the basis of this world that we are able to construct our sciences. This world of primary experience shows a constantly changing mien and we vary our own conceptions of it constantly. Our theoretical and practical activities result in conceptions and views which in turn affect our experience and, thus, the meaning of the experienced world is continually clothed with new layers of meaning. That which at first announces itself as a simple and immediate experience shows, upon closer inspection, that it contains elements of earlier activities of the mind. And that is why we must ask the question

19. *Ibid.,* pp. 55–56.
20. *Ibid.,* p. 56.

of where we are to find this genuine, pre-theoretical world of our pure experience.[21]

These sediments of our thinking on our experiences become especially clear when we talk about such things as constellations of stars or thermometers. On closer investigation, however, it appears that such sedimentary layers of meaning are found in practically all our experiences. That is why it is so difficult to describe what the original world of our experience precisely is. What is an 'original experience' and what is the 'world of original experience'? [22]

In the past many philosophers thought it easy to answer this question. All we have to do, they said, is give an exact description of that which announces itself in our immediate experience. Yet, we saw how our cultural and scientific experiences add layers of meaning to all that which appears to us. For the world which manifests itself in immediate experiences is already a cultural world; the objects which we encounter there are already interpreted and determined by our culture. This becomes especially clear when we consider such things as tools and other objects which are pure products of a culture. We speak, without hesitancy, about chairs and tables which allegedly present themselves *immediately* to our awareness. Yet, somebody from an entirely different culture would not be able to place these objects, just as we would stand uneasily in the presence of objects formed by other cultures with which we are unfamiliar. All these objects contain the sediments of the experience, the thought, the valuation, and the work of many generations. We fail to distinguish those sedimentations as such when we are immediately present to the object. Moreover, we also have certain *a priori* ideas concerning all 'natural' objects, which ultimately stem from our culture and with which we are so familiar that it would be very difficult to recognize them as distinct from the immediate data of our experience. We should be particularly mindful of the fact that in our culture objects are seen also from a scientific perspective. The sciences have influenced our vision

21. *Ibid.*, p. 56.
22. *Ibid.*, pp. 56–57.

of the world and intramundane things directly or indirectly. However valuable this vision proves to be we must realize that it is nowhere identical with the vision of the world as it presents itself in our immediate experience. All our seeing contains admixtures of meanings whose origins are unclear to us and which cloud our experience of things as they appear in their original light. Our task is, therefore, to turn away from the cultural world toward the world of original experience by means of certain reductive procedures. Only thus can we start to realize the task which we have set ourselves in regard to psychology.

Husserl mentioned this reductive procedure for the first time in his *Ideen* but it is only in his last work, *Krisis,* and in Landgrebe's posthumous edition of *Erfahrung und Urteil* that he came to a careful and detailed description of it. Also the term *Lebenswelt,* appears only in these later works and it is scarcely mentioned in his *Phänomenologische Psychologie.* Later we will speak in greater detail of the relationship between the world of our original experience and the *Lebenswelt* and the connection between the different types of reduction which Husserl distinguishes in his phenomenology. For the moment we want to concern ourselves only with this world of our original experience. Husserl felt that we could make this world accessible through the use of a special reductive procedure which would distance us from all that which our culture and the sciences have taught us concerning the world in order to give the things themselves a new chance to speak to us unmodified by the distracting noises of culture and science. Yet, to separate the world and things from their cultural and scientific admixtures will not necessarily suffice to bring out the essential structures of things. We must conceive of the world as the intentional correlate of our 'all-sided' orientation toward the intramundane beings and not as a world in and by itself, existing independently from our consciousness or presenting itself as a ready-made fact. Our phenomenological considerations show the world as correlative with world-consciousness and objects as correlative with object-consciousness. The phenomenological reduction aims to show

how object and world appear to consciousness in their original meaning. Only when we have succeeded in elucidating this original meaning can we begin to see how the cultural and scientific world arose out of the original world of experience.[23]

A first reflection will show that the world is always already given in our experience. Despite all changing opinions, all fluctuating thoughts and actions we always experience the world as the one and the same world to which all our actions and judgments are related. All the questions which direct themselves to the true being of this world presuppose this world already. The 'true' world we are accustomed to speaking about is already a product of higher mental elaborations of the world of our immediate experience. The world of our immediate experience is that fundamental domain out of which the 'true' world is built up by our scientific investigation. Yet, this primary world of our immediate experiences maintains a certain general structure which is unaffected by our later and fluctuating opinions of the world. What is this general and *a priori* necessary structure of the world?

It is very important for that which follows that we gain a very clear idea of what is to be understood by the expressions 'world of our experience' and 'experience of the world.' We notice, first of all, that during the act of perception, that which is being perceived announces itself as being immediately present to us as it itself, whereas in memory it manifests itself as having been immediately present to us as it itself. It is possible for objects to appear in our immediate presence without any exertion on our side; we suddenly and surprisingly find ourselves in the presence of an object. But there exists also a more active and conscious type of perception during which we expressly pay attention to a particular object that presents itself to us. In such an active and consciously performed act of perception we can focus atten-

23. Edmund Husserl, *Ideen*, vol. I, § 39, 52, 56; *Krisis*, § 28–55; *Erfahrung und Urteil. Untersuchungen zur Genealogie der Logik.* Redigiert und herausgegeben von Ludwig Landgrebe, Prag, 1939, § 7 - § 10. See also: M. Merleau-Ponty, *La structure du comportement*, Paris, 1949, pp. 232–237; *Phénoménologie de la perception*, Paris, 1945, pp. 64–77.

tion on a determinate object in our field of perception and
observe it carefully from all sides, and pay attention to all that
which is given through such an act of perception without, however, getting involved in judgmental, expressive, or theoretical
acts. But we leave out of consideration the question of whether
in that which we observe now, there still is something which
refers back to what we experienced earlier. In other words, we
take what manifests itself as being perceived and, therefore, as
present to us, just as it is perceived. It is of the greatest importance to realize that in this active and conscious perception of a
determinate object an immediately experienced world also manifests itself as a continuous and constant unity. From moment
to moment new experiences arise in which continually new,
perceived data can manifest themselves and yet all these new
experiences flow together without our conscious effort and
merge into a unity of experience that we can get hold of, manage,
and oversee. All perceptions and memories are somehow made
into a unity: in one single experience which links together all
these perceptions and memories, the world itself appears. It
sometimes happens that an actual perception does not fit into
this unity of experience; we then speak of an illusion or of a
deception. That which appeared to be real is not genuinely real.
In that case only a modification of our perception can restore
the original harmony. The expression 'the world of our immediate experience' thus refers to the structural unity of reality as a
whole inasfar as it manifests itself in the course of our experience in an harmonious way. The whole of our experience is
constantly moving and developing: the reality of our experiencing is, therefore, always something relative. In the progressive
movement of our experience there is always the possibility that
new evidence will show that, that which *is* true, turns out to be
merely something that *appeared* to be true; in that case the
content of the world of our immediate experience changes in a
corresponding way.[24]

One could make the remark here that our field of perception

24. Edmund Husserl, *Phän. Psych.*, pp. 57–60.

is always a limited one and that we, therefore, always have access to only a part of the whole of the world of our immediate experience. Thus, this world itself is, as such, not given in experience, but rather constructed by our thought. However, we can reply to this remark with a counter-question: is it possible to claim that, as far as the experiences of our single and individual object is concerned, we genuinely perceive a *thing* although that thing is always more than we perceive factually in an effective way? Is it possible that in the course of future experiences we will ever be able adequately to take possession of that thing? If in this case we can answer the first question positively whereas we have to answer the second one in a negative way, then the same holds true for the world of our immediate experience.[25]

With this remark and our counter-question, however, we have left the theme which immediately concerns us here, since neither one is really relevant for an explanation of the correlative concepts 'experience of the world' and 'the world of our immediate experience.' For, perception, memory, and even our global total experience precisely, and even necessarily, refer to a domain of things, structured groups of things, and even to the world in which all that is pre-given manifests itself as immediately present reality. All this is already presupposed to our actively being preoccupied with the world and, in particular, to each understanding, judicative, and theorizing activity.

An analogous example may clarify this problem. When we stand in front of a house we see a house even though our effective seeing is limited to seeing parts or one side of that house. The experience I have of this house carries with it the conviction that I can take different points of view in regard to this house and that I will, nevertheless, see this same house. This is not only true for things in the world; it is equally true for the world itself. I can look at this particular house; yet, implied in this look is also a piece of the street and a sky. My field of vision stretches out, as it were, toward an unlimited horizon which we

25. *Ibid.*, pp. 60–61.

call the world. In this consideration the concepts 'the experience of the world' and 'the world of our immediate experience,' are briefly indicated.[26]

What we are describing here is the world which appears prior to any theoretical inquiry and which, in its relativity, always is perceived and experienced with indubitable certitude *as being*. Certitude does not imply truth in this context; it refers only to that peculiar modality inherent in each perception which refers to the direct presence of a being that as such can be grasped in our immediate experience. Doubt exists only when we deal with a particular this or that; it never refers to the world itself. The world itself, therefore, is not problematic in that respect. In the flow of our universal experience the world continuously is the unshakable and universal ground of being on the basis of which all particular questions will be decided. It is to this world that all *natural* questions, all answers, and all sciences of facts refer.[27]

We carry the conviction that this world of experience contains somewhere a world-truth and that on the basis of our universal experience we can achieve a universal, theoretical knowledge that strives for objective and definitive truth. It is in this presupposition which itself is not a datum of our immediate experience, that every objective science takes its starting point.[28] If it is true that all the sciences of facts find their origins in the world of our experience, then we must also be able to find a radical explanation for the differentiations and the division of the sciences in the world of experience, and the domain covered by each science must correspond to a determinate value of the world of our experience.[29] And if the pre-theoretical world of our experience possesses a general systematic structure, then we must find this structure constantly reflected in every realm. This structure will, furthermore, co-determine the form and the content of the different sciences. It should, therefore,

26. *Ibid.*, pp. 61–62.
27. *Ibid.*, pp. 62–63.
28. *Ibid.*, pp. 63–64.
29. *Ibid.*, p. 64.

be possible to have a universal science of the world which would study precisely this universal structure. In addition, we could have the concrete sciences which would have as their tasks the careful description of the concrete and individual structures of the objects of our experience. These sciences would have to proceed on the basis provided by the general science of the world. And in case that structure of the world should contain several, universal structures of special types, the universal science of the world should have to imply various, correlated, special sciences.[30]

The question is now what we in general can say of the world as world of our immediate experience. The answer to this question can help us to determine accurately the full content of the concept 'the *natural* world of our immediate experience.' And this answer can be given only in and by a precise description of the correlation: experience and world-of-experience. Description now points to intuition. That is why we must place ourselves completely intuitively within our world-experience itself in order to see how the world of our immediate experience manifests itself there. In doing so we need not pay any attention to typical and particular characteristics, but must focus attention only on the most general structure of the world itself. This can be done only by penetrating the 'empty' horizons of the concretely experienced special structures and, furthermore, by uncovering these systematically in a genuinely intuitive way. This, however, can in turn be done only by investigating and rendering explicit all the references from our actual acts to other possible acts and their correlates. In this way we will find structures which we have already met before, but also other ones which we *now* can foresee and expect only.[31]

We can formulate this also in the following way. Taking our starting point in our experience of this concrete world in which we are living, we can try, with the help of our memory and imagination, to uncover the most general, typical characteristics of 'world-experience' and 'world of our experience.' Following

30. *Ibid.*, pp. 64–65.
31. *Ibid.*, pp. 65–66.

this procedure we uncover two basic insights: 1) There exists a general linking Gestalt (*Verknüpfungs-gestalt*) which connects all the manifold, divergent, individual realities into one totality. 2) All individual realities of the world possess a structure that has general applicability and validity. To speak more concretely, the linking Gestalt implies space, time, substantiality, causality, etc., whereas each concrete thing has its own spatial structure, its temporal aspect, its qualitative determinations, and its causal relationships.[32]

The procedure explained above makes it possible to come to a meaningful conception of the world. All the sciences of the world must ultimately refer back to that fundamental conception. All sciences which seek a solid foundation need to be based on this universal science of the world. This science of the world consists in a descriptive science of the most general structures of the world taken as it manifests itself in our immediate experience.[33]

The Method of Free Variation

ALL THAT we have said needs to be subjected to a critical examination. For our research has remained up to now within an attitude bound up with empirical factuality. It is this attitude that we must renounce now in order to elucidate the pure aprioric character of the science of the world. In our previous considerations we started with the facts of our experience and with the world which manifests itself in them. We asked there how the world of our immediate experience appeared to us when we considered it in general outlines. We asked for the universal characteristics of this world. In dealing with these questions we went beyond the individual facts in our quest for the essential characteristics of reality as such. Yet, we thought about these realities still as realities *in* the world. In this way the typical general characteristics of the world remained tied to the mode of experi-

32. *Ibid.*, pp. 66–68.
33. *Ibid.*, pp. 68–69.

encing demanded by our immediate presence to the world. The same can be said about the general structures of the world as a whole insofar as the future structures we seek to uncover remain dictated by that which we have experienced in the past. We notice, however, that although we started from empirical and hypothetical facts we, nevertheless, felt ourselves in the spell of a necessity that we did not experience in our presence to the original empirical facts. Thus, we found that the world is a spatial world. We were also drawn into the presence of other characteristics which were mentioned briefly. This inkling of necessity points toward an *a priori* in the sense of an apodictic generality which in itself must be open to further investigation. The territory that is merely suggested here must now be opened up for further critical exploration and verification.[34]

This transition from the level of concrete things to the level of the *a priori* in the sense mentioned, requires that we free ourselves from the domination of the factual. To the level of the factual belongs the real and factually experienced world with all the factual things which we encounter there. It is from this realm that we must divert ourselves in order to picture to ourselves other possible worlds and mundane things by means of the free play of pure imagination. In this manner we seek to ascertain the apodictically necessary *a priori* of the world of our immediate experience. In doing this we deny neither the facts of our experience, nor the real existence of the world which is therein revealed.[35]

To clarify further the above mentioned procedure we need to make a short digression and show how we arrive at an intuitive grasping of an *a priori*. The best method for grasping a particular *a priori* is the so-called 'intuition of essences' (*Wesensschau*) .[36]

The first description of this *Wesensschau* can be found in Husserl's *Logische Untersuchungen*.[37] This first tentative de-

34. *Ibid.*, p. 70.
35. *Ibid.*, pp. 71–72.
36. *Ibid.*, p. 72.
37. Edmund Husserl, *L.U.*, vol. II, 2, pp. 235–236.

scription of the ideation which originally occupied the central place in phenomenology, caused a great many misunderstandings. Husserl, therefore, tried to correct and clarify this method in his article entitled *Philosophie als strenge Wissenschaft*.[38] We find further elaborations and clarifications of this method in the *Ideen* [39] and in his *Phänomenologische Psychologie*.[40] Later Husserl continued this trend of thought in the *Cartesianische Meditationen* [41] and in his *Formale und transzendentale Logik* [42] where he tried to define the position and function of the eidetic reduction in its relationship to the other phenomenological procedures. The most exhaustive of Husserl's descriptions of this eidetic reduction appeared only much later in his posthumously published *Erhfahrung and Urteil*.[43] In the beginning, Husserl seemed to imply that ideation takes place on the basis of the particular experience of an individual of a certain class. Later we see an increasingly important role assigned to the imagination until ultimately Husserl saw the imagination as the essential factor in the revealing of the essences of things. We will limit ourselves in this chapter to the explanations given in the *Phänomenologische Psychologie* since we find there all that is needed for our present purpose.

In order to explain and justify the method of ideation, or the search for the essences of things, Husserl recommends that we start with a concrete fact which we then let freely vary in our imagination. We have to be careful to keep the free variations within the limits of possible individuals of the same type. The plurality of these variations which now appear, shows a certain unity, namely, the invariant essence of this type of thing. What is important here is the fact that no matter how we imagine the different possible variants of a certain type we, nevertheless, *necessarily* end up with an invariant essence which

38. Edmund Husserl, *Phil. str. W.*, pp. 315–319.
39. Edmund Husserl, *Ideen*, vol. I, pp. 12–17, 159–163.
40. Edmund Husserl, *Phän. Psych.*, pp. 72–87.
41. Edmund Husserl, *Cart. Med.*, pp. 103–106.
42. Edmund Husserl, *Formale und transzendentale Logik. Versuch einer Kritik der Logischen Vernunft*, Halle a.d.S., 1929, pp. 218–219.
43. Edmund Husserl, *Erf. u. Urt.*, pp. 394–398, 409–443.

can be grasped in immediate intuition once we are prepared in that way. All the imagined variations do overlap in a certain aspect; this is the general essence, the *eidos,* the *idea* in the Platonic sense of the word. Husserl makes use of this concept 'eidos,' without, however, attaching to it any metaphysical interpretation; he merely takes it to refer to the essences as they appear to us immediately in intuition.[44]

The factual reality from which we started no longer appears as one single possibility among an infinite number of others in the course of this process. Whether or not a particular variant actually exists is completely irrelevant as far as the *eidos* is concerned; the variants that ultimately point the way to the *eidos,* need only to be real possibilities of a particular species of things. The *eidos* is pure even only to the extent that it remains independent of the given world. In the natural attitude the experienced world is always presupposed as the universal and abiding basis for all our activities. The attitude required for a completely free and pure search for the essential (*Wesensschau*) is, therefore, incompatible with the natural attitude.[45]

When we consider the concept of *variation* and compare it to the concept of *change,* we find that despite their similarity they are essentially different concepts. We speak of change when we refer to a real thing that is affected by wear and tear, and subject to duration and development. Change refers to the transition from one phase to the next. Change, or the transition from one phase to the next, implies also a unity because it is this particular identical, individual thing that is subjected to the change: this particular identical thing survives all the manifold changes to which it is subjected. The unity, however, does not refer to the universal in the particular temporal phases; this unity precisely is the individual thing itself. True, it is also possible from another perspective to approach the phases themselves as variants; then we will see that change is impossible when the phases of the changing process do not belong together. A color changes into a color; it does not change into a tone.

44. Edmund Husserl, *Phän. Psych.,* pp. 72–73.
45. *Ibid.,* p. 74.

Each change takes place within the limits of certain given conditions which cannot be superseded. However, the species comes to the fore as *eidos* only when we stand back from our involvement in that which actually exists. On the level of pure imagination we can imagine possible variants of a concrete thing which takes part in the *eidos* and, therefore, possesses this *eidos* as 'law of necessity.' "All that can be subjected to variation carries within itself a necessary structure, an *eidos* and, therefore, a law of necessity." [46]

The procedure which we described is called intuition of ideas (*Ideenschau*) or ideation. We want first to summarize the most important steps of this procedure and then add some of the more important details. The fundamental step in this procedure on which all of the rest entirely depends is the formation of an open, endless multiplicity of variants of an experienced or imagined object. The open plurality does not, of course, command us to proceed indefinitely with the generation of variants of a particular thing. We do not need to project all possible variants. We need to form variants only to the point where we can truthfully say 'and so on at will.' [47] The intuition of the *eidos* takes place then on the basis of and is founded in the multiplicity of variants. The intuitive grasp of the *eidos* aims at the particular aspects which overlap each other in each one of the variants. These particular overlapping aspects bring about the synthetic unity which only allows us truly to speak of variants of one and the same thing.[48] We must then proceed to grasp this unity actively and immediately in our intuition just as this unity shows itself in the series of variants as unchanging unity. It is important to note that the complete series of the variants should remain present in consciousness; the intuition of the essence (*Wesensschau*) may never rest completely on the last of a chain of variants; the ideation must precisely hold its power in the fact that a particular invariant emerged from a particular

46. *Ibid.*, pp. 75–76.
47. *Ibid.*, pp. 76–77.
48. *Ibid.*, pp. 77–78.

chain of variants.[49] One could object that Husserl's appeal to the imagination seems unnecessary; why couldn't we rely on real individual cases to provide us with the needed variants? Husserl contends that an empirical generalization leads only to a generality, never to the *eidos*. This *eidos* can be reached only on the basis of an active, intuitive grasp and this intuition needs to include all of that which only an unlimited, free play of our imagination can provide.[50]

We should realize that it is possible to proceed from one single example and, nevertheless, ultimately reach more than one *eidos;* a particular red can lead us to the *eidos* 'red' and to the *eidos* 'color.' The intention of the variation determines which *eidos* we ultimately will find.[51] Ideas can even be used themselves as variants; it, thus, is possible to intuit an idea 'out of' many ideas. Thus, the *eidos* itself can likewise be subjected to variation. It is even possible to subject relationships, quantities, collections, or collections of relationships to this ideation.[52] Be this as it may, in all these ways we can come to an *eidos* that remains unaffected by any presuppositions of any real, factual occurence whatsoever. Such an *eidos* is to be distinguished from an empirical generality.[53] Furthermore, the intuition of essences is more than a mere vague speaking about, meaning, or intending. It refers to an active grasp in which I take a thing exactly in the way it is immediately present to me.[54]

It is essential in this method that we look upon the example from which we start as a pure possibility and not as a real thing: "in a free doing a certain indifference comes here into play in regard to reality and in this way that which manifests itself as real becomes transposed into the domain of imagination." The *eidos* does not have an extension which is formed by facts but rather one formed by pure possibilities. These possibilities can

49. *Ibid.,* p. 78.
50. *Ibid.,* pp. 78–81.
51. *Ibid.,* pp. 81–82.
52. *Ibid.,* pp. 82–84.
53. *Ibid.,* pp. 84–85.
54. *Ibid.,* pp. 85–86.

include real facts too, of course. However, the essential generality
precedes all questioning concerning facts. Essential generalities
constitute an *a priori* which precedes all facts and empirical
truths.[55]

In summary we can say the following concerning the intuition of essences (*Wesensschau*). We start from a particular observation of a known individual specimen of a kind of thing, a
meaning, act, etc. With the help of memory and also through
varying our position in regard to the object but, most importantly, by means of imagination we detect how we could vary
this object without violating its identity as this object, meaning,
or act. The contribution of our imagination is of great importance because it is precisely our aim to produce random variations which do not remain bound up with experience and the
experienceable world; the variants must remain free from positing the actuality of the object or act in question. This is evidently
accomplished best in imagination. During the process of comparing the variants, the unchanging aspects come to light which
form the necessary complex of characteristics without which we
cannot think of an example of this particular class of things.
This invariant comes about in a seemingly passive manner when
the objects of our many acts of imagination shift in front of each
other and cover each other partially. This passively constituted,
and as yet imperfect, content can then be grasped intuitively
through which we free the invariable, true, pure, universal and
always indentical essence.[56]

What we have said concerning the method of free variation
is already an example of a psychological description. We will
return to this later in greater detail. Yet, this method was not
intended here as an example of the new psychology toward which
we are directing our search in this book.[57] Free variation was
devised as an instrument that would help us to classify the
sciences of the world fundamentally. Ultimately free variation
would help us achieve a true description of what we now indicate

55. *Ibid.*, p. 86.
56. *Ibid.*, p. 86. See also: *Erf. u. Urt.*, pp. 410, 314–315, 204, 224, 397.
57. *Ibid.*, p. 87.

with the term 'spirit'.[58] We can then bypass all the traditional prejudices concerning psychology and psychological methods and we can reach a true insight into the essence, the subject matter, the method, and the system of psychology only by proceeding in the radical manner suggested above.[59]

As a purely eidetic-historical procedure the method of ideation has been applied for more than two thousand years to quantities and numbers. This long tradition implied to many scientists that this method could be meaningfully applied only to mathematical and logical entities: "Our description shows, however, that wherever and to what degree objectivities come to light originally and in an intuitive way, the method of ideation is to be applied . . . "[60]

Our first task is now to reveal the as yet vaguely outlined world in such a way that we can make use of *possible* experiences which will point the way to other possible experiences, so that we may reach an ever progressing and open total view of the world. We seek to reveal the world from the perspective of how it would be, how it must be when all the possible horizons that now remain undefined have acquired fuller determination and specification by means of appropriate, possible experiences. In other words we propose to apply the method of free variation to the world of our immediate experience in order in this way to find the most general structural concept of 'the world' as such.[61]

General Ontology of the World of Our Immediate Experience. Toward a Preliminary Description of the Subject Matter of Psychology

THE PRECEDING sections attempted to typify the science of our natural conception of the world as a universal, descriptive

---

58. *Ibid.*, pp. 87–88.
59. *Ibid.*, p. 88.
60. *Ibid.*, p. 88.
61. *Ibid.*, pp. 88–89.

science of both the pre-given world as well as of every possible world whatsoever. We, thus, prepared an as yet vague universal framework within which the *a priori* of all mundane sciences must find its place. Implied in what we said is also the observation that all goals and all problems which are posed by the mundane sciences possess a general and *a priori* type. Those who deal with these sciences would have to uncover this *a priori* if they are to come to a real and fruitful understanding of these sciences. It is impossible to fully develop here all the particular aspects of this general science which is concerned with the *a priori* of all the particular sciences. We attempt here only to give an outline.[62]

We start with uncovering the world of our immediate experience, thus with unveiling our factual experiencing of this real world. Let us suppose for a moment that we would know already what it means to say that the world is experienced and that it is present in its bodily reality every moment of our practical life. Our effective presence is, however, always limited to our perceptive field of the immediately perceived things here and now. We never are effectively present to all of the world. This limited field of perception which includes the directly bodily experienced realities is termed *field of proximity, (Nahfeld)*. This field of proximity is surrounded by a *marginal field (Umring)* of known and unknown things that are not clearly perceived. Surrounding the marginal field we find a *field of distance (Fernfeld)* which contains things which are completely unknown. The same holds true for every moment of the past. Many things which now are not yet experienced, will be perceived in future. It is for this reason that the most general structure of the world of our experience can be revealed only when we take into account our possible experiences.[63]

There is an unmistakable parallel between this problem concerning the evident structure of the world of our possible experiences, and the problems of Kant's transcendental esthetics and analytics. We need to stress in this context one point of

62. *Ibid.,* pp. 93–94. See also: *Ideen,* vol. II, pp. 27–54.
63. *Ibid.,* p. 94.

great importance, however. Kant expressly denies that the world can ever become the object even of our *possible* experience. Husserl's position is contrary to this point. It is true that the real individual objects are experienced first, prior to the experience of the world. Yet, in the experience of the concrete individual things is contained the experience of the world. Individual thing and world are inseparable. In our experience of the particular thing, the world is experienced as the horizon. This is precisely the point overlooked by Kant.[64] It is this particular point that makes us state that each and every intersubjective experience can be thought of only as being *in* the world. It now also becomes clear why each real object is placed in a context of space and time. The world appears originally only as a spatio-temporal horizon. Each particular thing partakes of this spatio-temporal horizon from which it cannot be separated and shows itself as a spatio-temporal, real thing. The world itself is but a concretely filled space and concretely filled time. We do not take into further consideration here the question of whether the world might not contain other universal structures in which the real objects would have to share.[65]

Up to now we have established that an empirical, descriptive, and eidetical analysis of the general structure of the world must begin with the contemplation of exemplary, real, and individual things. These individual things, objects, acts, etc., must be considered in their essential relationship to the world as horizon. We further remarked that no matter how or what the world may be, we are certain of one thing, namely, that it must be in such a way that the concretely experienced individual things fit into it.[66]

We must now consider the real and individual things of a world that remains still unknown in terms of its essential structures, and search there for the most general and apriorically necessary distinctions. Soon we will notice as the most fundamental distinction the following. On the one hand we find the

64. *Ibid.,* pp. 95–97.
65. *Ibid.,* p. 97.
66. *Ibid.,* pp. 98–99.

real, concrete, independent things and individuals in the largest sense of the word, such as chairs, tables, pipes, and people. On the other hand, we experience the dependent modes of these individual things, such as their size, form, and color. The independent things can be experienced independently of other things, the dependent modi presuppose the experience of substantial entities.[67]

If we follow this classification, then we must count such realities as collections, groupings, and configurations among the modi. Yet, when we think further about this result we become dissatisfied with this distinction between independent things and dependent modi. It seems that we might be more successful if we would make use of the concept of causality. Collections or groupings of things are not independent entities because they do not manifest themselves as unities which are causally coherent.[68] It, therefore, might be more accurate to say that independent things are constituted in such a way that despite all change or development they maintain and manifest a fixed form of causality. "Every thing is not only a unity of changeable characteristic properties but it is also subject to causal laws which as rules govern every individual thing of a determinate category." It is on this basis that we call the sun, a stone, a man, a society, a real thing.[69]

Within the framework of pure experience we find a further distinction between things of a higher order and things of a lower order. When we follow this scheme we place into the lowest order the single, individual things, which fail to appear as systems of things but instead manifest themselves as separate unities. A stone, a star, or a human being would be assigned to the lowest order. We set aside here the question of whether such individual things as we mentioned might possibly be revealed as a complex causally connected system of smaller entities. We limit ourselves here to saying that the world consists of single

---

67. *Ibid.,* pp. 99–100.
68. *Ibid.,* pp. 100–102.
69. *Ibid.,* pp. 102–103.

thing-realities which can form systems of a higher order. Each individual singular thing is a causal unity which maintains causal relationships with its surroundings; in the playful spectacle of changing causal relationships this individual thing is revealed as the substratum of fixed, causally determined characteristics.[70]

Another distinction which we note is that between the living and the inanimate things. Plants are usually thought of as living; since we do not experience plants as subjects, that is, as observing, striving, feeling beings, we, therefore, count them here among the inanimate things. We experience only human beings and animals as subjects of psychic life.[71]

A mere superficial consideration of the world brings us thus already into contact with the 'mental' and 'psychical,' as structural moments of the world of our immediate experience. Our task is to work out in greater detail this difference between the physical and the psychical so that we may reach the ultimate and *real* sense of the 'spiritual.' We may note here already that the physical and 'spiritual' are inseparably intertwined in the world of pure experience.[72]

The distinction between subjects and non-subjects manifested itself originally as a differentiation in the disposition of the things in the world. Only subjects were considered as living beings. The meaning of such words as 'soul' or 'psychical' remained still vague and elucidation was attempted only be means of examples. The psychical manifests itself immediately through such acts as perception, thinking, concluding, striving, the posing of goals, the striving after goals, etc. It further manifests itself in such enduring characteristics as nearsightedness, deafness, musical ability, good-naturedness, etc.[73]

It is noteworthy, however, that the beings which we characterize as 'psychical' do manifest also the characteristics of the physical. We experience human beings and animals as bodily-psychical subjects. We notice, also, that through the process of

70. *Ibid.*, p. 103.
71. *Ibid.*, pp. 103–104.
72. *Ibid.*, p. 104.
73. *Ibid.*, pp. 104–105.

death the bodily-psychical subjects are transformed into mere
bodily things. Although the psychical forms a unity with the
physical in all subjects we, nevertheless, can distinguish the two.
Both aspects of the subject have their own process of growth
which is bound to a certain style, even though these processes
influence each other.[74] When the body turns into a mere physical
thing, the psychical is destroyed, it turns to the realm of non-
being, or at least to the realm of not being *in* the real world.

Wherever we experience psychical life we experience bodily
being; the physical body can be experienced without the psychical. After death that which remains in the world is only the
bodily aspect of the subject. The bodily aspect, therefore, has
greater autonomy than the psychical.[75]

Closer analysis reveals further that we experience our own
body as the center of our bodily environment and as the necessary instrument for any experience whatsoever. We also experience our body as the primary, original body insofar as the
experience of our own body is a necessary condition for our
apperceptive experience of another's body. Insofar as our own
body is perceived it is seen as animate, as besouled. My psychological life is experienced by me only through my body as animate. It is here in my own body that I also experience the unity
of body and soul, this mutual interpenetration of bodily and
psychical events. It is here that I find the original source of the
meaning of body, soul, and animation. The experienced world
will remain present to me as long as my body retains this particular Gestalt and organic structure.[76]

I can experience other peoples' bodies and other peoples'
psychic life only inasfar as I can interpret this alien living body
which I experience, as a human being like me on the basis of the
analogy which exists between their and my own bodiliness and
on the basis of the fact that my own body is experienced as constituting a harmonious unity with my psychic life.[77]

74. *Ibid.,* pp. 105–106.
75. *Ibid.,* pp. 106–107.
76. *Ibid.,* p. 107.
77. *Ibid.,* p. 108.

As we have seen the term 'objective world' signifies inter-subjectively experienced world, or at least a world that can be intersubjectively experienced. The concept 'objective world' pre-supposes that each subject possesses his own world of experience, that these experiences can be exchanged, and that this exchange can result in intersubjective agreement. This concept requires also that we all agree that our own bodily being is anterior to any experience whatsoever, that it is given as 'original place of my own animating life.' Other peoples' bodies appear as 'places of alien psychic life.' No matter how we may vary the actually given world we, nevertheless, will always find the particular conditions which are implied in the apperceptive meaning of my own and other peoples' bodies, operating in our psychical life. It is clear that it would be impossible for us to experience my own and the other's psychical life if this life were not al-ready, in principle, related to our own bodily being. It is also clear that with the disappearance of our bodiliness in death the psychical has to disappear because then the apperceptive con-dition of the psychical experience is no longer fulfilled. We then must lose contact with our own and the other's psychical life because we experience this life precisely as that which animates my own and the other's bodiliness. Death, considered as a real event *in* the world can, therefore, not have the meaning of the freeing of a soul in which the soul would take off by itself and remain a reality in the world. From the perspective of the world, death means the destruction of the soul as soul *in* the world. The doctrine of the immortality of the soul must have an entirely different meaning if it is not to run counter to the mean-ing of the world as it is revealed by a universal and objective experience. And the meaning of this doctrine can indeed be different from what we described above because the sciences of the world cannot have the last word here.

Without viewing these problems in too great detail one will have become aware of the fact that all real animal and human subjects possess concretely two distinct yet interwoven aspects. These two aspects manifest themselves as being of different value. The bodily aspect possesses a higher degree of autonomy than the soul insofar as we can think about the bodily without the soul and not vice versa.

In the foregoing discussion we have tried briefly to describe the world of our immediate experience in its general style and structure as it appears to us in any experience whatsoever. There we found structures which are necessary because they manifest themselves in every experience. The extent to which these necessary structures reflect a purely eidetical, a purely absolute, and self-evident *a priori* cannot be appraised here without a thoroughgoing analysis of the experienced world. We are at this point not fully prepared to enter into such an analysis.[78]

For, what would really be required here is a descriptive analysis of the essential structures of the realm of the bodily, both as inanimate thing and as the substructure for our psychological life. In this context the all-encompassing causality as well as space and time would have to be described in detail. We could do something similar with the realm of the psychical. The problems which we would meet there would concern the specific nature and the characteristic properties, the unity and diversities of the psychical relationships as well as the interplay between the different psychological modalities.[79]

Moreover, we have by no means yet considered in great detail the structural split between the physical and the psychical. We need to go a good deal deeper to bring to light such ideas as 'pure physical nature' and 'pure spirit.' This work remains to be done.[80] It is of the greatest importance for our present purposes to reveal first the different forms assumed by the subjective, the psychical, and the spiritual as they appear to us in the world of our immediate experience. The fundamental mode in which the psychical manifests itself is the 'spiritual' in the sense of our psychic life with all its actualities and potentialities. Furthermore, we must realize that all artifacts incorporate something of the animal or human soul; the expressed 'spiritual' sense of things is not something that we find besides physical things, but instead is

78. *Ibid.,* pp. 108–110.
79. *Ibid.,* p. 110.
80. *Ibid.,* pp. 110–111.

grasped immediately together with the houses, chairs, and tables. This becomes particularly evident when we consider works of art, but it is also true for other cultural objects. Yet, all these objects that incorporate some human or animal 'spirituality' are experienced in a different way than we experience animals and human beings.[81] On the other hand, in addition to their psychic life with its actualities and potentialities, man and animal do have something in common with cultural objects insofar as they are influenced by their particular milieu and cultures.[82]

The world of our immediate experience shows, also, a slowly changing historical aspect. This aspect is explored in particular by the humanistic sciences in the strict sense of the word. These sciences must approach this historical aspect from two different perspectives, namely, from the perspective of the culture itself and from the perspective of the culture-creating subjectivity. Culture and subject form a unity of mutual implication. Every experience of a cultural object points in its own way to open horizons of meaning and reveals in its own particular way the still incompletely understood meaning that the thing embodies. The revelation of this meaning points to the things themselves as well as to the subject who uses them or who created them.[83]

We must now ask ourselves the question concerning the meaning of this spiritual aspect of cultural objects. We must also penetrate deeper into the relationship which this spiritual aspect maintains with psychical life. The psychical is the source of all spirituality. Cultural meaning is objectively experienced as connected with things on the one hand, and with people on the other. It appears in objects as a particular expressive style that 'belongs' to that particular object, while at the same time it 'belongs' also to the human subject who brought this meaning into being. The origin of the cultural meaning must thus be explained from the perspective of the creative subject.[84] But also my experience of cultural objects must be considered. Then it be-

81. *Ibid.*, pp. 111–112.
82. *Ibid.*, pp. 112–113.
83. *Ibid.*, pp. 113–114.
84. *Ibid.*, pp. 114–115.

comes clear that my experience of the cultural meaning itself presupposes an apprehending and interpretive act.[85] We conclude from this that cultural meaning is neither a physical, real thing, nor a psychical state or quality. Cultural meaning seems to refer to an 'ideal layer' belonging to a bodily reality. This ideal layer is itself distinguished from the bodily as well as from the psychical in the strict sense.[86]

Even though the world of our experience is everywhere enriched with cultural meaning, we can isolate this meaning and leave it out of consideration. A reductive procedure will make this possible and allow us to concentrate simply on human beings, on animals, and on animate things.[87] While proceeding further within the realm of this abstracting, reductive procedure we can then disregard all psychical living realities. We are then in the presence of the pure bodily seen as completely inanimate matter. We have now arrived at the concept of nature as it is narrowly interpreted by the physical sciences.[88] The method by which we exclude all subjectivity is of great importance since it gives us the possibility of accurately delimiting the area studied by the physical sciences. This method is of further importance since it leads to a better understanding of the methods used in the physical sciences. A science is constituted first by the unveiling of the horizons of experience, in which harmonious and real realities and possibilities manifest themselves precisely in the way they become evident in scientific observation and experiment. All the activity of physics is directed, therefore, towards the purely objective in the experienced, natural phenomena. The experienced nature must in this way be elaborated and theoretically determined in its pure objectivity deprived of every form of subjectivity.[89]

But what is this purely objective? And what is this subjective against which it is contrasted? When we omit from our consider-

85. *Ibid.*, pp. 115–116.
86. *Ibid.*, pp. 116–118.
87. *Ibid.*, pp. 118–119.
88. *Ibid.*, pp. 119–120.
89. *Ibid.*, pp. 120–121.

ations the psychical realm, we must consequently also leave the subjective out of consideration. With the omission of the subjective, all cultural meaning disappears. We must remind ourselves again at this point that the experiencing human being cannot be thought of separate from the world of his experience, and the world of his experience cannot be thought of divorced from the human subjectivity. The experienced world retains an intentional relationship with the meaning-giving human experience. This is also true for physical nature in its relationship to the physicist. Each and every physicist experiences from a particular position which is determined by his body. This bodiliness from which the particular position arises, brings in its wake a necessarily subjective orientation. The physicist ostensibly wants to leave this 'merely' subjective out of the picture. He, therefore, must seek to free himself from his particular perspective, of the particular conceptions that reach him by virtue of his being *this* particular person viewing the world from *this* particular stand.[90] He must seek to universalize his particularity. "That is why the objectivation of the objective searcher comes about by way of 'abstraction' and the objective itself which is investigated this way is something abstract." The subject matter of physics is obviously related to the physicist, but the physicist tries to abstract from that fact and seeks to direct himself exclusively to that which objectively appears.[91]

We may conclude that in the natural attitude we all share the conviction of an objective and definitely true world even though sometimes the reality which at first we thought to be *this way*, turns out to be *that way*. The unshakable belief in a real world is a necessary supposition for any science of the world.[92] We must realize at this point, however, that the natural attitude constitutes a pre-reflective experience. It is, of course, possible to reflect upon this experience. If we do just that we discover two realities which essentially imply each other mutually: the objective worldly reality and the reality of the experi-

90. *Ibid.*, pp. 123–125.
91. *Ibid.*, pp. 121–125.
92. *Ibid.*, pp. 125–126.

ence itself as the possessing of objective reality in the realm of the subjective. Close analysis of the phenomena of hallucination and other 'distortions' shows that the experience maintains a certain priority over that which is experienced. We will later return in greater detail to this particular problem.[93]

It is important to pay the most careful attention to the subjective elements, which despite all efforts remain embedded in the endeavors of the natural sciences. Such careful investigation will bring us closer to a real understanding of nature as investigated by the physical sciences and to a better appreciation of it as the end result of an abstracting procedure. Such an investigation will, also, gradually reveal the myriad forms the subjective assumes. Only in this way shall we arrive at a universal science of the subjective and genuinely understand the differentiations and specifications of the subjective in the different humanistic sciences.[94]

The realm of the subjective can be differentiated into two main parts. There is, first of all, the subjective experience which announces itself to one particular person; there is also the subjective experience which can be concretely shared by people, and which we term the intersubjective experience. These two realms usually run parallel, although this is by no means always the case. It is fruitful to make a further distinction between the subjective experiences shared by a community of 'normal' people and those shared by the so-called abnormal persons such as the blind, the deaf, etc. Pre-scientific nature is nature as it is normally experienced. Nature as it reveals itself through the sciences is the objectively true nature that can and must be experienced in this manner by everybody. "Natural science attempts theoretically to determine an objective nature opposite to the merely subjective experiences and the subjectively experienced world, which objective nature must transcend all the actual and possible subjective differences." [95]

93. *Ibid.*, pp. 126–127.
94. *Ibid.*, pp. 127–128.
95. *Ibid.*, pp. 128–129.

The 'abnormal' world of the blind and the deaf reveals another dimension of the psychical, namely, the psycho-physical or the embodiment of the psychical as a necessary condition for the purely psychical. For, deaf and blind persons have their own psychical life which is based on their bodily condition.[96]

The physicist who is only concerned with the pure *res extensa* rejects the subjective in all its various forms and appearances. The humanistic sciences must take the subjective as the object of study. It becomes easily clear that the many forms in which the subjective appears are, nevertheless, part of one underlying unity. It is by no means simple, however, to see *how* these different aspects of the subjective belong together and *how* it is to be determined within the different humanistic sciences. The answers to these questions have been pursued already for several hundred years and still no one has found a convincing solution.[97]

The knowledge of the physicist is directed toward the world out there, toward the realm of things in the temporal, spatial order which exert and undergo an exterior causality. Our analyses of this world must show clearly how the subjective, insofar as it is real, emerges from this world and how it remains bound up with it. Then it appears that we must make a distinction between the psychical of the lowest degree, which is characterized by passivity, and the typically psychical which is spiritual, personal and ego-oriented. The first of these two realms appears everywhere to be a necessary presupposition for the second one.[98]

For we must distinguish here two forms of animation, namely: 1) the animation of mere matter into a living body in which process the psychical is part by part incarnated into the body; we are here in the sphere of the psycho-physical; 2) the higher animation of this two-sided body toward the personal subjectivity which makes his presence known in his environment by means of his ego-activities. Animation in this sense refers to the way in which the 'spiritual' becomes situated in the world of

96. *Ibid.*, p. 129.
97. *Ibid.*, pp. 129–130.
98. *Ibid.*, pp. 130–132.

space. In a certain sense the spirit here becomes spatial, bodily reality. When we speak here of one reality we refer evidently not only to the co-presence of the spiritual to the physical with which it is bound up, but first and foremost, to the real causal oneness of the two. We must remember here that the '$\varphi\acute{v}\sigma\iota\varsigma$' and the '$\psi\hat{v}\chi\acute{\eta}$' are also causally connected in animals. It follows that we must not think of the world of objective experience as a pure unity of physical causality but as a unity of psycho-physical causality. Psychical activities are transferred to the 'phusis' and consequently to all of the physical world.[99]

We might raise the question of whether we need a more carefully analyzed distinction between causality and reality. What is the meaning of causality within the context of concrete, psychical realities within the spatial world? How does this meaning differ from the one we attach to causality as it applies to physical reality? We noted earlier that causality referred to the mutual interdependence of individual changes as they are given in our experience. This dependence that the parts show in regard to each other in itself determines the meaning of the whole object to which these parts refer. That is why the whole object maintains its identity despite the continual changes it may undergo by itself and also in regard to the surrounding world of objects. That is also why all things depend upon each other and are atuned to the changes which take place in each other.[100]

We can carry these insights over to animal and human realities. These realities are also knowable unities of experience given in the spatial world. They, too, are related to this world by means of physical bodies which in themselves are already realities. The animation of these physical bodies does not refer to some newly acquired psychical life that would hover in mid-air above the physical bodies. The animation of the flesh refers to a two-fold unity of the psychical with the physcial. We must conclude thus that human beings and animals also show in the multiplicity of their changes a certain causal style. This causal

99. *Ibid.*, pp. 132–133.
100. *Ibid.*, pp. 133–134.

style does not refer only to their physical bodies but also to the analogous realms of the psychophysical and the psychical.[101]

Causality, as it announces itself in the physical order, refers to a stable empirical regularity of co-existence and succession. This causality appears in the objective experience in the form of a definite expectancy. The empirically necessary co-existence and succession are in this context nothing but presumptions that need further experience before they can be accepted as real and true; the causality of the physical sciences is thus thoroughly inductive. This conception of causality also affects the typical characteristics of the physical things. Thus within the realm of our purely physical attitude one can investigate only physical characteristics which descriptively manifest themselves in the extensional states and changes of these states under the form of inductively causal regularities.[102]

How does this relate to the realm of psychical beings? We showed that the psychical enters the spatial world by means of a 'bond of annexation.' The psychical is by itself not extended, although it acquires extension through the bodiliness to which it remains tied. But what if the psychical, as such, possesses its own essence with its own typical causality which, although tied to inductive causality, nevertheless, is and remains of a spiritual order? The nucleus of this problem is the question of to what extent we are justified in considering the psychical realm in and by itself. Upon our knowledge of the very essence of the psychical all the rest will depend.[103]

We are sure, however, that the psychical is incorporated in the spatial world and that inductive causality must, therefore, *eo ipso* reach beyond the physical in order to include the psychical also at least in some sense. On the other hand, however, it is also true that the psychical is ruled by inductive causality only to the extent that it is tied up with the realm of the bodily as *res extensa*. We assume here that the psychical develops inductively in analogy with my body as I see it develop. This applies

101. *Ibid.,* p. 134.
102. *Ibid.,* pp. 134–135.
103. *Ibid.,* pp. 135–136.

in an analogous fashion to our knowledge of other living beings as well. We must finally assume also that, although the psychical possesses its own unique causality, it, nevertheless, shows the same typical regularity in all living beings.[104]

However, the psychical as such possesses its own characteristic way of being. That is to say the parallelism mentioned does not imply that the soul itself is exclusively a real unity constituted by inductive causality. Since Descartes, Hobbes, and Spinoza, such a view has been quite generally defended in psychological investigations. This view, however, is only possible on the basis of the prejudice "that every objective science possesses the same style and that correlatively each objective being, that is every objective spatial reality, must possess the typical characteristics of physical realities." This is absurd and this absurdity rests on an unexamined metaphysical presupposition. We want to stay away from these arbitrary prejudices and restrict ourselves instead to describing what, as meaning, we find in the world of our immediate experience. If we proceed along these lines we see that in our experience the soul, too, reveals itself as possessing an inductive structure, although this same experience reveals this soul also as *more than* a purely inductive causally constructed unity.[105]

We must thus agree with the psychological naturalists that we can learn much about the psychical from the physical body and from the perspective of the natural sciences. We deny radically, however, that the natural sciences can ever achieve a complete understanding of psychical life. The psychical has its own unique way of being and the natural sciences remain impotent precisely in the face of this. We leave unanswered the question as to what extent the psychical rightfully acquires a priority over the physical in another, transcendental attitude.[106]

The idea of a universal natural science as universal science of all spatial world-realities remains, nevertheless, acceptable. It is presupposed here that this unitary, all encompassing world

104. *Ibid.*, pp. 136–138.
105. *Ibid.*, pp. 138–139.
106. *Ibid.*, pp. 140–142.

is our single world of realities which remain causally connected with each other within the framework of the universal, spatio-temporal world-form. There is in this realm a place for the psychophysical and the psychical as we can clearly see from the example of physiology. A false naturalistic prejudice arises only when it is assumed that there exists nothing beyond that physical, natural reality, and when the psychical as such is denied any claim to having its own essence that needs to be investigated with methods that are appropriate to its own unique mode of being. That is the insight at which we arrive by means of an analysis of the general ontology of the world of our immediate experiences, i.e., a general eidetic science of the world of experience as such.[107]

Phenomenological Psychology as 'Regional Ontology'

AROUND 1925 Husserl felt that the subject matter of psychology could be determined only by taking one's starting point in the general eidetic science of the world of our immediate experience. In his view the same holds true for the natural sciences and the other positive sciences of the world. Husserl also refers to the general eidetic science of the world as 'the general ontology of the world of our experience.'[108] We conclude that the subject matter of the different sciences can only adequately be determined when we consider it in the light of such a general ontology. This ontology remains within the natural attitude and aims to reveal the unique being of the general structures of the world of our immediate experience and all the worldly objects that manifest themselves therein. This revealing must take place on the basis of analysis and description guided by intuition. Hus-

107. *Ibid.*, pp. 142–143.
108. C. Lannoy, "Phenomenologie, ontologie en psychologie in het werk van Edmund Husserl," *Tijdschrift voor Philosophie*, 11 (1949) 391–416, p. 405. See also: Edmund Husserl, *Ideen,* vol. I, pp. 23–24; *Ideen,* vol. III, pp. 1–53 and 77–92.

serl, furthermore, foresaw the development of so-called regional ontologies [109] which would have to follow once the general ontological structure of the world of our immediate experience had been investigated. These regional ontologies would examine the most general and necessary structures of the subject matter of the different sciences.

The most general structures of the world of our immediate experiences are substantiality, spatiality, temporality, and causality. The question here is how we can succeed in determining the general structures of the psychical, as such, on the basis of our insights into the fundamental characteristics of the world of experience. The task of dealing with this question falls to a regional ontology called *phenomenological psychology*. This phenomenological psychology must take its starting point in the insights of the general ontology of the world of our experience.

When we compare this with Husserl's earlier views we see a remarkable development. Landgrebe [110] notes that Husserl assumed in the *Ideen* (1913) that the different sciences all focus on a different aspect of the world of our immediate experience. These sciences express in precise concepts that which we find only vaguely and in passing in the pre-scientific and everyday experience. Each science has its own field of investigation but it does not acquire this field itself. This domain of investigation is immediately given in our pre-scientific experience. Thus our pre-scientific experience precedes *a priori* all sciences of experience and *a priori* predelineates their domains of investigation. In *Ideen* Husserl uses the term 'region' to refer to the totality of objects that any science approaches in its own characteristic manner.[111] He speaks of the region of physical beings, of psychophysical beings, of psychical beings, etc. The objects of a region all have something in common and this characterizes these objects as belonging to this region. These common characteristics are to be described with the help of categories which are char-

109. Edmund Husserl, *Ideen*, vol. I, pp. 23–26, 164–168.
110. L. Landgrebe, "Seinsregionen und regionale Ontologien in Husserls Phänomenologie," *Studium Generale*, 9 (1956) 313–324.
111. Edmund Husserl, *Ideen*, vol. I, pp. 13, 23–26.

acteristic of each region.[112] In these basic concepts are contained all aprioric presuppositions under which each multiplicity of beings given in pre-scientific experience can be understood as constituting a unitary region which can become the subject matter of one of the sciences.

Husserl speaks of *regional ontologies* to refer to those sciences in which the basic concepts of a particular region become clarified. Each science of experience which concerns itself with a particular realm of beings is thus based on such an ontology. In *Ideen* Husserl refers to these regional ontologies as *philosophical* sciences.[113] There he furthermore says that we must not think of these ontologies as necessarily preceding a particular science of experience. Such an ontology can only be developed by means of a retrospective reflection upon the conditions under which a certain group of beings could be distinguished and separated from the rest. A regional ontology actively searches for what an object must be in absolute generality and necessity if it is to belong to a region of beings studied by a particular experiential science. These ontologies, thus, have the task of finding the essential structures of each possible subject matter of a particular science. It is for this reason that Husserl speaks of these regional ontologies as sciences of essences which he contrasts there with the sciences of facts.

Be this as it may, when Husserl claims that every empirical science is to be founded in a regional ontology, this evidently does not mean that the regional ontologies should have to precede the empirical sciences in the order of time. On the contrary, it is Husserl's view here that regional ontologies can be built up only by starting from a subsequent reflection on the conditions under which such a domain of beings could be delineated. Regional ontologies explicitate what in unconditioned generality and necessity must belong to a certain object if it really is to be the object of investigation of the correlative empirical sciences; that is to say, regional ontologies must determine and describe the essential structures of every possible object of the different

112. *Ibid.*, pp. 26–29.
113. L. Landgrebe, *Ibid.*, pp. 314–315.

empirical sciences which deal with the entities belonging to the region in question. That is why Husserl also speaks of 'eidetic sciences' in contradistinction to 'sciences of facts.' On the other hand, however, it also follows from the foregoing that, although it is true that the regional ontologies come after the corresponding empirical sciences in the order of time, they, nevertheless, as eidetic sciences precede those sciences *de jure*.[114]

In *Ideas* now a *formal ontology* which makes abstraction from all the regional distinctions of the different objects, is put ahead of the regional ontologies.[115] It is the science which deals with the formal idea 'object-in-general.' Its subject-matter consists in the conditions under which anything whatsoever can be a legitimate object of man's thought and science, and under which, therefore, this object can be explained and described by every science. The fundamental concept or the basic category of this formal ontology consists thus in the empty 'object-in-general.' Although, on the one hand, one could say that this formal ontology is a branch of logic as universal analytic, it is, on the other hand, true also that it comprises the whole *mathesis universalis* (formal logic, arithmetic, pure analysis, set theory, etc.) [116]

The regional or material ontologies try to investigate all the conditions which from the point of view of their subject matters are necessarily presupposed in the different empirical sciences. They have to focus attention on the *eidos,* that is the universally operative and necessary essence of the objects of the empirical sciences. It is these essences of the different objects of the empirical sciences which are investigated in formal ontology in the reduced form of 'object-in-general.' The subject-matter of formal ontology does, therefore, not consist in the class of essences, but in a mere essence-form, which is indeed an essence, but a completely 'empty' one, that is to say, an essence which in the manner of an empty form fits all possible essences, and which

114. Edmund Husserl, *Ideen*, vol. I, pp. 23, 164–168. See also: L. Landgrebe, *Ibid.*, p. 315; C. Lannoy, *Ibid.*, pp. 408–409.

115. Edmund Husserl, *Ideen*, vol. I, pp. 23, 26–29, 140–141, 295.

116. *Ibid.*, p. 23.

in its formal universality has the highest material generalities subordinated to it.[117] However, the formal region is not on a par with the material regions; it is properly speaking no region at all, but the pure form of 'region-in-general' only.[118] Formal ontology therefore, investigates a completely new dimension of being, namely, the necessary conditions of 'being-object.'

Thus in 1913 it was Husserl's view that the being-structure on which the material ontologies focus all their attention, is not everywhere the same: different regions of being have different constitutions and can, therefore, not be described with the help of the same categories. Certainly, one can universally apply the categories 'object,' 'relation,' etc. But the structure which is expressed in these concepts common to all regions of beings, is merely formal. Therefore, the concept 'object in general' is *not* the supreme genus of which the basic concepts of the different material regions are to be the various species.[119]

At the time *Ideen* was written, Husserl had not yet developed a general material ontology of the world of our immediate experience as such. We also fail to find there the later idea that the subject matter of the material, regional ontologies must be justified from the point of view of a general material ontology of the world of our experience. Originally Husserl felt that these subject matters could be derived from the experiential sciences themselves. However, Husserl maintained in his *Phänomenologische Psychologie* what he had said in the *Ideen* concerning formal ontology. The concept of regional ontologies remains equally intact. In this later book only a new science makes its appearance, namely, the general ontology of the world of our immediate experience. This new science is of fundamental importance for the regional ontologies. With the introduction of this newcomer, all the relationships between regional ontologies and the corresponding, experiential sciences change radically.[120]

---

117. *Ibid.,* p. 27.
118. *Ibid.,* p. 27.
119. C. Lannoy, *Ibid.,* pp. 406–408.
120. See for instance: *Ideen,* vol. I, pp. 23–26; *Ideen,* vol. III, 23–24; *Erste Philosophie,* vol. II, pp. 212–218.

Husserl's description of the 'world of our immediate experience' such as we find it in the *Phänomenologische Psychologie* shows a good deal of resemblance to his later descriptions of the life-world.[121] However, there are a good many problems that we encounter when we try to compare these two concepts. We find, for example, that Husserl uses both terms in his *Phänomenologische Psychologie* whereas it seems that the life-world of *Krisis* seems to be identical with the 'world of our immediate experience' only.[122] In 1925 Husserl gives the following description of these terms. The world of our immediate experience is a world that is immediately given in consciousness. It includes only what is immediately perceived, that which we passively find present in its bodily selfhood and is to be taken, therefore, as completely deprived of any layer of meaning which refers to our active apperception and understanding. It will be evident that it will be very difficult if not even impossible to materialize such an experience of the world.[123] For it seems that such an experience has been realizable only by the very first human beings in the very beginning of their life as human beings.

Husserl refers in the same work to the life-world as a world which we constantly experience and in which we find furniture, houses, fields, gardens, tools, pictures, etc.[124] The term 'life-world' thus refers to the cultural world surrounding us, in which all the objects are determined to a large extent by science, technology, and culture in the large sense of the word. It follows that our life-world is very different from the life-world of primitive people, whereas the world of our immediate experience seems to remain the same for all people. The author Drüe feels that Husserl maintained the distinction between 'world of our immediate experience' and life-world throughout his career.[125] The same author asserts that the life-world of Husserl's work, *Krisis*, is of exactly the same content as the life-world described in

121. Edmund Husserl, *Krisis*, § 28—§ 55; *Erf. u. Urt.*, § 7—§ 10.
122. Edmund Husserl, *Phän. Psych.*, pp. 57, 111.
123. *Ibid.*, p. 57.
124. *Ibid.*, p. 111.
125. H. Drüe, *Edmund Husserls System der phänomenologischen Psychologie*, Berlin, 1963, pp. 72–81.

Phänomenologische Psychologie. We maintain, however, that the *original* life-world of *Krisis* has much in common with the world of our immediate experience described in the *Phänomenologische Psychologie.* But in *Krisis* this *original* life-world is to be distinguished from the life-world of our everyday life. Only if we maintain the distinction between these concepts can we come to a full understanding of the reductive procedure described in *Krisis.*[126] We will later return to this matter.[127]

Be this as it may, up to this point we have explained that we live within the natural world of our immediate experience. All our activities ultimately refer back to this world, including those which constitute the natural sciences. This world of our immediate experience encompasses all the objective, all that which can be intersubjectively established as true and real. Yet, all reality and all truth make themselves known only through subjects. On the other hand, however, this subjective element needs to be left out of our consideration when we seek to solve a scientific problem.[128]

We see thus, on the one hand, that the natural sciences, which remain within the natural attitude, seek to exclude all subjectivity. On the other hand, we also see that the subjective and the psychical form part of the world; the natural sciences are ultimately even brought about in and through subjectivity. How is it possible for the natural sciences to exclude the subjective while this subjective remains part of the world [129], and everything objective can be given only in subjective experiences? [130]

The physicist is not concerned with these problems. He excludes all the subjective from his considerations and proceeds to investigate physical nature. The psychologist, however, needs to wrestle with these problems: "how can the subjective become objective by means of exclusion of the subjective which, on the

---

126. Edmund Husserl, *Krisis,* § 38—§ 44.
127. See *Chapter VI,* second section.
128. Edmund Husserl, *Phän. Psych.,* p. 147.
129. *Ibid.,* § 26 and § 27.
130. *Ibid.,* pp. 147–148.

other hand, has its place only in the realm of the objective?" We see here an old question repeated: what is subjectivity, what is objectivity? The distinction between the two realms just as we find them within our natural attitude is still not fully clear, and it leads even to problems which seem to be insoluble. We need to make a distinction between the subjective as it relates to the objective prior to any thematization, and the subjective as it appears once it has been made the theme of psychology. Thus we must try to grasp the connection between the spatio-temporal world of objects and the unobjectified subjective. This problem can be solved only in an entirely new attitude. Within that attitude it will become possible to consider the psychical without its posing one single physical problem. Only from that attitude will it become clear what the real meaning of the humanistic sciences is. The problems which we found associated with psychology lead us from phenomenological psychology as regional ontology to transcendental, philosophical phenomenology.[131]

Before we turn to philosophy to seek a radical solution to our problem, we want to illustrate the above-mentioned new perspective by means of a concrete example. We will, therefore, proceed with a phenomenological analysis of an act of perception. In this analysis we attempt to bring to light those elements which prove to be essential to an adequate determination of the psychical, still our quest.

131. *Ibid.*, pp. 148–150.

IV ANALYSIS OF AN ACT OF PERCEPTION IN ORDER TO EXPLAIN THE ESSENTIAL CHARACTERISTICS OF REFLECTION AND THE VERY ESSENCE OF THE PSYCHICAL

Preliminary Description of Reflection

In his *Phänomenologische Psychologie* Husserl tries to answer the following questions. What is the proper subject matter of empirical psychology? Which methods should it use? How does empirical psychology relate to other empirical sciences? What is its relationship to philosophy? While trying to gain insight into these questions Husserl discovered a new science, phenomenological psychology, which is to be distinguished from empirical psychology. He characterizes this new psychology as an aprioric, eidetical, intentional, and descriptive science of the realm of the psychic. This penomenological psychology resembles empirical psychology in that both disciplines remain within the natural attitude. The task of this new psychology is to give a radical foundation to empirical psychology by explaining in intentional analyses the meaning and coherence of those aspects of the psychical that are measured and correlated by empirical psychology. Phenomenological psychology is thus to provide a basis for empirical psychology and make the results of that psychology truly understandable and meaningful. Transcendental phenomenological philosophy provides in turn the basis for phenomenological psychology.

Husserl's main concern throughout his many years in all his epistemological investigations was finally to arrive at some understanding of the essence of the psychical. To reach such an understanding Husserl felt that we must start out with a general eidetical science of the world of our immediate experience. In order to be able to explain the epistemological status of this general ontology of the world of our immediate experience Husserl distinguishes two main approaches to this world: the approach from the natural point of view and that from the transcendental point of view. Within the natural point of view he distinguishes a scientific and a pre-scientific attitude. The scientific attitude can be further broken down into an empirical scientific and an aprioric or eidetical attitude. The general eidetic science of the world of our immediate experience thus is an aprioric science that runs its course within the sphere of the natural attitude. This science approaches the most general and essential structures of the world of our immediate experience and of all the objects we find therein. It also has as its task the separation of the different regions of Being. Each region becomes the subject matter of a regional ontology and its corresponding empirical sciences.

The schematic and provisional description of the main themes of the general ontology of the world of our immediate experience already brought a sufficient number of elements to the fore to be able to delineate the subject matter of the natural sciences which, as we have seen, is to be explained further in the *pure* sciences of nature and the corresponding *empirical* sciences of nature. The subject matter of the science of psychology was indicated at that point only briefly by way of contrast. This must now be explained in more detail. In particular, we must now try to explain the difference and the mutual relationship between phenomenological psychology as the regional ontology of the psychical, and empirical psychology as the empirical science of psychical facts. In order to explain this important distinction and also in order to further elucidate some of the insights described in the previous chapter, we now proceed with a concrete illustrative example.

We have already mentioned that the subject matter of psychology comes to light only when we adopt an attitude of reflection towards the world of our immediate experience. What is meant here by this reflection? Husserl advises us to use as a point of departure the spatio-temporal experience of the physicist. The physicist grasps his subject matter through exclusion of the 'purely subjective.' His point of departure is the immediate perception of the *res extensa*. There reflection takes place only to the extent that we need to keep contact with that which we experience. Reflection keeps our attention fixated on the object of investigation. Another characteristic of the physicist's attitude is the primacy of that which I experience myself. The experiences of others come in secondarily. Nature is directly present to *me*. It makes no sense to introduce the differences between primary and secondary qualities at this point. This distinction will come later. The objects in front of me are experienced directly in self-evident completeness. The objects manifest themselves immediately in their properties, their changes, their relationships to other objects, etc. It is of importance to note here that the physicist pays no attention whatsoever to the subjective aspects of the different ways in which the objects present themselves.[1]

When I now consider my own perception it becomes immediately clear that it manifests itself as a unity of continuously succeeding phases. Each phase must be characterized as an experiential grasping of something. Perception is a whole of seeing and touching activities which extends itself in time. This continuity of my perception as a whole implies a multiplicity of changing acts and their contents. In each phase of the perception I take a slightly different perspective on the object which reveals certain of its aspects and keeps others hidden. The perceived thing itself is only present to me in and through these multiple perspectives, these different modes of being-given.[2]

In the different phases of my perception of this self-same,

1. Edmund Husserl, *Phän. Psych.*, pp. 150–151. The 'psychical' is characterized here by 'temporality' whereas the 'physical' is determined by the expression 'the spatial mundane.'
2. *Ibid.*, pp. 151–152.

spatio-temporal thing, I acquire a multiplicity of aspects which in the further course of my observation turns out to refer to one and the same thing. Through this multiplicity of acts and noematical aspects I 'intend to' and become clearly aware of one and the same thing. In the non-reflexive attitude I do not become aware of this. Only reflection reveals to me these manifold aspects and phases. It is also in reflection that I can look through the multiplicity toward the unity, and thereby see that all the phases of one perception overlap each other. Only in the reflexive attitude do I also become aware that the thing itself as such is never found in the sequence of phases of one act of perception. The object as such becomes manifest only by means of these subjective modes of consciousness. The reflexive attitude makes me finally aware of the fact that I never could experience an object without these modes of consciousness.[3]

We note something very similar when we focus on the different modes in which objects appear spatially. Changes in spatial orientation do not change the object itself. In the immediate attitude this fact remains hidden to me. The reflexive attitude on the other hand shows me that the unity of the perceived object cannot be separated from the modes of consciousness in which it appears; I find the object in reflection as the unity underlying the multiplicity of my varying conscious modes. All this was equally present, of course, in the non-reflexive attitude but it then escaped our notice. True, we experienced the different phenomena then, and yet we immediately led our attention past the different modes of consciousness towards the object itself.[4]

In addition to the reflection on the perceptual stream with its perspectivistic presentations of things we can also study how the constitution of the unitary pole comes about and how in a typical genesis it realizes itself with all its remarkable horizons of anticipation which seem to extend into infinity. The phenomenon which Husserl calls 'synthesis' is here again the most important theme of investigation. The visual aspects of a partic-

3. *Ibid.*, p. 152.
4. *Ibid.*, pp. 152–153.

cular object group together and constitute a unity inasfar as they possess a closed field structure which is given in immediate experience. This unity is not only present in our visual experiences. The same can be said about our sense of touch, of taste, etc. These different unities grow together into a unity of higher level, but the way in which this happens is not manifest in immediate experience. Only a study of the intentionality of the acts can reveal fully the unity, the synthesis that eventually takes place. Such a study will reveal that all the different data of the different fields become unified around one intentional act directed towards one and the same intended object.[5]

Such an exploration brings us outside the field of the natural sciences however. We approach that which the physicist leaves out of consideration as being 'merely subjective' and study it from an entirely different perspective. In view of the fact that this 'subjective' is incarnated in nature, the real problematic here is how we are to approach the link, the relationship, between the psychical and the physical. We are only indicating this problem here, but later it will be taken up again.

We began our investigation from the perspective of the natural sciences. Instead of remaining with that perspective, we proceeded to attend to what precedes the beginning and origin of every science of nature. We tried to see what is meant by a so-called 'perception' of a spatial thing such as a chair. Our description of the reflection focused on the subjective aspects of the conscious modes in which the object made its appearance. Our study of what was given in reflection did not concentrate so much on the object as it appeared, nor did we follow the particular direction which our consciousness naturally wants to follow. First and foremost we focused attention on the subjective modes of consciousness in which the perceived thing was present to us.[6]

We already dealt in the previous chapter with the differences between the physical and the psychical. Our purpose there was to shed some light on what constitutes the subject matter of

5. *Ibid.*, pp. 153–155.
6. *Ibid.*, pp. 155–157.

physics. Now we are again concerned with this distinction between the physical and the psychical, but our purpose at this
point is to delineate the realm of the subjective as a field for
further investigation. We need at this stage a closer scrutiny of
the act of perception. We will focus for the moment on the
object of perception in its different modes of appearance. Later
we will concern ourselves with the *ego-directions* which announce themselves in our perceptions.

Husserl is rather cryptic when it comes to the analysis of an
act of perception. His *Phänomenologische Psychologie* presupposes a good deal of knowledge in the reader. Based on Gurwitsch's investigations in this area we shall, therefore, add some
explanatory remarks and elaborations which we find elsewhere
in Husserl's works.

Systematic Analysis of an Act of Perception

IN THE foregoing section we saw that each individual perception
only presents a material thing partially and uncovers it from
one single perspective. To obtain a fuller perceptual experience
of a material thing we have to go beyond this single perception
and make additional perceptions of the same thing. Through
these multiple perceptions the thing presents itself from different sides, under varying aspects, in various orientations, and suc-
cessively unfolds its properties and characteristics. Yet all these
perceptions, the content of which may considerably differ, are
perceived as perceptions of one and the same thing. The perceived thing, therefore, can as being not be adequately grasped
in one of its individual, perceptual, partial presentations.
That is why we are faced here with the problem concerning the relationship between the individual, perceptual presentations, or *noemata,* and the perceived thing itself. It is not only
true that each individual perception actually must give us only
a partial presentation of the perceived thing: the partial presentation is also really *experienced* as such. Each individual
perception points as it were to other possible perceptions or

rather to a system of perceptions in which this particular one occupies a special position. On the other hand, we experience the various perceptions which may differ clearly in terms of their noemata, yet as belonging to one and the same thing. The unity of the thing is and remains a phenomenal datum that reaches us across the multiplicity of the *noeses* and the *noemata*.[7]

The material thing given in perception is thus seen to be experienced by means of a multiplicity of perceptual *noemata*. The individual perceptions reveal their object only partially. These two facts are based on an eidetical necessity which we might discover with the method of free variation.[8] When we apply this method on one or another act of perception, it becomes clear that each and every perception of anything what-soever is actually experienced as a phase in a certain process. And we also experience this phase somehow as a part that must be integrated into a larger whole. It appears that each phase somehow points to the other phases.[9]

The method of free variation can also be used to discover the *formal* structure of the perceptive process. Analyses of some concrete cases would show that the variations cannot be completely arbitrary as long as we remain bound to profiles of one and the same object. In order to explain that one becomes aware of one and the same perceivable thing, one must admit that there must be a certain concordance and harmony between the different possible acts in which we imagine the object to appear from ever new perspectives. This ultimately means that the *noemata* of these acts appear to be harmoniously connected with each other. We find here an explanation of the fact that each succeeding phase transcends the previous one but on the other hand, nevertheless, remains in harmony with it. All the different phases pass each other by while still maintaining a certain harmony between each other.[10] The individual percep-

7. Edmund Husserl, *Ideen* vol. I, pp. 91–98; *Cart. Med.,* pp 77–79; *Phän. Psych.,* 150–161. See also: Aron Gurwitsch, *The Field of Consciousness,* Pittsburgh, 1964, pp. 202–204.
8. Edmund Husserl, *Ideen,* vol. I. pp. 95–98, 368–372.
9. *Ibid.,* pp. 363–368; *Cart. Med.,* pp. 104–105.
10. *Ibid.,* pp. 366–367; *Cart. Med.,* pp. 87–89.

tive acts grow together into one process because the corresponding *noemata* of these acts fit into one coherent system. The fact
that the individual perceptive acts grow together into one coherent whole cannot be explained on the basis of their temporal
succession because the individual acts do not need to follow each
other in close or regular successions. The unification of the
partial perceptions does not relate to acts as psychical events
which take place in phenomenal time. This unification instead
has to do with the intentional correlates, with the corresponding
noemata.

The fact that the different perceptual presentations of one
material thing unify and form *one* noematic system also explains
why the onesidedness of each individual act is experienced at the
same time that it is overcome. The onesidedness inherent in each
one of the different presentations can only then be overcome
when the multiple presentations of the system gradually materialize in such a way that the thing manifests itself through a
multiplicity of aspects which despite their differences yet remain
in harmony with each other. Each individual perceptive act
reveals the object partially, and at the same time, points to other
acts in which the object is again partially revealed. This happens in such a way that the different aspects harmonize.

This pointing of one partial perception to the next can be
seen from two different perspectives. From the noematic point
of view these references constitute essential and fundamental
characteristics of the perceptual *noema*. From the noetic point
of view, however, these references appear as anticipations of
new acts which continue to accompany the actual perception.
The onesidedness of each particular act is thus not overcome
by the mere fact that they succeed each other in close temporal
proximity. The isolation of each partial act is conquered
through mutual implication, through mutual supplementation,
and confirmation. Husserl, therefore, speaks of perception as a
process of fulfillment (*Erfüllung*).[11] We could call this process
of fulfillment the sufficient condition for the possibility of the

11. *Ibid.*, pp. 333–335.

perceptive process as a whole. The coherence, agreement, and harmonious continuation of the *noemata* or appearances of one and the same thing, on the other hand, is only a necessary, not-sufficient condition of the possibility of the perceptive process as a whole.[12]

Each individual perceptive act shows us a certain aspect of an object in a certain *noema*. This particular *noema* points to others, whereas each particular act refers to other possible perceptive acts concerning the same thing. Since the *noemata* can succeed each other in an endless procession we must view perception as somehow always more or less arbitrarily ended and at least never truly completed. The perceptive process is, therefore, truly an 'open system' in which the object shows itself under ever varying aspects. From this we can draw the conclusion that all sciences which are based on perception are themselves ever 'open systems' which will never completely encompass their respective subject matters.[13]

When we seek to ascertain the reality of a spatial and mundane and, therefore, of a material thing, and not only of its possibility, then it does not suffice to appeal to all possible appearances whatsoever. For in that case one needs not only *noemata* which remain in harmony with each other, but those *noemata* should have to be given at once in one and the same perceptive experience in an effective way. Here we meet thus an essential imperfection in our perceptive process. The material thing shows only one aspect of itself at a time; we never *actually* perceive more than one particular aspect of such a thing. The other aspects can only be remembered or they can be anticipated. Seen from the noetic point of view this means that never can more than one link of the perceptive process as a whole be materialized.[14]

There are, therefore, a number of conditions that need to be fulfilled if the different perceptive *noemata* of a certain system are to manifest themselves as appearances of one and the same

12. *Ibid.*, pp. 91–98, 368–372; *Cart. Med.*, pp. 79–81, 89–91.
13. *Ibid.*, pp. 100–101; *Cart. Med.*, pp. 85, 97.
14. *Ibid.*, pp. 100–102.

material thing which in and through all these appearances continues to present itself as continuously identical. The internal organization of the system of *noemata* must thus maintain an internal harmony which will last throughout the perceptive process as a whole. That is to say its parts may not exclude each other and, furthermore, there must be an internal relationship of completion and continuation among the *noemata*. This unity of the system of *noemata* can hardly be thought of as being brought about by an extrinsic factor or by some extrinsic unifying principle. On the contrary, this organization itself is also an immediate phenomenal datum; the different appearances of one material thing are immediately experienced as harmoniously connected with one another.

Furthermore such a multiplicity can be organized in such a way only if the constitutive elements possess a relation of functional interdependence in regard to each other and to the whole. However, the thing is actually experienced only from a certain definite point of view; the actuality of an object can be seen to consist in the progressive actualization of a coherent system of interconnected *noemata*. We will return to this matter in greater detail. On the other hand, every *noema* refers to all the other *noemata* involved in a particular perceptive process. Every *noema*, therefore, is the observed thing itself which in this *noema* presents itself in a onesided way only; every *noema* realizes the noematic system as a whole in its own fashion. We can express this phenomenologically in the following manner: the experience of each particular appearance is a perception of the whole noematic system viewed from the position of one of the elements of the system. Only because of the actual reference of this *noema* to the other *noemata* is the actual appearance what it really is: the appearance of the perceived thing.[15]

Whether a thing actually exists is thus determined by the fact of whether in principle it is possible to perceive this thing adequately. For the perceptive experiences themselves are precisely the source of the existential meaning of things, as will be-

15. Aron Gurtwitsch, *op. cit.*, pp. 208–213.

come clear in greater detail in transcendental phenomenology.[16] Yet it is also true that these things are experienced as transcending our consciousness. But what is the meaning of this transcendence? To answer that question we must make a careful analysis of those acts in which the object precisely shows itself as transcending our consciousness.[17] We already made note of the fact that each individual perception can only be a perception of a spatial and mundane thing and, therefore, can be a phase of the perceptive grasp of that thing only when this individual perception becomes integrated within a systematically organized larger whole which must possess a determinate formal structure. When we are faced with a series of acts concerning one individual thing or concerning the world which mutually complement each other, which mutually 'fill each other out,' then it would be unreasonable to doubt the reality of those objects. But in that case one must posit also that all perceptible things and the world as a whole are essentially correlative to our acts of perception, that is to say, to certain processes of consciousness. They form identical unities which as such manifest themselves in and through multiplicities of acts which are in harmony with each other. These unities now depend upon consciousness to the extent that they are in the way they manifest themselves to us in and through the systematic groups of acts; that is to say, they must exist as having that meaning with which they present themselves in those groups of acts and which—as we shall see later—they even receive from these acts. Thus the necessary conditions which must be fulfilled by the system of acts if they are to be real experiences of real things, appear to be at the same time, the necessary conditions of the possibility of the real world. Thus these conditions appear to be transcendental conditions.[18]

In transcendental phenomenology we hold on to the following basic principle: each and every object must be viewed as the ever identical correlate of a multitude of acts and of systematic

16. Edmund Husserl, *Ideen*, vol. I, pp. 113–114.
17. *Ibid.*, pp. 110–113.
18. *Ibid.*, pp. 114–117, 329–333; *Cart. Med.*, pp. 64–77; *Form. u. tr. Logik*, pp. 205–208.

196 Phenomenological Psychology

processes of consciousness. The form this systematization will take depends upon the particular region to which the object in question belongs. Each real object corresponds to the idea of a possible act of consciousness which in regard to this object functions as the original, meaning-giving intuition which by the later multiplicity of acts must be completed.[19] This formulation seems to evade the question as to the inner structure which connects this multiplicity of acts into one process which has this one single thing as its object. When we call the object the correlate of these perceptive acts, then the object can be seen as the systematically ordered chain of the *noemata* which correspond to these acts. In that case we can call the *noemata* the *equivalent* of the object in question; the term 'equivalent' being thought of here as 'equivalent in terms of consciousness.' [20]

The real thing appears thus in the transcendental attitude as a systematic, ordered totality of all the appearances or perceptual *noemata* of that thing. The relationship between the mere appearance of a thing and the thing itself taken as a real thing is thus the relationship between a part of the noematical system and the whole of that system. We speak, therefore, of transcendental problems when we want to refer to the mutual relationship between the one identical thing and the manifold acts in which it appears to us. We move in the area of transcendental phenomenology when we want to account for an object in terms of consciousness, that is when we make the thing manifest itself as correlate of the acts of consciousness. The concordance, the harmony, the suitable continuation into each other of all the successive perceptual appearances of a thing form the necessary conditions for the perceptive process. All this also forms the necessary condition for the possibility of real things and for the possibility of the world of our experience in general.[21]

Perception, therefore, forms an open process in which it is

19. *Ibid.*, pp. 348–350; *Cart. Med.*, pp. 99–100.
20. *Ibid.*, pp. 375.
21. *Ibid.*, pp. 212–216, 348–350, 353–357, 363–375; *Cart. Med.*, pp. 77–81, 97–100.

required that the different phases of the process be in tune with each other; each earlier appearance must receive a confirmation and support from the following ones. But this does not take away the fact that successive perceptions can contradict earlier ones. On the basis of previous perceptions we have certain expectations concerning successive ones but these expectations are not always met. The openness of the perceptive process forces us to conclude that successive perception of anything whatsoever may, even of the world as a whole, in principle, force us to correct our expectation based on previous perceptions.[22] In the transcendental attitude the same rule applies when we speak concerning the Being of things and concerning the Being of the world in general. This should not be understood to mean that within the transcendental attitude the reality of the world would be denied, or even really doubted.[23] The Being of the world is indubitably certain but the meaning of this indubitable certitude must be understood in a radical way.[24] Every being has a complex tissue of acts and processes of consciousness that answers it and which enables this being to be adequately understood. Since the perceptive process is never truly completed we can say that only an *endless* perceptive process can give us an adequate and comprehensive grasp of that thing. To each real thing there corresponds such an endless perceptive process.

When in the transcendental attitude we speak of the presumed existence of real things we mean to indicate that our grasp on this thing by means of finite segments of the perceptive process as a whole is essentially inadequate and incomplete. Although a complete grasp on things can never truly be realized we nevertheless can form an idea concerning the totality to which our grasp refers. The word '*idea*' has here the meaning which Kant used to attach to it.[25] Thus also from the transcen-

22. *Ibid.*, pp. 106–109, 338–340; *Cart. Med.*, pp. 96–97.
23. *Ibid.*, p. 109.
24. G. Berger, *Le cogito dans la philosophie de Husserl*, Paris, 1941, pp. 93, 135.
25. Edmund Husserl, *Ideen*, vol. I, pp. 350–351, 365–368, 417–419.

dental perspective the 'thing-in-itself' can be shown to be an idea in this sense.[26] A consequent thinking through of the transcendental problems brings us necessarily into the domain of transcendental philosophy.[27] We want to return here, however, to phenomenological psychology and continue our analysis of a simple act of perception.

The perceptual *noema* is identical with the thing itself just as it is manifested in the perceptive act. In this *noema* we must make a distinction between all that is actually and effectively present by means of our senses, and what is not so present. While perceiving a house we never effectively perceive more than one side of this house; our actual perception concerns a house, not a certain plane displaying certain textures and colors. What is effectively perceived is interpreted under the impact of that which is not effectively perceived.[28] Both, the effectively and the non-effectively perceived aspects constitute the perceptive meaning of every concrete act. Sometimes those factors which are not effectively perceived are actually of a different order than the factors which are effectively perceived. It is thus possible for us to *see* that a feather is light and to *hear* that a car is heavy. In such cases, the non-effectively perceived can actually be of greater importance than that which is immediately perceived. We see that it is possible to drive a nail into the wood with a hammer even though nobody effectively performs such action at the time that we perceive the hammer.[29]

An analysis of the non-effectively given must take place and always remain within the descriptive orientation. It is important to note that this implies a purely static orientation rather than a dynamic one since we are no longer interested in what the next act may reveal concerning the object we are contemplating; we seek only to describe that which manifests itself in this particular instant both in a direct and in an indirect manner.

26. Edmund Husserl, *Cart. Med.*, p. 97.
27. See the third section of this Chapter.
28. Edmund Husserl, *Erf. u. Urt.*, pp. 27, 31.
29. Aron Gurwitsch, *op. cit.*, pp. 228–231, 234–236.

When we consider a particular perceptive act together with its *noema,* it soon becomes clear that each and every actual perception points to sensory aspects that are not effectively present to the senses at this moment. These aspects are more or less determined accordingly as the thing was more or less familiar to us. Every perceptual *noema* thus contains a nucleus which in the sensory experience is *immediately* given and this in turn points to aspects that are not immediately given. This immediately given nucleus of the perceptual *noema* is therefore surrounded by an horizon, an *inner horizon* in Husserl's usage.[30]

This inner horizon shows little differentiation in some exceptional cases, but the rule is quite the opposite. We not only perceive things as spatially determined objects which can be observed from a variety of different aspects, but we experience things also as belonging to a certain class. This is not to say that all perceptions of things are necessarily attempts to grasp that thing explicitly as an example of a particular class. For in the latter case we necessarily presuppose a universal concept which in itself is not part of the perception. Here, however, we must stick to the perceived thing as such taken in the fullness of its concrete being. Yet, the internal horizon of the object as such already contains a vague reference to the class to which this thing belongs. The indeterminateness of this horizon is always delimited by certain general traits which follow from the fact that the object in question is always *experienced as* belonging to this or that group of objects. This indeterminateness of the inner horizon thus is an indeterminateness within a general and immediately given determination. True, the references which lie contained in the internal horizon may sometimes appear vague, but even in that case a certain determination is given immediately. On the other hand, however, there is always a certain ambiguity contained in the explicitation of the inner horizon of a thing, but this ambiguity especially concerns the *manner* in which a particular type is materialized in a particular and concrete case. Here it is important to note again that in a

30. Edmund Husserl, *Ideen,* vol. I, pp. 100–101, 249–252; *Erf. u. Urt.,* pp. 26–37.

descriptive orientation we must restrict ourselves to the perception itself and its inner horizon.

Since in the initial phases of the perception the inner horizon is still undetermined, the subject is faced with an open field of possibilities. The actual perception does, therefore, not give the subject certain hints on the basis of which he might be able to choose between these possibilities. All the ambiguous possibilities contained in the inner horizon can be explicitated as long at least as they remain in tune with what is immediately and effectively present to the subject. Yet, none of these possibilities is more probable than the others. It is possible, however, to make a clear distinction between these open possibilities and what must definitely be called impossible on the basis of this inner horizon. But within the realm of open possibilities for this particular thing we do not find further clues that will help us to prefer one and reject the other possibilities. Thus the internal horizon is only helpful in making it possible for us to distinguish between the types of problems we may and may not pose on the basis of the effectively given; but we cannot get any indication as to the particular questions we should pose.[31]

The inner horizon of a thing is somehow co-determined by the past of the perceiving subject. When we are confronted with a thing we are familiar with, then it frequently happens that aspects which are effectively perceived actually give us information about that which we do not at this moment really perceive. When we are confronted with a completely unknown thing, we often can determine the class of things to which it belongs on the basis of our perception of other analogous things in the past. In psychology, associationism explains this phenomenon as resulting from the fact that that which is now perceived, calls forth certain images that appeared to have been associated with it in the past. The phenomenon of the inner horizon is thus seen in terms of associated images, while the act of perception is seen as an aggregate of sensations; and that which is

31. Edmund Husserl, *Erf. u. Urt.*, pp. 31–32, 93–112.

perceived becomes there the sum of heterogeneous elements which are connected with each other by simple juxtaposition. In this way, however, the intrinsic unity of the perceptual act remains an unexplained fact. Husserl rejects this explanation but his own interpretation of the given phenomena also remains unconvincing. This is due to the fact that Husserl remains caught in an unacceptable form of dualism in perception. In his further treatment of the phenomena of the inner horizon Husserl employs his well-known theory concerning the distinction between *hylē* and *morphē* which is of cardinal importance, according to him, in understanding consciousness. *Hylē* refers to sensory impressions, to sensations of pleasure or pain, to impulses and strivings. These impressions are as yet single elementary data, they lack as yet all meaning and all objectifying function. These *hyletic data* offer themselves as material for certain operative factors which bestow them with meaning. These operative factors are called the intentional forms, the noetical forms, or in short, *noeses*. The unity which results from the combination of *hylē* and *morphē* is an intentional act, that is an act through which the subject is placed before an object and in which the object presents itself in a certain mode which depends upon the *noeses* in question. Husserl acknowledges here specific factors which have a meaning-giving function; it is because of these factors that we are able to grasp a meaning and, therefore, an object.[32]

When considering a perception of something, we are to distinguish between the sensory impression as the rough material for sensory perceptions *and* the specific acts of intending, objectification, and apperception.[33] Husserl opposed traditional conceptions when he viewed apperception as a descriptive, specific, and irreducible moment of our conscious life.[34] In his view the objectifying and interpretive acts 'inform' and organize the *hyletic data* and bestow on them an objective reference. It is

32. Edmund Husserl, *Ideen*, vol. I, pp. 207–216, 218–221, 228–232, 241–252.
33. *Ibid.*, pp. 210–216, 241–249.
34. Edmund Husserl, *L.U.*, vol. II, 1, pp. 380–387; *Ideen*, vol. I, pp. 241–249.

only in this way that these data start to play a role in the perceptual manifestation of the object in question as it appears in the concrete intentional act.

The objectifying perceptive apperception maintains a certain relationship with the grasping of the meaning of our words.[35] Both rest on an interpretation of the already present *hyletic data* by means of special meaning-giving acts. Husserl makes note also of the difference between the two.[36] In the perceptive apperception the *hyletic data* acquire a noetic form and in and through the intentional act which is constituted in this way there appears then a particular object in the mode of a perceptual presentation. In the grasping of the meaning of a word, there takes place a second interpretation which takes the form of an act which will provide the word with a definite meaning. In other words, in the first case the hyletic data are constitutive elements of the perceptual *noema,* whereas these data are not constitutive elements of the meaning of a word.

In other words, Husserl maintains a dualistic position in regard to perception. It seems that the organization of the perceptual *noema* is entirely ascribed to *noetic* factors; taken by themselves the *hyletic data* are amorphous, without structure and organization. Husserl bases this view on the fact that the given data lend themselves to more than one manner of interpretation.[37]

The perceptual *noema* is identical with the perceived thing itself in the exact form in which it immediately appears to the subject by means of a certain perceptive act. In this *noema* thus are contained: 1) all the attributes of the thing which are effectively and immediately given in our sensory experience; 2) all the attributes which play a role in the perception even though they are not exactly given in that form; 3) all the aspects under which the thing in question could appear, insofar as these aspects are actually referred to in that which is effectively present to the perceiving subject.

35. *Ibid.,* pp. 61–74.
36. *Ibid.,* pp. 74–77.
37. Edmund Husserl, *Ideen,* vol. I, pp. 247–248; *Erf. u. Urt.,* pp. 99–100.

The perceptual *noema* thus contains only that which is effectively and immediately given together with the inner horizon. The perceptual *noema* is therefore characterized as the meaning of the perception inasfar as this itself is already given in that perception.[38] Implied in such a conception seems to be the idea that the meaning of a perception is not an exteriorly derived ingredient that needs to be added to the sensory data as such. This idea seems, in turn, to lead to an interpretation of the perceptual *noema* as a complex unit of meaning. If Husserl had stressed this idea, he probably would have been able to avoid the dualism to which we referred earlier. Be this as it may, it is time now to return to our analysis of the perceptive act.[39]

Each and every perception reveals its object in an incomplete manner. From a noetic point of view this means that each perception includes anticipations of other perceptive experiences in which the object could be revealed under different aspects. We noted before that the implicit elements of the inner horizon never remain completely undetermined. In a very similar sense we note now that the anticipations of other perceptive experiences are never completely *empty*. Anticipations always are anticipations of something, and this "something" always meets the general requirements of a certain organization, however indeterminate this may be in particular details. Thus the indeterminacy on the side of the perceptual *noema* corresponds on the noetic side to anticipations of possible future determinations in new acts. On the noematic side we observed a mutual interdependence, a mutual determination of the constitutive elements of the inner horizon of the perceptual *noema* itself. The noetic consideration, on the other hand, reveals this indeterminacy as a pointing from the present perception to future perceptions which will gradually complete the actual perception of the thing.

38. *Ibid.*, pp. 223–226, 249–252.
39. Aron Gurwitsch, *op. cit.*, pp. 265–273; J.-P. Sartre, *L'être et le néant. Essai d'ontologie phénoménologique*, Paris, 1948, pp. 23–27, 372–383; M. Merleau-Ponty, *Phénoménologie de la perception*, Paris, 1945, p. 464.

All that which is implicitly present in the actual perception gradually becomes explicit while the perceptive process proceeds. The incompleteness of every perception stems, noematically considered, from the fact that the object of perception is present only in some profile (*Abschattung*). This same incompleteness stems, noetically considered, from the fact that the perception refers beyond itself toward possible future perceptions.[40]

It is clear that there must exist a close tie between a perception and the anticipations of future perceptions contained in it. To see this close tie only in terms of simultaneity would be a gross over-simplification. We must remain in touch with the fact that it is perceptions that are being anticipated. In these perceptions certain aspects and properties of the thing will be given which—although they are now not yet given effectively—nonetheless co-constitute the perceptual *noema* that corresponds to the present perception.[41]

Not every perception is effectively accompanied by *explicit* anticipations; the anticipations can be in a formally implicit stage. Yet, each and every perception can be further explicitated, and during the process the perceptual *noema* can be revealed without being changed in any way. For explicitation refers to the process in which the constituent elements of a thing are revealed without the addition of new elements.[42]

Husserl speaks in this connection about potentialities of consciousness. The actual perception of a thing implies certain anticipations which point to further possible experiences of the same thing. The actualization of these potentialities is experienced as something that in the last instance depends on the subject. We can reach beyond the actual aspect under which we perceive something and turn to another aspect under which we might observe the same thing. We experience this anticipated

40. Edmund Husserl, *Ideen*, vol. I, pp. 100–104; *Cart. Med.*, pp. 83–86; *Erf. u. Urt.*, pp. 26–36.
41. *Ibid.*, pp. 201–203.
42. *Ibid.*, pp. 177–181.

perception as a possibility which we can freely actualize just by moving ourselves bodily to another location. The indeterminacy of the constitutive elements of the *noema* refers to this freedom of the perceiving subject. And the perceiving subject knows that it can bring about the further determination of the thing. This effective determination of the as yet indeterminate constitutive elements can come about only by means of appropriate activities of the perceiving subject.[43] We must in this connection become aware of the importance of our body, or rather of the importance of the consciousness of our body. This consciousness plays an important role in the perceptive experience of things. This consciousness of our body forms a *constant* although marginal datum of our total consciousness; as such this consciousness of the body relates at the same time to our present bodily attitude under which we observe the object and to the many other possible attitudes which we could assume.

From this it follows that we must differentiate two types of potentialities; both types do differ to an extent but also are narrowly related to each other. First of all there is the possibility to explicitate the perceptual *noema*. Besides this possibility we have the ability to investigate that which we perceive with ever new acts, with ever new *noemata*. It is especially during the actualization of the latter that the object acquires its progressive determination.

In a given perception the perceived thing appears under a certain aspect. This aspect was already implicitly present as a co-determinant in the perceptual *noemata* which corresponded to earlier perceptions. This aspect is in turn co-determined by other aspects under which the thing can or will manifest itself in future perceptions. This mutual referring brings about a gradual binding together of the perceptual *noemata* until a systematically related group is formed. This group constitutes, in terms of consciousness, the equivalent of the thing in question. Each separate *noema*, realizes the whole system in its own man-

43. *Cart. Med.*, p. 82; *Erf. u. Urt.*, pp. 34, 88.

ner and in its particular place in the group; this explains how
each individual *noema* can represent one and the same thing
and can be experienced as such.

We can express this noetically as follows: the different perceptions mutually confirm and strengthen each other during the
perceptive process as long as no corrections or revisions take
place. Ultimately these different perceptions fit into each other
as phases of a unitary process. The inner coherence of the
process is based on the effective fulfillment of the references to
other perceptual acts of the same process which as anticipations
were implied in previous perceptions. The perception as a
whole manifests itself in this way as a process of fulfillment of
anticipations. Since there is no absolute guarantee that this
process of fulfillment will stretch out into infinity, it follows that
things and also the world as a whole only have a presumptive
existence. The world and the things are therefore essentially
contingent and in this sense depend for their Being on consciousness.[44]

It also becomes clear that the unity of the total process forms
a systhesis by means of identification. The unity of the perceived
thing, however, reaches us as being given throughout different
perceptive acts. This unity therefore is not the result of certain
special acts which as such could be distinguished from the other
perceptive acts. Our consciousness of the identity of the observed thing is tied to the experience of the mutual implication
and mutual strengthening of the different partial perceptions
of the same system.[45] The problem of the identity and thus of
the substantiality of the thing is by no means exhausted by
these remarks. However, we will not further pursue the problem
of the relationship: *cogito cogitatum,* as it relates to the perceptive act. Our first task in this chapter was to explain the essential
aspects of the reflexive attitude in order to prepare ourselves
in this way for a discussion concerning the subject matter of
psychology.

44. *Erf. u. Urt.,* pp. 93–94; *Ideen,* vol. I, pp. 115–116.
45. *Ideen,* vol. I, pp. 91–95; *Cart. Med.,* pp. 77–81; *Ideen,* vol. I, pp. 329–
330.

Yet, we do not want to leave our analysis at this point without having said a word about the intentional method which we used in our analysis of an act of perception. The intentional analysis is without a doubt the preferred phenomenological method. The original function and meaning of this method consists in the uncovering of the implicit potentialities of the actual states of consciousness. It is the general method used in the explicitation of meanings and consists in the unraveling of those constitutive elements which lie buried in certain actually given meanings.[46]

When applied to the perceptive process the intentional analysis rests on that which is immediately but still only implicitly present in our actual experience. If we want to uncover the 'meaning of a perception' we must try to explicitate the internal horizon.[47] This procedure has a noetic and a noematic side.[48] From the noetic perspective the method requires that we describe the internal horizon as an uncovering of anticipations of possible, new, still potential perceptions: the actual perception must therefore be seen in connection with the whole system of those acts which in some way can be connected with this particular perception.[49] Now we have seen that the real thing is constituted into an objective unity through the concatenation of the perceptions which form a systematically interrelated group. We saw also that the thing itself is something that manifests itself progressively in perception, and, thus, derives the meaning of its existence from these systematically interrelated partial perceptions. Intentional analysis of a particular perception therefore entails research into the contributions of this particular perception to the constitution of the thing which manifests itself in this perception.[50]

To subject a perception to an intentional analysis, therefore,

46. *Cart. Med.*, pp. 83–86; Gaston Berger, *op. cit.*, pp. 45–46, 79–88, 106–117.
47. Edmund Husserl, *Cart. Med.*, pp. 83–86.
48. These analyses are sometimes called 'noetico-noematic analyses'. See for instance: P. Ricoeur, "Méthode et tâches d'une phénoménologie de la volonté," in *Problèmes actuels de la phénoménologie* (Ed. H.L. Van Breda), Brugge-Paris, 1952, 111–140, p. 115.
49. Edmund Husserl, *Cart. Med.*, p. 85.
50. *Ideen*, vol. I, pp. 212–215; *Cart. Med.*, pp. 85–86.

always entails considering it in a transcendental way. The reference of this perceptive act to the total process in which the thing is constituted, is essential here while, on the other hand, the total process itself is no more than an explicitation of that which the partial perception already implicitly contains within its inner horizon.[51]

The Transcendental Problem

WE ALREADY touched on the transcendental problem in our noetico-noematical analysis of a perceptive act. This problem turns out to be of great importance for a radical explanation of the very nature of the reflexive attitude and it is of equally great importance for our research into the subject matter of psychology. It is, therefore, really worth our while to examine this problem more closely. In order to pose the problem clearly we must repeat a few points which we discovered in the previous section.

We have already pointed to one of the most remarkable phenomena of perception, namely perspectivity. This perspective character can be seen to belong also to the whole of the perceptual field. We shall now shift our attention from the individually perceived thing to its spatial horizon. This spatial horizon is to be distinguished carefully from the inner horizon. That is why we want to indicate it with the expression 'outer horizon' even though this outer horizon contains more than spatial aspects as we will see later.[52] The natural attitude already reveals a group of perceived things as surrounded by a perceptual field which as perceptual space contains all the separate spatial things and in which each thing has its own qualitativily determined place. Only from these concrete things is the open space as horizon experienced.

---

51. Aron Gurwitsch, *op. cit.*, pp. 292–295.
52. Edmund Husserl, *Phän. Psych.*, p. 161; *Ideen*, vol. I, pp. 57–62; *Krisis*, pp. 163–167. See also: L. Landgrebe, *Phänomenologie und Metaphysik*, Hamburg, 1949, pp. 42–49.

In the reflexive attitude it is possible for us to move in analogous fashion from the thing to the totality of all the perceived things surrounding it, or from the perspective of the thing to the perspective of the given totality. Again we meet here with a problem of synthesis: how is this total perspective constituted out of the separate perspectives of the separate things? And how is space visualized in this totality? [53] Again we also meet here with two different kinds of elements. First of all we meet with the objective data which we perceive directly in the perception of spatial things. Secondly, we meet with the hyletic data of the immediate experiential data as such. These latter data have, as we saw previously, their own Being although, on the other hand, they are not objective beings. The hyletic data are not even perspectives although they become perspectives by means of our intending acts which provide them with the 'subjective function' of being appearances of an objective being. We can grasp these hyletic data directly only in the reflexive attitude without paying attention to the fact that an objective spatial being appears through them. Our seeing of an object becomes possible only because we experience the hyletic visual data which receive their perspectivistic character as a result of our intending acts. It is thus because of these acts only that these data can appear to us as manifestations of this or that thing. We should try to apply these observations to the problems of perceptual space.[54]

Previously we contrasted the perceptual data given in both the direct and the reflexive attitude insofar as they relate to spatial worldly things. We thus learned to distinguish the spatial-objective from the subjective manner in which the perspectives are given. In addition to what was said already in the beginning of this chapter we must realize now that each momentary perceptual space manifests itself *in* the visual field of experience as the invariable form in which all visual forms of the profiles are ordered. By the expression, 'perceptual space' is here to be understood either the primordial field of perception itself or in

53. Edmund Husserl, *Phän. Psych.*, pp. 161–163.
54. *Ibid.*, p. 163.

other cases the primoridal spatial field as the fixed general form of the perceptual spaces which manifest themselves in these momentary perceptual spaces.

Concretely speaking we notice, thus, on the side of the subject a visual field with the sense qualities which extend themselves throughout the perceptual space and therein constitute the various particular *Gestalte* which, thus, are to be taken as concretely informed qualities. We call these the visual, sensory data. The form of the visual field remains constant despite all changes which take place within it, and turns out to be two-dimensional while the space occupied by the perceived things shows itself as three-dimensional. It is, nevertheless, correct to say that objective space is represented in a two-dimensional space. Similar problems should be studied for the other non-visual spheres. Our sense of touch in particular offers many problems since this sense is without perspectivity, at least without perspectivity in the real sense. Ultimately we need to come up with concrete indications of how we put the different data together in such a way that the experiential datum as a whole emerges at the same time that the sensory space as a whole emerges.[55]

Be this as it may, there are subjective data which cannot be objectively perceived by means of *Abschattungen* of other data, yet which taken by themselves should be free of all the characteristics of consciousness. These subjective data fulfill an important function in that they can form the nuclear contents of certain functional characteristics in a variety of ways. By means of the nuclear contents these intentional functions make other objectivities become conscious which are to be distinguished from the functions themselves.[56] Earlier we called these functional characteristics the *intentional functions,* whereas we referred to the nuclear contents such as color-data, sound-data, smell- and taste-data insofar as these are thought of as purely subjective rather than psychophysical, as *hyletic data.* These hyletic data form the material for the functions of consciousness.

55. *Ibid.,* pp. 164–166.
56. *Ibid.,* p. 166.

The function in which and by means of which the subjective data of a perception are transformed into the perception of a spatial-objective thing thus forms a very special case. According to Husserl it will be possible to pose the problems of immanence and transcendence correctly and bring them—in principle at least—to a solution when we make use of the above described subtle distinctions and differentiations.[57]

It should be clear at this point that we can mean a variety of things when we say that 'something' is perceived. First of all, the thing itself is immediately and directly perceived. When we reflect upon the perceptive event it becomes clear that we can also say that subjective modes of appearance are perceived. We further can assume two different attitudes towards these modes of appearance. 1) We can approach them in such a fashion that we do not lose hold of the thing in the particular appearance; the modes of appearance are then precisely seen as modes in which this thing appears. 2) We can also focus more exclusively on the hyletic data and renounce in this the thematic interest in the thing itself. For, hyletic data can be experienced without any interest in the fact that they point to an object, even though the orientation of those data toward the objects evidently still exists.[58]

It is thus still possible to make a distinction between the sphere of real things, the sphere of the perceived, spatial field, and objective temporality on the one hand, and the purely subjective appearances as the sphere of the subjective and the flowing temporality of the modes of appearances themselves on the other. This fundamental distinction can be observed in all our acts of knowing and striving.[59]

But then it is possible also to distinguish two types of temporality: the endless, objective time seen as the 'form' of the objective world, and the subjective time as the 'form' of all subjective entities which is experienced as 'flowing reality.' One of the most important problems of phenomenology consists in

57. *Ibid.*, pp. 166–167.
58. *Ibid.*, pp. 168–169.
59. *Ibid.*, pp. 169–170.

explaining how in the subjective, flowing time which is characteristic of the appearance of a thing, not only the spatio-temporal
but also the objective duration of spatio-temporal reality is
constituted.[60] Dropping this question for the moment we now
only posit that there are two forms of temporalities and two
kinds of temporal objects present in any perception whatsoever.
Our perception now is called 'external perception' as long as it
is oriented toward the objective, spatio-temporal reality. The
internal perception is directed towards the purely subjective.
The object of this internal perception is the immanent which
is characterized by subjective time.[61] Let us now focus attention
for a moment on our internal or immanent perception which
thus is directed towards the subjective and its characteristic
immanent time. There it will be clear that that which is perceived *in* this mode of perception is an individual something.
The individuality, the uniqueness of this 'something' follows
from its own temporal determinations, whereas it furthermore
appears as tied to other equally individual entities. We now
speak of the stream of experiences to point to the stream of all
the subjective data of our experience, the perspectives and appearances, as the stream of immanent-temporal objects which are
concatenated into a harmonious unity. All that which we perceive in the immanent temporal sphere as being individual,
immanent, temporal, exists only as something flowing. This is
also true for sensory data, for every single appearance of something, and for each and every intentional experience as such. It
is important to state here once more that everything that is
experienced in this sphere is observed without any possible perspectivity [62] and without any possible internal horizon [63] "The
immanent is adequately grasped without any anticipation of
what ought first to be given in other perceptions." In this case
it is impossible, therefore, to perceive one and the same thing

60. *Ibid.*, p. 170. See also: *Ideen*, vol. I, pp. 196–199; L. Landgrebe, *op. cit.*,
pp. 75–80; Q. Lauer, *Phénoménologie de Husserl*, pp. 188–194, 324–330.
61. Edmund Husserl, *Phän. Psych.*, pp. 170–171.
62. *Ibid.*, p. 171.
63. *Ibid.*, pp. 171–172.

in more than one way. Neither do we find here a tension between the subjective and the objective. For this 'objective' precisely is the flowing subjective inasfar as it presents itself in one or other perception.[64]

Taken within the realm of the purely immanent, any intentional experience consists of two real parts, namely the hyletic data contained in it and the typical characteristic of being the perspective of something objective by means of intentional acts. Besides this, however, we find in this obviously pure subjective experience also somehow the object which is represented therein in a perspectivistic way. However, the object does not form a *real* part of this subjective experience because the intentional object appears in all phases while the phases insofar as they differ cannot share and contain real moments in common.[65] *Really* immanent are only the appearances, the hyletic data, the characteristics of being 'consciousness-of-something,' but the object which is 'meant' in these moments is itself not part of the real immanent. The separate, visual, hyletic data of the stream of experiences must be unified in a special process which we call *synthesis*. This synthesis can be based on the hyletic unity of the data themselves as long as we talk about data associated with *one* sensory organ. There also exists, however, a synthesis between visual unities with similar tactile and auditory unities. This unity cannot be based on the hyletic unity of the data; the synthesis is derived here from the intentional directedness of all data toward one and the same object.[66] It follows that the synthesis of the flowing stream of appearances must possess this characteristic trait that it forms a real synthesis which, nevertheless, consists of phases which in turn are based on something unreal. This unreal element in the phases of the synthesis is the 'meant' object. Thus the spatial object is inseparable from the intentional synthesis of the appearances thereof, and it is immediately present in this intentional synthesis as an ideal identical pole in which each phase is contained as *its* intentional

64. *Ibid.*, pp. 171–172; see also: *Ideen*, vol. I, pp. 95–98.
65. *Phän. Psych.*, pp. 172–173; *Ideen*, vol. I, pp. 218–226.
66. *Phän. Psych.*, pp. 173–174; *Ideen*, vol. I, pp. 196–199, 291–293.

object, while, on the other hand, the object nonetheless remains identical in all the phases. In analogous fashion this is true also for every objective property of the object.[67]

We find something similar in every other intentional act. For what in manifold modes of consciousness is always consciously present as the same is (purely taken just as it is consciously present) an ideal correlate in the synthesis which materializes within the immanence of the intentional experience. However, this conscious object, though inseparable from this synthesis, is nevertheless like something which in comparison with the immanent data manifests itself as something 'irreal' or, in other words, something which is relatively transcendent.[68]

A special type of transcendence manifests itself here: every purely subjective object transcends the manifold, synthetically connected modes of consciousness of that object. In this 'relative manner of speaking' immanence and transcendence are thus not entirely mutually exclusive. Yet, when we look closer we will see that this which at first announces itself as 'relative' ultimately will point to a deeper, a more fundamental, even absolute distinction between immanence and transcendence.[69]

An object is called absolutely transcendent only when it can manifest itself in itself merely as the unity of the appearances of the subjective, although it cannot itself appear in the immanent sphere as an experience. We should note here that this transcendent as such can never appear in the sphere of the physical sciences: the immanent as well as the transcendent appear only in the pure humanistic sciences. It is true, of course, that nature when opposed to the subjective must be seen as absolutely transcendent; which means that nature as such cannot appear in the stream of experience in a real manner.[70] Generally speaking, the transcendent, therefore, is the 'unreal' moment in the subjective stream of experience: it transcends this stream of experience. Yet, we can also take the position of the scholastics

67. *Phän. Psych.*, pp. 173–175.
68. *Ibid.*, p. 175; *Ideen*, vol. I, pp. 223–226.
69. *Phän. Psych.*, pp. 175–176.
70. *Ibid.*, p. 177.

and call the object immanent precisely because we are conscious of it. We could from that perspective also speak of the object as subjective, and place it for that reason in the domain of the humanistic sciences. This 'immanent' object is only partially given in each separate phase of the stream of experiences, although in each phase it is always 'meant' in its totality. We therefore must make a distinction between the perceived object that I experience as real and bodily in its adequacy and the perceived as precisely the correlate of the perception. The perceived forms then an ideal pole only, which is not included in this perception in a real way but is taken only as that which appears in it as 'meant.' A spatial object as bodily and real is therefore transcendent in a double sense: it is not immanent in the stream of experiences (for immanent in this sense are the real moments only) and it is further transcendent as the ideal pole of the stream of experience as such.[71]

We now turn from the consideration as to how the unreal pole comes into Being and go instead to the actual structure of this pole. This pole seen as object manifests itself as the always identical which persists from the beginning to the end in the perceptive stream and only becomes further determined as far as its properties and characteristics are concerned. The object itself is an ideal pole that appears as a substratum in relationship to its own characteristics. This substratum-pole cannot exist as such by itself, and is only what it is by virtue of the ever changing, continuous determination of these characteristics and aspects. Without this it is a non-substantial and merely ideal pole. Every characteristic is by itself also an ideal pole in an analogous way; it is a constantly appearing identical entity in the stream of the corresponding, continuously succeeding perspectives. These, likewise, are nothing in and by themselves; they are what they are only as characteristics of the substratum-pole in question.[72]

If we look closer we are forced to conclude that each perceived spatial thing, as it makes its appearance as a bodily being in this perception as continuity of perspectives, is in each

---

71. *Ibid.*, pp. 176–179; *Die Idee*, pp. 32–39.
72. *Phän. Psych.*, p. 180; *Ideen*, vol. I, pp. 320–323.

phase of the stream of experiences more than a pure substratum of the complex of those properties of which we are aware at the moment. For if this were not the case we would have to find a different object in each succeeding phase, and, in case the object would remain the same, it would have to gain or lose characteristics when moving from one phase to another.

We must add to this substratum-pole an empty horizon which will help us to understand how the object can *a priori* make its appearance in each succeeding phase. For each object is already taken in advance as a determined object before it becomes really determined in and through special perception.[73] We must conclude, therefore, that each appearing object has an horizon of as yet unknown characteristics which are to be revealed later. We want to stress once more that when we speak of this empty internal horizon, we are not speaking of nothing. This horizon is a typical characteristic of the substratum-pole itself; it appears there as an actually present emptiness. This emptiness is constantly, and by necessity inadequately filled during the perceptive process as a whole so that there is always an endless horizon left over. Thus the internal horizon does not function as a determining characteristic of the substratum pole; it is an empty horizon of characteristics. However, we saw already that it is this empty horizon which provides the perceptive process with direction, with a *telos*. For, it provides the general frame within which the further determinations of the object must be placed. It also throws light on the fact that each phase of the total process refers to possible other phases and that the already perceived characteristics of an object point to possible other characteristics. The internal horizon thus provides the foundation for the characteristic expectancy which pervades each phase of the perceptive process, while, at the same time, it helps us understand why this expectation proceeds in a certain direction.[74]

We see again with renewed clarity that the object with its objective characteristics is not simply a thing that maintains

73. *Ibid.*, p. 181.
74. *Ibid.*, pp. 181–182.

itself statically throughout the whole process of subjective experiencing. We can only think of the object of our perception as something that is transcendent in regard to the structural pattern of the stream of the experience of perspectives. The object itself is not present as flowing but it is the enduring, identical substratum-pole within the stream.

There is still one problem left that necessarily must be discussed in this context: how is it possible that such concrete perception grasps the object as bodily present, whereas on the other hand it reaches also beyond this object in a transcending movement? [75] The external object is in our perception as a bodily being present only as intended and meant, but it never is a ready-made immanent datum of that perception. From start to finish this object is intended as possessing a transcendent meaning, as provided with an horizon of meaning which in principle will always remain open. It is meant as a substratum for the determinations which are already realized in perception and as a substratum for all the determinations which can be realized *ad infinitum*. This bodily present object of which we are conscious in our transcendent perception is only something meant that has a certain sense which already has been partly realized but, on the other hand, never will be realized in an adequate way. A determinate sense can contain within itself an infinity of meanings, which are present as foreshadowings of possible realizations in ever new conscious acts.[76]

These future realizations are not *really* foreshadowed in each phase of the perceptive process; this foreshadowing is itself a system of multiple meanings which permits us to question the perception in such a way that always new possibilities can be developed. But that which then is brought to light is not entirely new, it follows from an explicitation of the original, conscious meaning in which all the new meanings can be recognized. The intentional object of the external perception shows us as the first form of being-as-intentional-object how an object of intentionality or even an object of a perceiving intentionality is noth-

75. *Ibid.,* pp. 182–183.
76. *Ibid.,* p. 183.

ing else but meaning, intended sense. It also shows how this
meaning encompasses infinities of mutually interrelated meanings, although on the other hand, it does not encompass these
as real parts. The object of our perception gains its meaning by
means of the meaning-giving activities which come about
throughout the chain of appearances; it itself, however, is never
given in an adequate way; it is intended only. But the intended
sense as such is itself also intention inasfar as it itself, partly
fulfilled already and partly transcending, refers and points to a
determinate fullness of meaning. We therefore must distinguish
two moments in the object of our perception taken as the meaning which in this perception is intentionally meant: as Being-
there the object of our perception is something merely meant
and every certainty in its regard may soon end in doubt, in
illusion or in naught. Besides this, there is the purely objective
meaning for which the question concerning a Being-there is
completely irrelevant and which consequently cannot be
doubted. It will be evident that this objective meaning includes
the inner horizon mentioned above.[77]

We can now come closer to an understanding of the transcendental moment of the object of our perception and of how
the concepts of 'transcendence' and 'immanence' in the strict
sense are to be understood. A hyletic datum as such, not yet
considered as a profile of an objective being, is the perceptual
object of each original reflection which directs itself to it. This
form of perfection equally finds its perceptual meaning in the
object, thus in this datum. This perceptual meaning appears as
certain, indubitable being. Such object is to be termed immanent; its givenness is adequate; there is no horizon here. These
objects finally are real parts of the immanent time in which they
flow. Their givenness is called adequate since these objects are
completely realized in every phase of the perception.[78] The objective meaning of the transcendent object is, in contrast, realized
in a way which essentially is incomplete, insofar as it always and
necessarily reaches beyond the perceiving realization of the act

77. *Ibid.*, pp. 184–185.
78. *Ibid.*, p. 185.

here and now. We could formulate this in still another way: the immanent and adequate objectivity is a real datum of the perception, and it is so only during and as long as the perception lasts. A transcendent datum in an *idea* which as reality is given in an original but necessarily inadequate way because of which it always and necessarily reaches beyond that which already is effectively realized in this concrete transcendent perception. The adequately perceived is apodictically evident; the transcendent object cannot be given in apodictic evidence and certitude.[79]

The transcendence of outer perception poses a number of great problems. Before we can deal with these problems we need to discuss first the two basic attitudes, which can be assumed in respect to perception. Thus we must try to explore the real meaning of the phenomenological reduction. The natural attitude is the attitude which we assume in our daily activities and also in our scientific endeavors. Within the natural attitude we can assume a *direct* and a *reflexive* attitude. When we direct ourselves to the domain of the subjective and immanent by means of the reflexive attitude, we are practicing phenomenological reduction. It is by means of this procedure, and by means of this procedure alone that we can get hold of phenomena in the phenomenological sense. This reduction is characteristic for both phenomenological psychology and phenomenological, transcendental philosophy.[80]

Briefly summarized we could say that in the phenomenological attitude we are interested only in the subjective. We see our outer perception precisely as a subjective experience and are concerned with the real and ideal contents which are necessarily and inseparably connected and bound up with these experiences. The object forms part of these but only insofar as it has been 'intended' and 'meant' in this act. This attitude places the object between parentheses, so to say; it is no longer the object as such. We reach this attitude only when we freely renounce and take

79. *Ibid.,* pp. 186–187; *Ideen,* vol. I, pp. 350–351.
80. *Phän. Psych.,* pp. 187–188.

distance from every possible transcendence of objective Being. In the *natural attitude,* which precedes the other attitudes in time, our interest is precisely focused on objective Being. While in this attitude we believe in objectivity.[81]

The natural attitude opens up the possibilities for all objective knowledge and science; it also leads us to all *praxis* which is related to the world. The *phenomenological attitude,* on the other hand, opens up the possibility for an entirely new science of pure subjectivity. In this science we only speak about experiences and modes of consciousness; all objective being is taken merely as 'meant.' This does not mean, however, that in the phenomenological attitude and the natural attitude we cannot be concerned with the same topics. The difference in treatment boils down to the fact that in the phenomenological attitude we no longer stand "on the ground of the world, objects, and worlds of objects." 'World,' 'object,' and 'world-of-objects' are no longer taken as referring to real beings in the proper sense of the word.[82]

The pure description which we attempted in our treatment of our perception, already functions in the realm of the phenomenological attitude. This description offers doubtless many difficulties to the reader who is accustomed to thinking within the realm of the natural attitude. The difficulties were compounded by the many subtle differentiations which we needed to introduce along the way. Despite this complex treatment we are in no way justified in thinking that this treatment of subjectivity is complete. We saw this subjectivity through an analysis of an act of outer perception only, and even our treatment of perception itself asks for a great many more subtle differentiations than we are able to give in these few pages.[83]

The phenomenological attitude demands essentially: the placing between parentheses of nature, of the objective world in general, of all the objective, physical sciences, and the exclusive focusing on the subjective and on the question "of how

81. *Ibid.,* pp. 189–190.
82. *Ibid.,* pp. 191–192; *Die Idee,* pp. 17–26.
83. *Ibid.,* pp. 192–195.

the subjective in forms of intentionality makes the objective become conscious." The next question is how true and genuine science is possible on the basis of this new phenomenological attitude.[84]

Our previous analysis of an act of perception forms in itself only one of many possible themes of phenomenological psychology. It nevertheless affords us some insight into the question which we posed just now. In this analysis we saw that phenomenological psychology can be seen as a science concerned with the revelation of pure, inner reality. This science is based on the so-called phenomenological attitude, on an entirely new kind of perception and thinking. The purpose of this science is to "unveil the 'matrix' of all knowledge, the 'matrix' of all appearing objectivity before the intuiting eye of the mind." The ultimate purpose of this science is not the construction of a new metaphysics; phenomenological psychology has as its task only the foundation of an empirical science. This psychology itself, however, is an eidetical science on the bases of intuitive sources.[85] Its point of departure is self-observation: "an intuiting self-experience." Psychology thus becomes "self-knowledge of the mind, first in the form of an original self-perception which phenomenologically purified brings to light its own hidden Being and life, and then in the form of a strict science founded on this experience." The subjective must appear therein as "that subjectivity which in a conscious way constitutes for itself all forms of objectivity" and all this in the passive stream of the experiences themselves as well as in the active, objectifying achievements.[86]

The descriptions and analyses of phenomenological psychology are precisely so difficult in that we are naturally oriented towards the realm of the objective whereas here the reflexive attitude must be acquired. Our analysis of an act of outer perception showed these difficulties to a sufficient degree. Part of the difficulty in following this analysis must be sought in the in-

84. *Ibid.*, p. 192.
85. *Ibid.*, p. 193.
86. *Ibid.*, pp. 193–194.

sufficiently explained phenomena of the 'outer horizon,' of the 'world,' and of the constitution of 'nature' in the realm of the subjective. The most important omission in our analysis concerns, however, the orientation of the subject. Our next task is to deal with this important topic.[87]

Analysis of Perception Insofar as It Relates to the Perceiver Himself

IN OUR analysis of an act of perception up to now we only paid attention to the perception "as the course of the appearances of an object" which in addition, we considered also in its relation to other objects.[88] To perceive meant to experience appearances and to experience through these appearances that which appears as well as that which was 'meant' and intended. Yet, perceptions do not fall out of a blue sky; we only have things appear to us when we actually perceive. Apart from the question whether this perceiving act occurs involuntarily or rather is the consequence of a deliberate act of the ego, one must note that an act of perception has its own characteristics that need careful studying. We do not merely have empty appearances. The point at issue here is to perceive the appearing of a thing visually in a seeing, and tactically in a touching subject, since only in that way does one have these or those appearances.[89]

In an exemplary fact we discovered here a necessity which in turn points to an *essential* necessity. The study of this essential necessity reveals our body to us as a unity of sensory organs. For perception as such cannot be adequately studied without paying attention to the part which our body plays in it. At first glance it seems that my body is merely given as a thing. However, such a view places our analysis immediately in a vicious circle from which we cannot extricate ourselves. A pre-psycholog-

87. *Ibid.*, pp. 195–196.
88. *Ibid.*, p. 196.
89. *Ibid.*, p. 196.

ical consideration of the body reveals the body both as thing and as a specifically determined body. These two mutually connected intentionalities should therefore be subjected to careful study. To do this we would need a new intentional analysis in which the kinesthetic systems of hand movements, head movements, etc. would constitute themselves intentionally, and in which they then would fit themselves into a total-system. Such an analysis would ask also a further elaboration and explanation of the specific nature of kinesthetic processes as subjective experiences. It would need a further explanation for the fact that each part of the body does move in an objective-spatial sense as well as in a more properly kinesthetic sense. Finally, it would need a further explicitation of the entire unique nature of the body, both as spatial thing and as habitual organ of subjective functioning.[90] We also meet in such an analysis an entirely new form of causality, namely somatic causality which needs further explaining.[91] It can further be seen that we must make special demands on the phenomenological reduction in such an analysis because we are not concerned here about the body as a thing-in-nature, but as a center of active, objectifying functions which make their appearance when we reflect upon our outer perception.[92]

Another topic which is of the greatest importance here concerns bodily abnormalities since these abnormalities and anomalies influence the constitution of the objective, of nature, and the world. Yet, in spite of all this we can already say that these phenomenological investigations of the living body in their interwovenness with a phenomenological study of the physical thing constitute the fundamental sections of a phenomenology of nature, that is to say of the phenomenological explanation of the subjectivity as constituting nature in itself by means of its experiencing activities.[93]

Taking our starting point in outer perception we thus con-

90. *Ibid.,* pp. 196–197.
91. *Ibid.,* pp. 197–198.
92. *Ibid.,* p. 198.
93. *Ibid.,* p. 199.

tinue to discover new topics for further research. Some of these
topics concern the phenomena of retention, of recollection and
remembrance, of expectation.[94] In these types of experience
which are closely related to perception we soon meet again with
the important problem of temporality. Husserl only points to a
number of important questions concerning temporality and
time-consciousness which should not be omitted from an adequate analysis of perception. Among these questions the
problems concerning 'protension' and 'retention' occupy an
important place. Husserl makes it clear at this point again that
phenomenology has opened up entirely new perspectives in the
realm of temporal phenomena which had not even been suspected by classical psychology.[95] A complete analysis of perception should also include a study of the relationship between
perception, memory, and fantasy. In our analysis we will pass by
these particular topics in order to concentrate on the so-called
'ego polarization' which is of central importance in perception.[96]

Our foregoing analysis has stressed only the noematic side of
all intentional relations. Up to now we stressed the object as it
manifested itself in its objective meaning, in its modalities of
Being, and in the subjective modes in which it made its
appearance. In all these considerations we touched in passing
again and again on the perceiving ego. But instead of turning
from the objects to the appearances we can also turn straight
from the objects to the self, since it is this self which executes
the acts through which it possesses these objects. The stream of
subjective experiences already receives a certain polarization
from the side of the object insofar as every object of the stream
appears as belonging to our world. The stream of immanent
experiences likewise forms a unity, namely, immanent life itself
as pole-system. Opposed to this in characteristic contrast, stands

94. *Ibid.*, p. 200.
95. *Ibid.*, pp. 200–203; *Cart. Med.*, pp. 79–81.
96. *Ibid.*, pp. 203–206; see also: Edmund Husserl, "Vorlesungen zur Phänomenologie des inneren Zeitbewusstseins (Hrsg. v. M. Heidegger) in *Jahrbuch für Philosophie und phänomenologische Forschung*, 9 (1928) 367–498,
pp. 382–426.

the polarization toward the ego. Starting from anything that announces itself as an object we can turn our reflection in two directions: we can reflect on the experiences in which the object is constituted or we can reflect upon the lasting self-identical ego which underlies these experiences. And this ego is the subject of all experiences as well as the subject of all objects seen as the unitary pole of its own intentionalities. The ego itself, however, is not an experience. Just as we have demonstrated earlier with the object of experience, we fail to find the self in the real stream of experiences, neither as experience, nor as real part of an experience, nor as real moment of an experience. Only in reflection does it become clear that all experiences and all the objects contained in these experiences refer to the self-same ego. In such a reflection, which itself is again an experience, the ego becomes the object of itself.[97]

The most remarkable aspect of all this is that a universal synthesis is at work throughout the stream of experiences and throughout all that which is formed in it as stable and enduring. On the basis of this synthesis the ego appears and reappears as identity-pole in regard to all that which appears as object. In the explicit reflection upon the self, however, I am both subject and object at the same time.[98]

The ego about which we speak here is evidently not this human being, this ego here in this world, but rather the pure ego of the described phenomena. Yet, this self is not a dead identity-pole, it is an ego which undergoes emotions and which poses acts. In order to see this more clearly we must consider more closely the acts of the ego. The ego poses acts: I experience while perceiving. I 'consider' an object, I catch in memory something that already is passed, I try to recall something to my mind, I relate this object to other objects, I compare them and point to similarities and differences, I judge something to be beautiful or ugly, I imagine something as threatening, I wish it had been different. I can change any object; I can want it or

97. *Phän. Psych.*, pp. 206–208; *Cart. Med.*, pp. 99–121.
98. *Ibid.*, p. 208.

realize it. In all these cases the self is always present as an immediately recognizable center.[99]

Every act, therefore, is to be characterized as an act which issues from an active ego. It is presupposed here, however, that a passive intentionality in which the ego does not dwell yet, has already before constituted an object in itself which affects the ego-pole and determined it into an 'act' (*Actus*). On the other hand, however, every actuality in the way it is brought about by the ego, as something that is achieved by it, is thus immediately itself an experience which inserts itself in the same stream of experiences as the one to which the passive experiences belong.[100]

This continually enriches the world of objects. Once this richer world is constituted it can in turn affect the self anew and motivate it to new deeds. This in turn results in new objects being constituted by the ego which then again take their place in the world of the ego. It is therefore not true that the ego turns itself passively to an already pre-given world, nor is the ego a purely perceiving ego. It is by means of the ego's comparing, that similarity is constituted; it is because the ego produces ties between objects that there can exist such a thing as relationships among objects, and such relationships are both of a theoretical as well as of a practical nature. Also these relationships have their own original manner of appearances and therefore are truly perceived. But this original manner of appearance issues from the activity of the ego even though the entities related were already pre-given in a passive way. Thus also these objects are only present to the ego insofar as they have been actively realized by itself. And once these objects are realized the ego can forever re-direct its attention to it, it can bring these objects to mind, recall them, use them as reference-points for further acts of combination and comparison.

In this manner we can get an idea of the ego as source of logical, axiological and practical products. It is not our intention

99. *Ibid.*, pp. 208–209.
100. *Ibid.*, p. 209.

to focus on the objective entities of the 'spiritual' order which in this manner are added on to the world of the ego. We seek rather to know how to gain some insight into the peculiar changes which occur in the ego itself as a result of this process. The pure ego-pole is numerically and identically the same; it is the one and only center of the total, pure subjectivity into which we have already gained some insight. We saw already how an object remains numerically identical throughout a series of interconnected appearances. Yet, the object continues to be determined by ever new contents which then come to belong to the object. The ego shows much in common with this. And yet, the ego is not a thing-object which constitutes itself as a unity of appearances, or as a substratum of objective characteristics. The ego carries out activities. But the ego is not an empty ideal point where the different lines of its activities and their objects intersect with each other. The ego is also a pole of habitualities. Habitualities have a mode of being which is quite different from that of the properties of objects. Habitualities are determined by the fact that the self has already executed certain acts which from now on belong *historically* to the ego. A particular decision made by the ego transforms the ego into somebody whose mind is made up in regard to this or that. The ego can henceforth consider itself as having made such and such a decision. The ego has a history and in this history it provides itself with an habitual reality without the identity of the ego fundamentally being affected. Let us suppose that I see a spatial object for the first time. I will study the object carefully so that I can form a clear concept of it. When I encounter the same object a few moments later, I do not experience it any more as something new but as something already known. The knowledge which I gained during my first seeing of it is therefore not a momentary knowledge that remains locked up in this particular act; this knowledge, on the contrary, remains with me as a sort of constant conviction. My following acts which concern the same object really yield no new knowledge but merely strengthen my original conviction concerning the object. This same phenomenon can be experienced clearly when we study for the first time a certain method by which a mathematical proposition can be proved. When later we return to this method we meet with more than a mere memory of having previously proved this or that. Nor is what I meet merely a new belief in what has been proved before. For I notice also that my conviction concerning this particular type of proof has remained unchanged; it has become my steady possession.[101]

The ego, therefore, has no thing-like characteristics; as such, it only has the mode-of-Being of a particular subject who has formed certain permanent convictions. This subject forms its conceptions first on the basis of his own personal insights and activities. Yet, this subject also lives in community with other subjects and receives from them certain insights and convictions. However, the convictions which are formed in this manner are not the immediate product of the ego. The ego follows in the footsteps of other egos, it directs itself in response to the convictions and motivations of others.[102] The ego in this case does not think, value, or act on its own accord, but follows the suggestions of others. Yet, in all this there is room for the self to assume different attitudes, with respect to the opinions, acts, and thoughts of others. It can accept passively the convictions of others but it also can try to account to itself for the convictions it has accepted by means of extrinsic considerations. I also can achieve real insight and personal motivation. Yet, in all these cases in which I make other's convictions my own, I experience these not as passing experiences; bur rather I possess them as definitely belonging to the ego.

It is clear that we should study this matter more carefully and at greater length than can be done in these pages. A more complete treatment should include topics concerned with the genesis of someone's personality or character, with the characteristic traits of someone's individuality, etc. A very important theme concerns the problem of our identity experience. Despite

101. *Ibid.,* pp. 209–212.
102. *Ibid.,* p. 212.

the constant flux of acts, convictions, and decisions I experience myself constantly as one and the same person.[103]

What we have said so far, however, will suffice for a first impression of the realm of the ego. When taken in its concrete unity this ego could be called a *pure subjectivity* or a *monad*. 'Monad' or the 'identity of the ego' are not used here as metaphysical concepts but refer to the unity inasfar as this manifests itself in phenomenological analyses of the type indicated above.[104] Phenomenological analysis is originally a statical analysis in which relatively isolated phenomena are studied. This analysis tries to describe all the immanent real and ideal in their essential relationships. Subsequent to this analysis a genetic investigation should follow in which both the active and passive genesis should be studied, in which the monad unfolds and develops and through which the 'monadic self' acquires its personal unity, in which it thus becomes the subject of a partly passively pre-given and partly actively constituted world, and in which it also becomes the subject of a history.

This analysis should further concern itself with the nature of intersubjectivity. The question concerns especially the exact course traveled by the ego which enables it to move from its position as *my* subjectivity to that of 'alien' subjectivities.[105]

The pure phenomenology whose meaning we tried briefly to describe with the help of an analysis of an act of perception can also be called a 'pure psychology' insofar as it is concerned with pure subjectivity. There are, however, a great number of sciences which go by the name 'psychology.' All these sciences are closely related to each other and, as we shall see later, to pure phenomenology. All the sciences which up to now have been called 'psychology' are related to the world and as such are sciences of the world.[106] The sciences of the world fall into two broad categories: a) the 'natural investigation of the mind,' to which belong physiological and naturalistic psychology, and

103. *Ibid.*, pp. 212–214.
104. *Ibid.*, p. 216.
105. *Ibid.*, p. 217; *Cart. Med.*, pp. 121–177.
106. *Ibid.*, p. 222.

b) the personalistic study of the humanistic sciences. To the latter belong the empirical sciences of the person, the community, and the 'objective mind.' [107] The first group of sciences deals with the soul as temporalized and spatialized in physical nature; it deals with the soul as causal *'annexus'* of the physical body. It deals with those human and animal characteristics which can be derived inductively from the spatio-temporal manifestations in physical reality. These sciences seek the characteristics of the physical-organic-bodily realm, the specific somatological and the corresponding psychological phenomena.[108] It is clear that this inductive procedure presupposes a certain view on the very essence of the soul.[109] It is precisely the task of phenomenological psychology to yield this insight concerning the essence of the soul.[110]

Be this as it may, within the realm of the natural attitude other humanistic sciences can be formed which all are essentially different from the physical sciences in methodology. These sciences could take up such topics as the person, the manifold ways in which persons can form communities and groups, the different relationships maintained by persons; also, such topics as culture, technology and the *Umwelt* [111] can be treated by these sciences of the natural attitude. All these sciences, however, presuppose an eidetical science of the very essence of the psychical. Husserl assigned this scientific task to phenomenological psychology.[112]

We must make note of the fact that phenomenological psychology is not really a radical science in the full sense of the word. Husserl attributed to phenomenological psychology the task of laying the foundations for empirical psychology and the other possible sciences mentioned above. Yet, phenomenological psychology must in turn depend on a transcendental science, phenomenological philosophy, for its own foundations.

107. *Ibid.*, pp. 217–221 (passim).
108. *Ibid.*, p. 217.
109. *Ibid.*, pp. 217–218.
110. *Ibid.*, p. 218.
111. *Ibid.*, pp. 219–221.
112. *Ibid.*, pp. 221–222.

We must return later to this problem of the relationship between phenomenological psychology and phenomenological philosophy. Husserl does not tell us much about this in his *Phänomenologische Psychologie*. He returns to this problem in his later treatises and there deals extensively with this relationship without essentially changing the point of view adopted in *Phänomenologische Psychologie*.

V PHENOMENOLOGICAL PSYCHOLOGY. ITS RELATIONS TO EMPIRICAL PSYCHOLOGY AND TRANSCENDENTAL PHILOSOPHY.

The Encyclopedia Britannica Article and the 'Amsterdamer Vorträge'

Husserl remained throughout his life preoccupied with the relationship between phenomenology and psychology. The problems involved in this relationship were never far removed from his mind as we can see clearly in all of his writings starting with his *Habilitationsschrift*. We see this concern in the *Philosophie der Arithmetik* and especially in the *Logische Untersuchungen*. At first Husserl did not succed in finding a satisfactory basis for his original ideas. Around the years 1906 and 1907 Husserl discovered the necessity of a transcendental philosophy as we saw in *Die Idee der Phänomenologie* and other works and notes from that period.

With this discovery the necessity of distinguishing phenomenology and psychology manifested itself for the first time. In the later *Logos*-article we see the further development of a more balanced and matured view concerning the relationship between psychology and phenomenological philosophy. In *Ideen I* the accent is on a radical foundation for the transcendental phenomenological philosophy, but already in the second part of the *Ideen* Husserl has returned to the problems involved in the relationship between psychology and phenomenology. In the nineteen twenties the relationship between the two sciences 'of the subjectivity' begins even to occupy a central place in Husserl's thinking. It is also then that we can observe a gradual crystallization of the idea of phenomenological psychology as a transitional science between classical empirical psychology and trancendental philosophy. This idea can be traced as far back as the first part of the *Ideen*. Husserl lectured about this topic in the year 1925. The topic is taken up again with some slight modifications between 1926 and 1928. In the *Encyclopedia Britannica* article concerning phenomenology Husserl assigns an important place to the questions dealing with the relationship between psychology and philosophy. In the *Cartesianische Meditationen* we see a return to the topic of transcendental phenomenology proper, although even here we find a number of discussions about the relationship between psychology and phenomenology. In Husserl's last work there is again a central focus on the problems of psychology.

In this chapter we shall try to get a well-rounded overview of the most important ideas on our topic as they were developed by Husserl between 1925 and 1928. For this purpose we shall in particular make use of a series of the drafts for an article on phenomenology prepared for the *Encyclopedia Britannica*. In the chapter to come we shall deal with the new perspectives which were opened up by Husserl's *Krisis*.

The editors of a new edition of the *Encyclopedia Britannica* asked Husserl in 1927 to write a short article about phenomenology and the phenomenological movement. Husserl must have welcomed this opportunity to make phenomenological philosophy known outside the borders of Germany. He, no doubt too, was stimulated by the challenge again to formulate his main ideas concisely and clearly in a necessarily short article. Husserl wrote the first draft in conjunction with Heidegger shortly before the summer vacation of 1927. This draft betrays a certain haste and tenseness. During that same vacation a second draft was drawn; Heidegger framed the first part and Husserl wrote the rest. The completed second draft was then sent to Heidegger who spent part of that summer in Messkirch; the annotated manuscript was returned to Husserl on October 22 of that year. Husserl then sat down to write a definitive text which, however, turned out to be too long. Another shorter version was subsequently produced and sent to Salmon for an English translation. The editors still felt that this article would occupy too much space in their encyclopedia and Salmon was asked to cut the text as much as possible. In Husserl's view Salmon's precis was not a success. From April 7th to the 17th, 1928, Husserl reworked the third and fourth draft of the article and the resulting text served him as an outline for his series of lectures on phenomenology at Amsterdam. This text is by far the better of the five drafts for the *Encyclopedia Britannica* article. It was later entitled *Amsterdamer Vorträge*.[1]

It was Husserl's intention in this text to explain in concise form the essential aspects of phenomenology.[2] However, he was still very much preoccupied with those problems of phenomenological psychology which had occupied his mind since 1925. We can also find in this work the traces of an inner struggle over the question of whether he should or should not devote an entire volume to 'pure psychology' as soon as possible in order to be able again to focus all his attention on transcendental philosophy. He must have felt that this would be possible only after he had definitely clarified the problems of phenomenological psychology. Informative in this respect is Heidegger's letter of October 22, 1927 to Husserl. Heidegger wrote that in his view the course of their discussions on phenomenology had clearly shown that Husserl ought to publish his larger studies on phenomenological psychology as soon as possible. Heidegger was of the opinion that there were at least two reasons why this had to be done. First of all, it would be very difficult to convince somebody of the necessity of a new discipline, phenomenological psychology, as long as one is not able concretely to

---

1. W. Biemel, "Husserls Encyclopaedia-Britannica Artikel und Heideggers Anmerkungen dazu," in *Tijdschrift voor Philosophie*, 12 (1950) 246–280, p. 246, note 1; see also: W. Biemel, in *Phänomenologische Psychologie: Einleitung des Herausgebers*, p. xv, and *Textkritische Anmerkungen*, pp. 590–592.
2. W. Biemel, "Husserls Encyclopaedia-Britannica Artikel," p. 246.

show him what is involved. Secondly, Heidegger said, you will be free again to concentrate completely on the radical explanation of the transcendental problems.[3]

Husserl did not follow Heidegger's advice. In the *Cartesianische Meditationen* and especially in his last work he chose from the thoughts which had occupied him throughout his university lectures between 1925 and 1928, only those which in his view were ready for publication.

The *Amsterdamer Vorträge* consists of two large parts. The first part concerns itself with pure phenomenological psychology. It discusses its subject-matter, its method, and function. We are particularly interested here in the treatment this essay gives to the relationships between empirical and phenomenological psychology. The second part deals with the meaning of phenomenological psychology with respect to the transcendental problem and the relationship between phenomenological psychology and transcendental phenomenological philosophy. Husserl originally intended to write a third part which would have given a short survey of transcendental phenomenology itself as the universal and radical science 'in absolute foundation.' The table of contents of the *Amsterdamer Vorträge* shows that Husserl intended to use the fourth draft of the *Encyclopedia Britannica* article as a basis for this third part.[4]

Pure Phenomenology—Subject, Method, and Function

THE STRUGGLE of both philosophy and psychology for a strict scientific method resulted around 1900 in a new science with a new method for philosophical and psychological research. This new science was called phenomenology because it presents a radicalization of the phenomenological method which was proposed at the end of the 19th century by physicists and psychologists such as Mach, Hering, and Brentano. Mach and Hering had

3. *Phän. Psych.,* p. 601.
4. *Ibid.,* p. 349, and pp. 296–301.

delivered a strong critique against every form of theorizing which uses concepts that are far removed from actual experience and also against one-sidedly mathematical considerations which in fact prevent a really clear insight into the realm of the physical phenomena. Among the psychologists we find analogous concerns as far as the psychical phenomena are concerned. The radicalization of the methodological tendencies which we find in these thinkers finally resulted in a new method for purely psychological research in the field of psychology and the closely related area of epistemology. Phenomenology also leads to a new manner of approach for specifically philosophical problems. In dealing with these problems phenomenology finally revealed an enlarged view on what constitutes science and scientific endeavor.[5]

During the further development of this new phenomenology it became necessary to distinguish between psychological phenomenology as the fundamental science for all psychological disciplines and transcendental phenomenology as the fundamental science in philosophy. Modern psychology is the science of the real psychic happenings which occur within the objective-real world. 'Psychic' here means everything that refers to the self and that which is inseparably connected with the self. Thinking, feeling, willing, etc., therefore belong to the realm of the psychical as do capacities and habits.

In our experience the psychical manifests itself as a dependent sphere of Being which always maintains a relationship with a more fundamental realm of Being, namely, physical reality. Psychology is therefore an independent branch of the more concrete anthropology or zoology which includes the study of the physical and the psycho-physical.[6]

The world of our experience as a whole is differentiated in an endless multiplicity of concrete individual realities. Each individual reality must, apart from all possible super-structures,

5. The text of the *Amsterdamer Vorträge* is found in *Phän. Psych.*, pp. 302–349. See for the remarks made: *Ibid.*, pp. 302–303.
    6. *Ibid.*, p. 303.

possess physical, bodily reality. We can denude each real object of all the determinations which are not strictly physical and thus arrive at what is called 'physical nature.' But already in the purely physical as such, we find a determinate, essential structure governed by laws. Each concrete worldly object has its own nature, its own bodily reality; and all these worldly objects together form an harmonious unity. When we look upon this from a methodological point of view we see that it is possible by means of an 'abstracting experience' to focus only on the physical aspect of things and the world as a whole. The experience of the world when it is thus strained through my abstracting activities can then be organized into a self-contained theoretical science. It is thus that physical sciences, including physical zoology and biology, come into being.[7]

The question is now whether it is possible to build up a science of the psychical in a similar manner. Is it possible to approach the psychical through a similar process of abstraction in which we leave out the physical? To what extent then is it possible to constitute a pure psychology? It is immediately evident that the existing empirical psychology cannot be considered a *pure* psychology since it also deals with physical elements. Whatever a pure psychology may tell us about the realm of the psychical we must not forget that the pure psychical with which one is concerned there manifests itself in a spatio-temporal world. We have no access to the psychical except as it is revealed and determined in a spatio-temporal world. But space and time belong originally and immediately to the realm of physical nature. All that which falls outside this realm, nevertheless, has to 'pass through' it, if we are to experience it. This observation shows us that it will never be posible to draw a clear line through the field of empirical psychology which would separate *purely* psychological research from psychophysical investigations. In other words, it is impossible to build within empirical psychology as an objective science of facts a separate, sharply delineated

7. *Ibid.*, pp. 303–304.

niche for pure psychology. Empirical psychology concerns itself with concrete, real beings and points in these concerns to the realm of the psychophysical and the physical.[8]

Yet, a pure psychology is not an idle, impossible endeavor. An empirical psychology which really strives towards strictly scientific concepts actually is in need of such a psychology. How else could we achieve concepts that would truly express the essential aspects of psychical phenomena? And what is to be thought of an empirical psychology which lacks concepts expressing the general and essential aspects of the psychical? And how are we to arrive at such concepts without an aprioric, eidetic science of the purely psychical as such? It is with this particular science that we want to concern ourselves in the following pages. Such an aprioric and eidetic science of the psychical runs parallel to *pure* physics, not with the larger field of physics as a whole. Pure physics concerns itself only with the essential and *a priori* aspects of any natural phenomenon whatsoever.[9]

Aprioric truths are hard to come by. Their revelation as essential truths in apodictic insight, requires an immediate presence to the source of intuition. It will be a difficult task to lift these truths from their sources without falsification or distortion. What is required is a methodic study which will gradually and carefully uncover the many-faceted horizons in such a way that the psychical constitutes itself in an original and concrete way. "That is why the real foundation of our guiding ideal requires an aprioric and pure psychology by means of which we are able to return to our intuitive experience, to an intuition which is methodically prepared and adequately uncovered and disclosed. For only in and by such an intuition does the psychical manifest itself immediately in its characteristic and essential 'selfhood.' " [10] The central focus in this process is not so much on that which is concretely experienced. The concretely experienced merely functions as an example of all that could

8. *Ibid.,* pp. 304–305.
9. *Ibid.,* p. 305.
10. *Ibid.,* p. 306.

similarly be experienced. Instead we concentrate on that particular aspect which remains constant in the flux of experience
when we shift from one example to the next.

We see here that the study of the exemplary, the possible,
and the real experience is of great importance for the development of a pure psychology. A special method for the study of
these experiences is an absolute necessity. An important consideration in this respect is the fact that we can only focus on
psychical events when we approach them *reflectively*. In our
normal every day attitude the psychical runs its course without
our attending to it reflectively; there is a certain anonymity to
our psychic life; it is not experienced by itself, nor is it grasped
in its unique and proper aspects. Each experience in the every
day attitude turns immediately to that which is perceived, remembered, willed, etc. It is only in reflection that we avert our
glance from the immediate thematical content in front of us
and confront instead psychical life itself in all its different
modalities, characteristics, and horizons. Another important
fact is that whatever is revealed by our reflection possesses the
characteristic of intentionality. Intentionality manifests itself as
the essential characteristic of psychical life. Furthermore, whatever appears, appears to someone. All appearances refer to a
subject to whom they appeared. They refer in particular to
certain moments of the psychical life of the subject in which
these appearances manifest themselves as appearances of something. We therefore are referring to both the subject and the
object when we talk about an appearance.[11]

It is true, in a certain sense, that in every experience something manifests itself to the subject to the extent that he is
aware of it. If this is true we would consider as the fundamental
characteristic of the psychical the phenomenality seen as typical
of the appearance and the appearing. In that context we could
describe pure psychology as phenomenology or rather aprioric
phenomenology. This science would also study the 'I-subjects' in
their individual and social aspects, but it would see these sub-

11. *Ibid.*, pp. 306–307.

jects only as subjects of such and such a phenomenality. But let us return to the question of how we can shed light on the pure phenomenological experience. Phenomenological experience is understood here as a type of reflection in which the psychical reveals itself in its typical aspects. Such a reflection is here evidently to be understood as performed with theoretical interest and as methodically materialized. For only in this way will the specific life of the ego which continuously flows on, intuitively unfold itself in its essential components, in its all-sided horizons.[12]

The first question which we must pose in this connection is that of how we can proceed here in a methodical fashion and realize *pure* experiences which will reveal the essential and typical aspects of psychic life. The concept *pure* refers here to two qualities. The experience of which we speak must first of all remain free from all those psychophysical and physical elements with which the psychical is *essentially* connected. Whatever we can learn by means of physical and psycho-physical considerations must be suspended. We must seek to remain true to the purely phenomenological experience and try to clarify all that which appears to us in that experience. Here, there are grave obstacles in our way. How do we realize such a pure phenomenological experience and how do we proceed from these experiences to a uniform and pure field of psychic experience which fails to imply anything that does not strictly belong to the essentially psychical? Another requirement which we must meet is that we must remain free from any prejudices which find their origin in our contact with other sciences. These prejudices could blind us to the essential and the typical which is revealed in our phenomenological reflection.[13]

These two requirements attached to the concept of pure phenomenological reflection are so difficult to meet that in Husserl's view we cannot find in the whole of modern psychology an intentional analysis which truly fulfills both. Even Brentano did not succeed in this although it was he who ac-

12. *Ibid.*, pp. 307–308.
13. *Ibid.*, pp. 308–309.

corded the concept of intentionality a central place in psychology and who sought to base all of psychology on a systematic and descriptive analysis of consciousness.[14]

The prejudices of which we spoke a few lines ago have their origin in the wide-spread preconception that psychology has to follow in the methodological footsteps of physics and chemistry. Descartes was the first to defend the thesis that the method used by psychology should be essentially identical to that of physics. Hobbes, Locke, and Hume continued this line of reasoning and were supported in this by practically all professional psychologists after them. Even Brentano could not entirely free himself from this form of naturalism. Even those who after Brentano strongly rejected a naturalistic psychology fell in some respects victim to this naturalism. Gestalt psychology, for example, is still basically a form of naturalistic psychology. The principle mistake of naturalism in psychology becomes clear only when we pursue a purely phenomenological experience to the end, an experience in which the very essence of intentional life manifests itself in a consequent all-sidedness and evidence, and consequently can be submitted to a pure description.[15]

At the root of this confusion lies an equalization between immanent temporality and objective, real time. Objective time is the 'extensional' form of objective realities and in particular of their structural basis, physical nature. Psychical experiences either taken singly or taken as a whole, do not by themselves manifest the unitary form of coexistence and succession which as such is typical of the spatio-temporal itself. An essential aspect of the psychical is that it manifests itself as a flowing within the unity of the stream of consciousness. This aspect does not form a genuine parallel to the spatio-temporal of physical nature. An intentional anlaysis of immanent temporality brings out both the strong and the weak points in the simile of the flowing stream. This analysis also clarifies why all real analogies between an analysis of consciousness and a physical, chemical, or biological analysis and therefore, also those between conscious-

14. *Ibid.,* p. 309.
15. *Ibid.,* pp. 309–310.

ness and nature, are of necessity invalid and void. The physico-
logical concepts of thing, characteristic, whole, part, connection,
separation, cause, effect, action, etc., all find their ultimate foundation in the real, in nature, in the *res extensa*. In the transfer
from the physical to the psychical these concepts lose their
original meaning. As psychological terms these physical concepts
are mere empty shells; what remains of them are merely formal
logical concepts.[16]

There are still other difficulties which are essentially connected with the realization of a purely phenomenological
experience. We saw that it will be necessary to get rid of all
the prejudices induced by our contact with other sciences. Even
the most self-evident tenets of logic must be left out of consideration since they are already interpreted in a too one-sided
way from the viewpoint of the physical sciences. In our analysis
we only hold on to what the phenomenological reflection offers
us in consciousness and to what appears there truly in a genuine
self-evidence. We thus must try to focus exclusively on the
phenomenological experience without paying any attention to
what appears in this experience as factual actualities. The
phenomenological experience now is first of all a self-experi-
encing. All other forms of experiencing the psychical find their
root in this immediate self-experience. This holds true also for
the experience of someone else and of society. It is for this
reason that in phenomenology the method of pure self-experi-
encing, of thorough-going phenomenological self-revelation, is
dealt with in such great detail.[17]

The difficulty in this analysis lies in the fact that we must
leave out of our considerations all that which relates to external
experience which necessarily refers to the physical. But how
can this be done? We observed before that all experiences are
experiences of something, of the world, and that each reflection
presupposes a direct experience of the other.[18]

In order to realize a pure phenomenological experience of

16. *Ibid.,* pp. 310–311.
17. *Ibid.,* pp. 311–312.
18. *Ibid.,* p. 312.

my conscious life, in order to make this consciousness in its
pure and unique Being the universal theme of my research, I
must 'put between brackets' as being not psychical the general
thesis of our natural attitude according to which the real world
about me is at all times known as a fact-world that has its Being
out there. In doing so the thesis of the natural attitude is still
experienced as lived, but I make no use of it any more in order
exclusively to focus attention on the psychical as such.[19]

Yet, I cannot deny that all consciousness is indeed consciousness of something. And in our direct experiences that which we
are conscious of is the natural world, the real, spatio-temporal
world. It is thus impossible to describe the essential aspects of a
perception or a memory without reference to *what* is perceived
or remembered, without describing the concrete objects of these
determinate activities. It follows that not just any reflection on
consciousness suffices to reveal to us the psychical in its essential
Being and purity. First of all we must put out of action our
natural belief in the reality of the world and place in brackets
whatever it includes respecting its Being-status. As phenomenologists we should become disinterested bystanders watching our
own conscious life. It is only in this manner that it can become
a pure theme in our experience. Instead of living in the world,
instead of investing it with our worldly interests, we must actually observe our life as somehow being conscious of this or that,
as somehow being interested in itself. If we did not do this we
again would be referring to the non-psychical world. In this
epochē consciousness remains a consciousness and this consciousness remains consciousness of something. The fact that
every consciousness manifests itself as consciousness of something
is precisely the essential aspect of consciousness as a psychic
datum. That which we are conscious of, however, is not to be
taken as such; that is to say what we experience is not to be
taken as a being in the real world but exclusively as that which
is intended by consciousness. The object as being in the real
world must be placed in brackets.[20]

19. *Ibid.,* p. 312.
20. *Ibid.,* pp. 312-313.

The phenomenological reduction is essentially determined by these considerations. It is of importance to note here that in this reduction in addition to the noetic, the noematic also, is maintained and even as an endlessly fruitful theme of phenomenological description. It is precisely through the phenomenological reduction that for the first time intentional objects are liberated as essential constituents of our intentional experiences.[21]

The phenomenological reduction also has its consequences for our attitude toward the ego of our conscious experiences in that here, too, the human and the animal as real fall away. When by the *epoché* real nature is reduced to a noematic phenomenon, the real human ego of the natural attitude is reduced to a pure psychic life. This is to say, within the realm of the reduction the ego no longer manifests itself as a real being in the real world which in this world lives its mundane life, but only as the center of the intentional activities which are correlative to the intentional objects mentioned.[22]

The consequent uncovering of the *noema,* that is the object meant as such, can be turned into a consideration and analysis of the related *noeses,* of the different acts in and through which the ego is conscious of something. Besides these, the ego as center is something special; it is the *ego* in the *cogito,* the 'I' which phenomenologically remains identical throughout the diverse acts. The ego is the center from which flow all the different acts and toward which stream all the different affects. In both these respects this phenomenologically pure ego as center forms an important and comprehensive theme which is closely intertwined with all other phenomenological topics.

To the specific egological topics which are phenomenologically relevant belong the faculties and habits of the ego, also. The first and most important topic remains, however, the analysis of the pure life of the ego itself in its diverse modalities. And in this research concerning the life of the ego as well, it is

21. *Ibid.,* p. 314.
22. *Ibid.,* pp. 314–315.

essential to move in both the direction of the *noema* and the *noesis*.[23]

In these analyses concerning the life of the pure ego we see manifest itself the fundamental and essential distinction between the mode of Being of consciousness in its phenomenological purity and nature as it is given in our natural attitude. This distinction is clearest in the ideality according to which the noematic contents are included in every conscious act. One can, therefore, also say that this difference consists in the typical synthesis which makes each consciousness-of into a unity and connects it with other conscious acts, making a unity of *one* consciousness in this way. All forms of synthesis ultimately go back to identity syntheses. Let us try to explain this briefly.

In every conscious act we are directed toward an object, we 'intend' it and reflection reveals this to be an immanent process characteristic of all experiences. To be conscious of something is not an empty having of such a something in consciousness. Each phenomenon has its own intentional structure which analysis shows to be an ever-widening system of intentionally related, individual components. The perception of a house, for instance, reveals a multiple and synthesized intention: a continuous variety in the appearances of the house, according to differences in the points of view from which it is seen and corresponding differences in perspective. Observation of the stream of these noemata and of the manner of their synthesis, shows that every phase is already in itself a consciousness of something, yet in such a way that with the constant entry of new phases the total consciousness, at any moment, is a consciousness of one and the same house. In this it is implied that in every conscious act we are referred to an indeterminate number of similar experiences of the same house and, therefore, that in the noema of a certain individual act there are already implied references to other aspects of the same house which in this individual act are already predelineated as real or possible as-

23. *Ibid.*, p. 316.

pects of the house in question. The same holds true for every conscious intentional act. As we have seen, it is in this way that the real essence of an intentional relation becomes manifest: that of which I am conscious in every intentional experience is a noematic pole which refers to an open infinity of always new intentional experiences in which this house would appear as identically the same. This means that the noematic pole is not really but only ideally contained in the different possible experiences.[24]

In Husserl's view we should have to take up again our previous discussion of the intentional analysis. However, since in my view we need not enlarge upon this theme further in this context, we shall limit ourselves to one general concluding remark.[25] Intentional analysis, seen as the explicitation of the intentional meaning of our experiences, forms a type of analysis that should be clearly differentiated from other known analytical procedures. Intentional analysis is essentially an interpretative, noetico-noematic procedure. In this interpretation we are especially concerned with the different forms of synthesis, the temporal syntheses being the most important ones. Intentional analyses aim originally at a pure egological descriptive phenomenology. This phenomenology must later branch out to constitute a phenomenology of intersubjectivity. This discipline concerns itself with a critical analysis of our experience of others and community.[26]

We do not have a real science as long as we remain in our analysis within the sphere of ordinary experience and as long as we are caught up in particular, isolated facts and the empirical generalities which can be derived from them. We already pointed out that we can not have a pure phenomenological psychology which is at the same time a real factual science. It is possible to have an empirical psychology as a factual science, but this presupposes an eidetic descriptive study of the purely psychical. Such a study, in turn, cannot be made without the help of an

24. *Ibid.,* p. 316.
25. *Ibid.,* pp. 316–319.
26. *Ibid.,* pp. 320–321.

eidetic reduction. We have already discussed the eidetic reduction and we will therefore suspend a further treatment of the
process of ideation and turn instead to the treatment of the
role of phenomenological psychology in respect to empirical
psychology.[27]

Phenomenological and Empirical Psychology

LET US presuppose now that we are already placed in the realm
of the purely psychical by means of the phenomenological reduction. Let us also assume that with the help of the intentional analysis and through ideation we have already gained an
insight into the essence of the psychical in all its diverse modalities. All concepts which we are able to form in this sphere are,
just as aprioric concepts, expressions of an essential and necessary style which governs all real and possible forms of factual
psychic life. All that which can be thought, in fact is bound up in
this particular style and is bound to the concepts which are
fashioned under its influence. All empirical psychological concepts relate to these primary concepts in the same sense as all
concepts in physics relate to those developed by general,
aprioric, pure physics. The aprioric truths founded in these
concepts, therefore, possess an unconditioned, normative validity in regard to the purely empirical domain of the purely
psychical.[28]

Comparing now phenomenology with the larger field of empirical psychology we observe that phenomenological psychology
forms the unconditional and necessary foundation for a
strictly scientific psychology. This scientific psychology could be
the exact analogue of physics. The exactitude of physics rests in
the last analysis upon an *a priori* that is characteristic for
physics, or rather on an *a priori* system of forms characteristic
of any possible thinkable nature as such. We find this system in
pure geometry, in pure mechanics, etc. The vague realm of the

27. *Ibid.,* pp. 321–324.
28. *Ibid.,* p. 324.

empirical partakes of essential necessity if one theoretically relates the facts of experience to this *a priori* of the possible forms. It is through this procedure that the method of physics materializes its task of transforming vague concepts and rules into 'exact' laws. The fact that it is the quantitative as such which forms this *a priori* of physics and that this quantitative can be expressed in measures and numbers relates to the essence of nature as nature.[29]

Exactitude is required of each and every science including empirical psychology. Here also we need all-encompassing fundamental concepts. The experiential domain of psychology possesses its own typical *a priori* structure without which we cannot think of an ego or a relationship between egos in a community, in view of consciousness and object. Eidetical phenomenological psychology reveals this *a priori* in all its aspects and dimensions belonging to the *noema* and the *noesis*. It provides us with the basic concepts, the *rational* founding concepts which must govern and rule any psychology imaginable.[30]

We must not forget, however, that psychology is the science of the psychical as it manifests itself as a real moment in the given world and thus as a part of nature itself. That is why empirical psychology must maintain ties with the aprioric sciences which found the different physical disciplines. In other words psychology is partly founded on the *a priori* of the psychical and partly on the *a priori* of nature itself. It even rests ultimately on an *a priori* belonging to the realm of the psychophysical as such. This particular realm, however, has not been scientifically investigated up to now.

As we have said before, a pure phenomenological psychology is only possible and meaningful if it is conceived as an eidetical science. A genuine and exact psychology which follows the pattern of the rational, mathematico-physical sciences can still be called a phenomenological psychology in a larger sense, if at least it deals with the real psychical, expressed in concepts based

29. *Ibid.*, pp. 324–325.
30. *Ibid.*, p. 325.

on the eidetical phenomenological doctrine of the essence of the psychical.[31]

It is not necessary to explain here at length how a phenomenological psychology in the strict sense of the term could also study man's knowledge and even the sciences. This could give rise to an elaborate epistemology and a theory of science, which would not truly belong to the realm of philosophy since the study would take place from the perspective of the natural attitude. Otherwise, such a theory of science would come very close to a philosophy of science. Only a 'Copernican Revolution' would be needed to give such a phenomenology a transcendental meaning. This 'Copernican Revolution' comes in the form of a transcendental reduction in which we place between brackets what is presupposed by every positive science, namely the belief in the existence of a natural and self-evidently real world. Instead of the world, it is consciousness, subjectivity as such, that in the transcendental attitude is posed as absolute.[32]

Phenomenological Psychology and the Transcendental Problem

WE NOTED already several times before that the task of a pure phenomenologigal psychology is not limited to providing a basis for empirical psychology. Phenomenological psychology also can be seen as preparing the way for a transcendental phenomenological philosophy.[33]

Historically viewed it is quite clear that phenomenological psychology did not really grow out of empirical psychology. Phenomenological psychology came into full being during the beginning of this century, but we can find early traces of its development in Locke's thinking about the foundation of psychology which formed a stepping-stone for the analogous endeavors

31. *Ibid.,* p. 326.
32. *Ibid.,* pp. 326–328.
33. *Ibid.,* p. 328.

of Berkeley and Hume. We find already the first traces of a systematic phenomenology in Hume's *Treatise*. In this work Hume is trying to launch a systematic research into the area of our pure experiences. Hume did not have access to the eidetic method and moreover he was unable to evade the pitfalls of a contradictory sensualism. We see further that starting with Locke, in classical English philosophy the concern with the purely subjective was not determined by psychological factors and motives. The 'inwardly turned psychology' was supposed to solve the transcendental problem posed for the first time by Descartes.

The way in which Descartes got on the trail of the transcendental problem is generally known. In still undeveloped form we find in the *Meditationes* the idea that the objectively real and also the world as a whole can appear as such only to the extent that they form the actual or at least the possible *cogitatum* of our own *cogitationes*. The objectively real and the whole world appear as being there only insofar as they form the experiential content of our own experiences.

Another one of Descartes' widely known thoughts concerns the idea that real Being is only a title for real or possible, cognitive achievements. This thought has become one of the basic themes of modern philosophy and it has to a large extent determined its specific style. Starting from the position assumed by Descartes one can turn in two directions. Descartes himself went in the wrong direction and this prevented him from posing the transcendental problem correctly. From then on he was doomed to lose himself in transcendental pseudo-problems. Descartes reasoned as follows: the experiencing and knowing subject has nothing to hold on to but itself. Knowledge operates in pure immanence. The evidence of the *ego cogito*, of pure subjectivity, of the internal experience precedes all other evidences and is always presupposed. But the immediate question arises as to how the knower can ever get beyond the immediately evident sphere of consciousness. Descartes believed that it is possible to move from my consciousness to a world which transcends my consciousness by means of mediate modes of reasoning.

The fact that such a view is absolutely untenable needs no further elaboration here.

After Descartes, the transcendental problem remained in the dark for several centuries. It seems that several generations of philosophers became lost in the problem concerning the reality of the world. Yet, Descartes had the great merit of sensing the real problem and preparing the ground for it. He was the first in the history of philosophy who focussed attention on the universal subjectivity and the way consciousness 'possesses' the world. We could also see his method of doubt as a first attempt at uncovering transcendental subjectivity. His theory can be called the first transcendental theory and the first transcendental critique of the universal world-experience as a basis for a transcendental theory and critique of the objective sciences.

The unsuccessful posing of the problem aggravated by a faulty solution to it led to the transformation of the pure ego into a pure spirit, into a *substantia cogitans.* The ego became a real and self-sufficient soul (*animus*) attached by means of causal connections to a self-sufficient bodily substance.

Locke failed to see the perspectives opened by Descartes' *Meditationes,* nor did he grasp the fact that this work introduced a radically new attitude toward the world and the soul. Locke sees the ego *a priori* as pure soul, as 'human mind.' He felt that a systematic and concrete research of the human mind could ultimately answer all theoretical epistemological questions, provided this research were based on evident inner experiences. Locke deserves our praise for placing these questions within the context of a systematic, epistemological horizon and for relating them to the ground of internal experience; yet we cannot overlook his failure to grasp those questions in their transcendental meaning. Locke understood this internal experience as *psychological* experience. It is thus that he became the founder of psychologism which tries to accomplish the contradictory task of building a transcendental philosophy on the basis of a non-transcendental psychology. During the centuries following Locke psychologists wrestled with this problem without ever being able to come to real grips with it. Neither the early psychology which arose on the basis of philosophical interests, nor the later empirical psychology were able to make a sharp and clear distinction between the natural attitude and the transcendental attitude. Without such a disinction the problem of psychologism can never truly be approached.

In this regard Brentano already offered certain advantages in that he saw the necessity of an eidetical, descriptive psychology. Especially his formulation of the phenomenon of intentionality certainly represented an important break-through in this respect. Yet even Brentano did not escape psychologism in that he failed to see the transcendental problem clearly. This problem can only be correctly posed and subsequently solved when we start with a clear insight into the transcendental sphere about which both Descartes and Kant already spoke. But to do this we need the transcendental reduction. In the solving of the transcendental problem as proposed by transcendental phenomenology, it becomes clear, moreover, that we need a new theory of science. The epistemological conceptions of Leibnitz, Bolzano, and Lotze seem to lend themselves to the requirements of phenomenology.

But leaving all this out of the picture for a moment we see that a true scientific psychology would stand or fall depending on the *radical* conquest of psychologism in which both its internal contradictions as well as its important kernel of truth would be revealed. Psychologism maintained itself for such a long time chiefly because of the essential ambiguity of the concept of 'subjectivity' and all other concepts connected with the idea of subjectivity, as soon as the transcendental problem comes into focus. This ambiguity which binds psychological and transcendental subjectivity together can be dissolved completely when we are aware of the difference between phenomenological psychology and transcendental phenomenology. We could characterize the first as the fundamental psychological science and the other as the fundamental philosophical science.

It now becomes also clear how phenomenological psychology can be seen as an excellent point of departure for transcendental, phenomenological philosophy. But let us start by posing the transcendental problem as sharply as possible. The adequacy with which this task is fulfilled determines the success or failure of the next task which asks us to determine the nature of philosophy and the nature of philosophy's relationship with psychology. The truth of this observation is amply illustrated by the history of modern philosophy and psychology themselves.[34]

The transcendental problem relates universally to the world as a whole and all the positive mundane sciences. Yet this problem lies in an entirely different dimension from the universal problem of the natural attitude where it is being approached from different angles in the different positive sciences. We will see the clear emergence of the transcendental problem only when we move out of the natural attitude of the pre-scientific and scientific world and turn instead in an entirely new direction.

The natural attitude reveals to us a world which is self-evidently real, a world that is at hand and bodily present. This world reveals itself in our experience in ever increasing completeness, and invites, as it were, our theoretical mastery of it. Whatever *is* for us belongs directly or indirectly to this world. We are not limiting ourselves here to things and subjects, but we speak also of 'irreal' objects such as linguistic meanings, scientific theories, and 'ideal' products of art. These objects are in the world as 'irreal' determinations of realities which are to be attributed to them, as the meaning of physical sounds, the meaning of physical signs, the sense of real marble, etc. Together with these real and 'irreal' determinations the world as world-at-hand forms the general theme of our natural, practical, and theoretical interest; it is in the last analysis also the general theme of the positive sciences.[35]

The need to break through the natural attitude towards a radically different one arose in philosophy the moment that universal theoretical questions were posed which were directed to the *universum*, to the world as *omnitudo realitatis*. The need increased when it became clear that the world in its Being and in its essence appears *in* consciousness as something

34. *Ibid.*, pp. 328–331, 246–270.
35. *Ibid.*, pp. 331–332.

that appears to and is 'meant' by this consciousness. *Whatever* meaning the world offers us appears as a meaning which is 'contained' *in* the interiority of our own experiencing, thinking, and valuing life; it is a meaning which constitutes itself in the subjective genesis of our own consciousness. When I claim that something is real, this claim is formulated by and in my consciousness and every evidence which is able to substantiate this claim is and remains within the realm of consciousness regardless of the question of whether this evidence has its origin in experience or in one or another theory. This holds true also for the world as a whole, even if we take it in the sense of the totality of all things which 'in and for themselves' are what they are whether or not man is conscious of them.[36] However, as soon as we relate the world in its full universality to the subjectivity of consciousness we note that this world acquires a certain dimension of incomprehensibility. For then it becomes clear that the 'being-for-us' of the world as a world which in evidence can be brought about only in a subjective way needs further explanation. We have already seen several times that world and consciousness continuously maintain a relationship of intentionality. But this fundamental insight alone cannot show that it is possible for consciousness, for instance, to keep a stable and abiding object constantly present in its 'bodily selfhood' throughout a series of continuously changing perceptions, whereas, on the other hand, this object manifests itself as transcendent in regard to these perceptions and, therefore, constantly must manifest itself as a being which is 'in and for itself.' How is it to be explained that in a present recollection I can be conscious of a non-present object as 'having-been'? How can this 'I have seen this before' be contained in an evident way in an 'I remember it right now'? How is it possible that the perception of a material thing which shows this thing to me immediately as being 'bodily' present, nevertheless implies that the thing 'in and for itself' is more than what is effectively given in this concrete perception? How are we to understand that 'the world' is and remains al-

36. *Ibid.*, p. 332.

ways more than the totality of all our actual and even possible experiences will show us? How is it that all that our total experience can effectively present to us, keeps promising an infinite *plus ultra?* In general we can say, therefore, that the world becomes immediately incomprehensible as soon as we replace our naive way of being practically and even theoretically present to the world, by a questioning attitude which focuses attention to the *how* of our conscious achievements. Even our natural reflection is not able to clarify this incomprehensibility. This incomprehensibility also implies our own mode of Being. For every real and *a fortiori* every ideal world should receive meaning and validity in and through our conscious life; and yet, we ourselves too belong to this real world. Thus, as being in the world and as having a mundane meaning man is again referred back to his own consciousness as to that in which this mundane meaning originally is constituted. It seems that this strange situation can be explained only by questioning our own conscious life and the world inasfar as it becomes conscious in it; for the world as well as consciousness itself ultimately seem to derive their meaning and existence-claim from nothing but our own conscious life. But how can we question our own consciousness in this respect and, at the same time, prevent ourselves from getting caught in a vicious circle?

But before penetrating this problem further we need first to take one more decisive step by means of which we will be able to bring the transcendental problem to a genuinely fundamental level. The relativity in regard to consciousness just mentioned does not only operate with respect to the factual world. It applies equally to any thinkable and imaginable world whatsoever. When we now by means of the method of free variation transform this factual world into an arbitrarily thinkable world, we ourselves undergo an analogous transformation in that our concrete, factual consciousness changes into a possible subjectivity. And the particular world we imagined, then becomes the *Umwelt* of this possible subjectivity as the world of its possible experiences. In this way the transcendental problem concerning

the world leaves the merely factical behind it and changes into
an eidetic problem which only can be solved in an eidetic, and
aprioric theory.[37] One could evidently use an analogous approach to the ideal world of the sciences and to the factual,
theoretical subjects.[38]

As is shown above, an aprioric, phenomenological psychology
which consequently remains within the sphere of the phenomenological reduction, is able to reveal the typical essence of
psychic subjectivity in its eidetic generality. From this it seems
to follow that such a psychology could radically describe and
differentiate all the different forms of evidence and also the
essential form and structure of all possible worlds of experience.
It could perhaps also clarify all possible systems of universal
experience and all the sciences founded upon them, in whose
immanence a possible subjectivity constitutes for itself the meaning of a world that is based on 'objective truth.'

It looks thus as if the aprioric psychological phenomenology
would be able to unravel the transcendental problem. We must
remember here, however, that this psychology is still a positive
science which therefore remains within the realm of the natural
attitude. In this science "the" world is already presupposed as a
constant world-at-hand. Thus, this world is and remains the
general and thematic basis for this science. Psychology seeks to
find out about souls and communities of souls which are encountered in this natural, presupposed world. The phenomenological reduction is of use as a psychological method only in
so far as it helps to isolate and determine the purely psychical.
Even in eidetic phenomenology the psychical retains the mode
of Being characteristic of intramundane beings. The souls to
which it directs its attention remain souls of concrete human
subjects within the real, spatio-temporal world. Phenomenological psychology as such therefore is not able to advance a
solution of the transcendental problem.[39]

In the transcendental attitude we become aware of a certain

37. *Ibid.*, p. 334.
38. *Ibid.*, pp. 332–334.
39. *Ibid.*, pp. 335–336.

contrast; on the one hand there is the anonymously functioning subjectivity which for us constantly constitutes new objectivity and on the other hand, there is the objectivity which is always pre-given precisely on the basis of that constitution; it is this objectivity which we call the world. This world also encompasses people and their souls and their human conscious life. When we focus on the ever continuing relationship between this pre-supposed world and that functioning subjectivity we see that human beings, too, merely are intentional 'products' which as far as their objectively real meaning and their validity as beings is concerned are constituted *in* this subjectivity.[40]

The very study of the correlation between constituting subjectivity and constituted objectivity brings us outside the realm of the positive sciences. This becomes immediately clear when we realize that our question does not only concern the general nature of the correlation itself but also directs itself to the phenomena which become possible on the basis of this correlation. For we must ask here also how all the universal structures of the world can be explained in their relationship to this correlation and how the constitutive achievements of consciousness can be brought to light which are able to explain how this world-for-us becomes evident in its meaning and Being-status. In the positive sciences both the Being and the intelligibility of our world are always presupposed and are left out of any subsequent scientific activity. Their task consists only in explaining this pre-given world in objective truth. Moreover, the most fundamental question does not ask about the objective truth of a real world; the most original question directs itself to the correlation between constitutive consciousness and constituted objectivity.[41]

The transcendental question presupposes also that which *every* question presupposes, namely: "an unquestionable ground which contains all the means necessary for its solution." [42] When we ask this question in regard to our factual world we presuppose our own Being and our own conscious life in whose

40. *Ibid.*, p. 336.
41. *Ibid.*, pp. 336–337.
42. *Ibid.*, p. 337.

functioning this world receives the meaning of being this determinate world of these determinate objects of experience. When we raise the question from the eidetic point of view we come into the presence of a thinkable world in its aprioric generality. But this thinkable world again is necessarily related to a variant of our own subjectivity which is equally freely thought by us. And this subjectivity is, in turn, conceived as that subjectivity which constitutes the world mentioned. In the background the factual 'I' and 'we' do still play a role insofar as it is we ourselves who think this possible world as constituted by this possible subjectivity. It is now of the greatest importance to see clearly that this world and especially the subjectivity in which it is constituted is not yet the unquestionable ground we are looking for in our attempt to solve the transcendental problem.[43]

For the universal domain of all that which is transcendentally problematic stretches as far as that which from a transcendental point of view appears as being naive. Thus this domain entails the entire allegedly real world. This is why the reality of this world needs to be placed between brackets. In the transcendental attitude we must refrain from making any judgment concerning real objects and the real world, even though and especially when these judgments seem self-evident. Those judgments would be meaningless here, because they would be in contradiction with the meaning of the transcendental problem as such. It follows that all the positive sciences must also fall within this transcendental *epoché*. Again we see how it is impossible to base a transcendental philosophy on psychology or even phenomenological psychology, since both these disciplines are positive sciences. The subjectivity which finally constitutes all objectivity is neither the subjectivity of empirical psychology, nor the one of phenomenological psychology.

We can speak here of a certain subject doubling. From the perspective of psychology human beings are psychophysical subjects of a psychic life in the world. From the transcendental

43. *Ibid.*, p. 337.

perspective men are subjects of a transcendental and world-constituting life. In order to understand such paradoxical statements,
we must recall how phenomenological psychology succeeded in
elucidating pure psychical subjectivity starting from the human
besouled-bodily subjects which are living in the world. The
phenomenological-psychological reduction formed the essential
method to bring to light the very essence of the psychical and
that of pure subjectivity. To understand truly the nature of
transcendental subjectivity we must in analogous fashion apply
the new transcendental reduction in order to fully understand
its real meaning. In order to gain a deeper insight into the
problem of subject-doubling we would do well here to make a
careful comparison between the phenomenological-psychological
reduction and the just introduced transcendental reduction.[44]

Psychology as a positive science studies the psychic subjectivity which belongs to the always pre-given, spatio-temporal
world which for this psychology remains the only valid one. As
an eidetic science phenomenological psychology seeks the *logos*
of the psychical. Its thematic basis is a thinkable world, that is to
say the world which is now thought to be real and really pre-
given. The phenomenological-psychological reduction forms a
psychological method by means of which it becomes possible to
determine and delimit the real psychical, especially in its aspect
of intentionality by means of an inactivation of all the transcendental 'positings' which become realized in this intentional life.
This psychology remains, nevertheless, a positive science because
it retains the validity of the natural apperception of the world.
As soon as this latter aspect is inactivated we enter the realm of
transcendental phenomenology, and with it a 'Copernican revolution' is set in motion which affects the whole of our life, including the practice of psychology by the psychologist. Such a
revolutionized psychology can no longer speak about 'the' world
nor can it deal any longer with the realities-at-hand which belong
to this world. Such a psychology views the world and any other
possible, imaginable world *merely as phenomenon*. Instead of

44. *Ibid.*, pp. 337–340.

viewing the world as presupposed, the psychologist becomes a transcendental spectator, to whom this world-possession, this manner in which the world or any other world appears in regard to its meaning and Being-status becomes unfolded in experience and in the analysis of this experience.[45]

Psychological experience, even purely phenomenological experience, is and remains a mundane experience. It is only after the application of the transcendental reduction that we come into contact with the transcendental experience in which there is no longer question of a really spatio-temporal, mundane Being. In psychology the phenomenologist as man-in-the-world always remains part of the subject matter under investigation. The phenomenologist is no longer this 'I,' this human being, after the transcendental reduction. He himself is placed between brackets as a human being, he is nothing but phenomenon. He is now the phenomenon for a transcendental 'I,' for that "life of the 'I,'" which manifests itself as the last functioning subjectivity, the hidden function of which was precisely the universal apperception of the world. That which in phenomenological psychology retains a psychological-real meaning is transformed in transcendental phenomenology to mere, pure phenomenon.

There is here clearly a strict parallel between the transcendental sphere and the phenomenological-psychological sphere. In the same way there is a clear parallel between the transcendental *epoché* and the phenomenological-psychological reduction. We can formulate this as follows: "the transcendental ego and the transcendental community of egos taken concretely together with its full transcendental life is the transcendental parallel in regard to the ego and the community of egos in the usual sense taken concretely as pure psychic subjects with pure psychic lives." [46] Yet, the transcendental ego is not the same as the natural ego, even though they are not completely separated either. To go from one to the other we merely shift from one attitude to the other.

Seen from the perspective of the transcendental attitude an

45. *Ibid.*, pp. 340–341.
46. *Ibid.*, p. 342.

identification comes about between phenomenological-psychological subjectivity and transcendental subjectivity. The ego as absolute being is not an objectively-being ego; it is precisely the absolute ego-subject. This ego now finds in the last and absolute instance, in its own life which constitutes all objectivity, itself as an object, as content of a self-objectivation or self-apperception which, as actively endowing this ego with its own real meaning, belongs to its absolute Being.[47]

The interwovenness of the mundane ego and transcendental subjectivity can only be seen from the perspective of the transcendental attitude since it is solely here that we see that the two corresponding experiential spheres overlap even in regard to the most vital relevant details. It is therefore to be expected that eidetic phenomenological psychology and transcendental phenomenology will exhibit analogous overlapping areas. Once we have formed an eidetic, phenomenological psychology of universal subjectivity and universal intersubjectivity which remains within the sphere of the natural attitude, we can transform this into a transcendental phenomenology by means of a free, transcendental reduction. The reverse is also possible, of course. The only difference here is that seen from the side of phenomenological psychology we cannot see transcendental phenomenology as necessary and *a priori,* although in the reverse process this is evidently the case.

Up to now we have generally spoken about the ego-logical, phenomenological psychology. This science needs naturally to be worked out into a positive, eidetic phenomenology of intersubjectivity. The analogue of this should take place within the sphere of the transcendental attitude. Only transcendental intersubjectivity is the absolute ground of Being from which all objectivity, all objective, real Being, all objective, ideal worlds derive their meaning and value.[48]

It should now also become clear why, from a pedagogical point of view, pure phenomenological psychology forms such an excellent introduction into transcendental phenomenology. We

47. *Ibid.,* p. 343.
48. *Ibid.,* pp. 343–344.

can now also understand why psychologism was able to maintain itself historically for such a long period. The force of this movement hid in an essentially transcendental 'guise' which was unmasked 250 years after Descartes when the possibility and the actual meaning of the transcendental reduction became clear. The failure of a radical understanding of transcendental subjectivity or of the transcendental reduction, resulted in a failure to see the methodic separation between transcendental and psychological subjectivity. Only after the transcendental and the phenomenological reduction is understood does it become clear that the 'supra-mundane' subjectivity which constitutes the world and which forms the subject matter of transcendental philosophy must be distinguished from the pure subjectivity which forms the theme of eidetic phenomenological psychology *and* from the intra-mundane subjectivity which forms the topic of investigation for empirical psychology.[49]

Now it also becomes clear how these two sciences can develop in relative independence from each other. We could, for example, pose the transcendental problem, apply the transcendental reduction, and achieve a transcendental experience and an eidetic interpretative explicitation without consulting psychology. The first volume of *Ideen* in which this procedure is followed forms the direct proof of this contention. It is also clear from the *Phänomenologische Psychologie* and the *Amsterdamer Vorträge* that we can explain the subject matter, the method, and function of phenomenological psychology without an overt reference to transcendental problems.

There are great advantages to an introduction into transcendental phenomenology which proceeds from the side of phenomenological psychology, because it offers the possibility to explain separately the two great difficulties which are inherent in transcendental philosophy: first of all the difficulties necessarily connected with a proper understanding of the method of pure 'inner' experience, difficulties with which one already has to

49. *Ibid.,* pp. 344–346.

cope in phenomenological and empirical psychology; next, the difficulties essentially connected with a proper conception of the transcendental problem and method which supersede every form of positivity.[50]

50. *Ibid.,* p. 348.

VI PHENOMENOLOGICAL PSYCHOLOGY IN 'KRISIS'

The Meaning of Husserl's Last Work

By the time Husserl came to Freiburg he had already established his name as a philosopher. In his *Logische Untersuchungen* (1900–1901), the *Logos*-article (1911), and especially his *Ideen* (1913) he had laid the foundations of a new phenomenological philosophy. A variety of scholars and students joined him in this phenomenological movement and subsequently recorded their thoughts in their own philosophical journal called *Jahrbuch für Philosophie und phänomenologische Forschung*. Through this journal the phenomenological movement exercised considerable influence on philosophy between 1913 and 1938. The phenomenological method did not only find application within the realm of philosophy, for also a number of positive scientists used this method with considerable success. When we consider this early phenomenological movement we are struck by the independence and originality of most of its members. This is why already in the very beginning of the movement we see the suggestion of different directions and trends. Only a very few of Husserl's followers remained completely faithful to the master.[1]

In 1916 when Husserl was appointed as full professor of philosophy in Freiburg he was already enjoying an international reputation. Yet, in the midst of this success he was in a grave

1. H. Spiegelberg, *The Phenomenological Movement*, vol. I, pp. 124–125; E. Fink, "Die Spätphilosophie Husserls in der Freiburger Zeit", in *Edmund Husserl: 1859–1959*. (Ed. H. L. Van Breda and J. Taminiaux), Den Haag, 1959, pp. 99–115, p. 99.

philosophical crisis. This is why he could not publish the second and third parts of the *Ideen,* and why he directed all his energy toward realizing his ideal, which was to lay the foundations for a truly radical philosophy. Throughout all this he remained convinced however that it would be the task of phenomenology to form the basis for philosophy and the sciences, and that the phenomenological method in principle was able to come up to the requirements demanded for a genuinely radical science.

The concepts 'knowledge' and 'science' had become more and more problematic in Husserl's thinking. Yet, he remained convinced that the field of 'pure consciousness,' which had been opened up by means of the phenomenological reduction, was the domain in which each and every object, process, movement, and objective relationship had to find its ultimate origin. But an investigation into the subjective constitution of all objects brought him into contact with ever new, unsuspected, fundamental difficulties and problems. Innumerable detailed analyses of that period tell the story of how he tried to penetrate these problems and to find a radical solution for them. Husserl himself scarcely published any of these very valuable analyses. In his lectures he only rarely referred to them. The three larger works which he wrote in Freiburg have more or less the characteristics of an introduction. "Within the perspective of a determinate problematic these works were meant to bring natural consciousness in the realm of the dimension in which the analyses of the manuscripts take their starting point." [2] In these works Husserl returned to the great problems which had occupied him since 1887 and tried to approach them anew with the insights he had gained in the meantime.

In his *Formale und transzendentale Logik* (1929) he tries to show that traditional logic forms a correlative bi-unity of a formal apophantic logic and a formal ontology. He also shows how each formal, logical *a priori* needs to be radically founded in the subjective constitution of meaning through transcendental

2. E. Fink, *Ibid.,* pp. 99–101.

subjectivity. Husserl felt that the problems of which he spoke in the *Logische Untersuchungen* could find here, at least in principle, a definitive solution. In the French edition of the *Cartesianische Meditationen* (1931), Husserl returned to the question of how we "can question back from the intramundane objects of knowledge and the hidden worldlihood of the human modes of knowledge to that consciousness which constitutes all sense and meaning." [3] He indicates here in a very condensed and somewhat enigmatic way, how the unsolved problems of *Die Idee* and *Ideen* could be adequately solved. In his last work *Krisis* he returns once more to the problems which were first posed in the *Logos*-article. After the radicalization of logic and epistemology, he tries here to bare the hidden roots of a general theory of the sciences in a consequent radicalization of his originally rather naive theory of science. Yet, the three works which we mentioned ultimately have no other purpose than to bring about an introduction to transcendental phenomenology [4] by means of a typical gradually more and more radical criticism of the traditional conceptions.[5]

The *Krisis* book is remarkable especially in that it tries to solve the problems of theoretical knowledge and science by means of a careful analysis of our pre-scientific life, that is, our life as we live it everyday and as we experience it prior to every theoretical experience. The *Lebenswelt* forms a complex system of relativities hard to understand; it is the world as it appears to us immediately in our individual and social experience. It is here that objects appear in their color, in their sensory qualities, in their 'practical' meanings. This *Lebenswelt* forms an extensive domain of 'subjective' phenomena, which encloses all objects as they are experienced immediately. The scientific worlds arise out of this world and then occupy a position in opposition to this 'subjective,' 'practical,' and always relative world. The sciences try to overcome the 'subjective,' the 'practical' and the relative

3. *Ibid.,* p. 106.
4. *Ibid.,* pp. 104–105.
5. *Ibid.,* pp. 101–108 (passim).

just as they try to conquer the magical and mythical. They try to grasp the objects in a purely 'objective' manner with the help of the method of the mathematico-physical sciences or by means of the critical methods of the humanistic sciences. This 'objectivity' becomes the ideal of all theoretical scientific thought which wrests itself loose from the *Lebenswelt*.

No doubt the sciences transcend the *Lebenswelt* in this manner, but in this transcendence the *Lebenswelt* is also concealed without this being noticed. It is this failure to notice the concealing action of the sciences which resulted in an 'objectivism.' In this 'objectivism' the naive subjectivity of the *Lebenswelt* has been conquered but at the price of losing clear contact with certain basic patterns of the *Lebenswelt*. This is why the theories of science fail to see that a radical explanation of the basis of science requires a 'subjective explanation' which in turn is rooted in the transcendental analysis of transcendental subjectivity. Husserl's approach to this problem takes place on three separate levels: 1) the naive-mundane phenomena of the *Lebenswelt* itself; 2) the level of objectivism of the sciences which in principle remain within the domain of the pre-supposed, and pre-given, really existing world; and 3) the level of transcendental subjectivity which precedes and in its conscious life constitutes this world, and in and through which all objects of the *Lebenswelt* are formed as well as all possible thinkable substrates projected by the sciences. It looks as if a dialectical structure announces itself here: the immediate subjectivity of the things of the *Lebenswelt* is denied by the mediate objectivity of the objectivistic sciences while this objectivism must in turn be denied by a transcendental subjectivism of phenomenology. Husserl, however, kept complete distance from such a dialectic. To him this work was but an introduction to the innumerable detailed analyses which he had completed at that time and which had forced him to accept such a view.[6]

Husserl chooses as a point of departure for this work the

6. *Ibid.*, pp. 106–107.

" 'break-down-situation of our own time' which came about because of a break-down of science itself." [7] Only a completely executed phenomenological philosophy could overcome this crisis. In this respect Husserl refers to his ideas of 1923 and 1924 which he had expressed in *Die Idee einer philosophischen Kultur* [8] and in *Erneuerung*.[9]

When Husserl speaks here of a radical crisis he refers to a crisis in the self-understanding of man, in particular to a crisis in the way man understands and interprets himself in his relation to the world and to the ground of its Being. The understanding of this relationship is what gives man his guide lines; it helps him to determine his own place as a being among all other beings. It is on the basis of his knowledge of this relationship that man can determine his own attitude in the world with assurance. When this self-understanding collapses it is not only the technical-scientific explanations which break down, but it entails also a failure in every 'practical' orientation in the world. At the root of the disintegrated self-understanding lies objectivism. Husserl sees objectivism as the conviction that the ultimate truth of the world and the truth of the interrelatedness of all beings can be expressed clearly in the concepts and sentences of the objective sciences.[10] This conviction is based on the belief that all beings can truly be represented in our objective-scientific knowledge without leaving an unassailable residue. It presumes that human reason can completely grasp that which is immediately experienced and that it can place this experience within a conceptual context in such a way that nothing is left

7. Edmund Husserl, *Krisis*, p. 59. See for the following: L. Landgrebe, "Die Bedeutung der Phänomenologie Husserls für die Selbstbesinnung der Gegenwart," in *Husserl et la pensée moderne*. (Ed. H. L. Van Breda and J. Taminiaux), Den Haag, 1959, pp. 216–223 (and 223–229).

8. Edmund Husserl, "Die Idee einer philosophischen Kultur. Ihr erstes Aufkeimen in der griechischen Philosophie," *Japanisch-Deutsche Zeitschrift für Wissenschaft und Technik*, 1 (1923) 45–51. See also: *Erste Philosophie*, vol. I, pp. 203–207.

9. Edmund Husserl, "Erneuerung. Ihr Problem und ihre Methode," *The Kaizo*, 1 (1924), pp. 84–92.

10. L. Landgrebe, "Die Bedeutung der Phänomenologie Husserls," p. 217.

undissolved by knowledge, praxis, or technology.[11] Human reason is thought of here as the power that, even though incapable of creating the world, nevertheless can faithfully reproduce the design of the world by means of its own concepts. It thus becomes possible to act upon the world and to predict its changes on the basis of calculations. In this approach the world loses its characteristic of world in which man always *lives already,* in which man finds himself. Instead, this approach stresses that which came into being as a result of man's knowledge. The world of the sciences, therefore, turns more and more into an artificial world in which we find less and less of all that which is not of man's own making. In such a world man turns into an artificial object that is nothing but the result of its own scientific self-project. Reason is no longer conceived as the power to reveal that which is as truth 'in and by itself'; it is now rather seen as an instrument for the scientific self-production of man in a world of his own making. Husserl expressed some of these thoughts in connection with what he calls the phenomenon of 'meaning-deprivation' which in his view is the necessary consequence of the mathematico-physical sciences and their technical applicability.[12]

Husserl saw the bankruptcy of this scientific objectivism long before it was more widely accepted. And he was not content to sit down and enumerate for us a list of factors responsible for this bankruptcy, but actively sought a solution to remedy the situation. Personally, he felt that the phenomenological method would be the one method which could bring about the changes in attitude and in understanding which were needed to truly overcome this philosophical and human crisis.[13]

In order to evaluate the possibilities of the phenomenological method in this direction, we need to contemplate the phenomenological reduction once more. This reduction assumes a new form when seen from the perspective offered in *Krisis*. Phenom-

11. Edmund Husserl, *Krisis,* pp. 18–20.
12. L. Landgrebe, *Ibid.,* pp. 217–218.
13. *Ibid.,* p. 218.

enological reduction starts by placing between brackets everything that has its origin in philosophic conceptions and scientific
theories and thus is only an explanation and interpretation of
what really is. This maneuver is made in order to unveil that
which is originally and immediately given in consciousness. The
horizon in which the world of everyday appears is always already
determined and often distorted by philosophical and scientific
explanations. To place these explanations between parentheses
means to start with the concepts used in everyday language and
from these concepts to question back to the original intuition
from which they originally derived their meaning. The word
'intuition' is not used here in the sense of 'observing' or 'looking
on,' but rather refers to a form of intercourse with things, in
which and through which we come into immediately experienced
contact with these things. It follows that the objective scientific
explanation of the world is really a special *modus* of contact
with things which turns out to be by no means the most original
one.[14] When the reduction is understood in this context we see
that it represents a going back 'behind' the scientifically explained world, back to the world of our pre-scientific, immediate
experience. A philosophy which is concerned with an original
intuition of the world must use the naive modes of language
and expressions of everyday-life. Difficulties often arise when we
try to adapt everyday language to phenomenological research.
This difficulty can be solved in a particular reflection: "It will
gradually become clearer and finally it will even be completely
evident that the right return to the naiveté of life in a reflection
which, at the same time, transcends this naiveté, is the only way
to conquer the philosophical naiveté which necessarily is implied in the scientific character of traditional objectivistic
philosophy." [15]

Our return to the world of immediate experience thus cannot
be completely exhausted in naive descriptions. For this return
cannot be executed without reflection on that which is experienced just as it was immediately experienced. We must thus try

14. Edmund Husserl, *Krisis*, p. 133.
15. *Ibid.*, p. 60; L. Landgrebe, *ibid.*, pp. 219–220.

to capture in reflection the subjective achievements of the experience itself, and ultimately also the necessary conditions of the possibility of experience which are to be found in the experiencing subject itself. If it is true, as Kant maintains, that the task of transcendental philosophy is to reflect upon the conditions which make experience itself possible, then we must characterize phenomenology as a transcendental philosophy. Kant's transcendental philosophy restricted itself to the study of those conditions which make possible the emergence of the beings which constitute the subject matter of our objective-scientific knowledge and determination. In this way, however, Kant refers the given things exclusively to man as a *theoretically* knowing subject. Husserl, however, seeks the conditions determining a much more basic experience which precedes the theoretical scientific world-experience and which forms the most fundamental mode of our life in the world. This more basic experience is furthermore itself a necessary condition for the emergence of the scientific experience. Husserl thus is concerned here with the necessary conditions which together make the 'life-worldly' experience possible as such. The conditions which determine the possibility of this life-world experience are couched in structures which precede our theoretical-conceptual thinking in terms of objective categories. These original structures are those which as the temporalization of temporality and as the determinations of the original space constitution are related to the subject as a bodily sensory being in the world. It is these structures which determine the passive presence of that which is experienced prior to any active theoretically knowing determination.[16]

In the reduction Husserl thus seeks to return from the objective realm of the sciences to the realm of the subjective in which the condition for the possibility of any experience whatsoever is to be found. That is to say, he seeks to return from what is objectively determined back to transcendental life. This return can be characterized on the one hand as the completion of

16. L. Landgrebe, *Ibid.,* p. 220.

the Cartesian foundation of philosophy upon the apodictic evidence of the *ego cogito*. On the other hand this return must also be seen as a radical conquest over objectivism to which Descartes' philosophy finally has led. The phenomenological reduction, when seen in this light, does not represent the last point which the modern philosophy of subjectivity is able to reach but it rather constitutes the starting point from which that philosophy can be conquered and transcended.

True, on the level of which we are speaking here, every constitution of whatever being in the experiencing achievements of the constituting subjects is only a passive constitution. This, however, points to the fact that the constituting, transcendental subjectivity, that is to say absolute, transcendental and constituing life, on this level of our analysis is not a completely autonomous Cartesian *ego cogito*, but constitution here rather is an event which occurs *to* the subjectivity. Also in this case this event is already oriented toward reasonableness, but the 'reason' which operates here is as yet not distinguished into a theoretical, a practical, and an aesthetic reason.[17] Thus the phenomenologist engaged on this level of analysis does not see reason as the totality of all conditions which enable us by means of thinking to determine the originally meaningless material which reaches us through the senses. Reason refers here to that which *a priori* makes this original experience possible and that which enables us to gain access to a truth which always is already present and to which we are subjected. Seen in this light, reason no longer is the power to project and to master, it rather is the power to observe, to receive, to be present-to. This remark is true in an absolute sense for all possible levels even if we here identify reason with objective scientific reason.[18]

This approach to the phenomenological reduction reveals that the truth of that which appears to us cannot be found, as objectivism wants it, in its objective determinableness which refers to a purely theoretically knowing subject which stands

17. Edmund Husserl, *Krisis*, p. 84.
18. L. Landgrebe, *Ibid.*, pp. 220–221. However, I do not subscribe to Landgrebe's attempt of reconciling Husserl's view with the ideas of Heidegger.

opposite to it. The reduction teaches us that the truth of the world cannot be found in its entirety in the world determined by the sciences. The pre-scientific world opens up the possibility for the explicitation of certain general structures which are given in our original experience, namely the structures of the *Lebenswelt*. In our pursuit of these structures we encounter an unconditional, general *a priori*. This is the positive side of this reduction.[19]

The meaning of the universality of this *a priori* differs of course from that attached to the laws and concepts of the objective sciences. The concepts by means of which we express this *a priori* are not objective concepts but concepts in which we ourselves are involved. These concepts therefore do not leave unaffected what is uncovered in them, but rather change this in the process of bringing it to light. The logic underlying this philosophical way of speaking about things has as yet not been fully worked out.

The road taken by phenomenology is one of recall which leads man back from the world which in objectivism confronted him as a strange object, to himself, and which, furthermore, shows him the region where consciousness and world merge inseparably. Phenomenology warns us beforehand that the ego which we will meet in this inseparable unity of subject and world is not only a knowing-ego, nor is the world given in this unity only the world of objective scientific knowledge. Furthermore, the truth which we find within this unity can never be possessed completely and it is the task of phenomenology to prepare man to accept the consequences of this fact. We refer here also to the possibility inherent in phenomenological reduction to bring about a complete personal change in attitude.

We can already conclude from Kant's *Kritik der reinen Vernunft* that we cannot uncover the ground of all beings by means of our theoretically objectifying, scientific knowledge. Phenomenology adds to this that the ground of all beings cannot be reached by means of postulates of practical reason either, at least

19. *Ibid.*, pp. 221–222.

not if we really want to go back from the artificial world which has been constructed by means of our objectifying thought to the 'true' world of immediate experience. The process of uncovering the ground of all beings cannot start from a position which defines man as rational subject only. The point of departure for such a venture is man in his full concreteness (which includes his thinking, striving, and his moral activities as well as his sensory-bodily being) and also the way in which this concrete man uncovers the richness of the world in its intuitive fullness. Only if we choose this as a starting point can we hope to uncover a really true world.[20]

With this last remark we are already running ahead of Husserl's thought proper as we find it in *Krisis*. It seems that Husserl never took the pains to fathom the depth of these remarks as Heidegger has done. From the very beginning Husserl is primarily concerned with a still deeper and more fundamental level of contemplation to which we only can gain access by means of the transcendental reduction. Before we turn specifically to this matter we want to discuss briefly the concept of life-world (*Lebenswelt*).

Description of the Life-World

THE STUDY and editing of Husserl's unpublished works revealed a number of fertile ideas of which that of the life-world is, in the opinion of many scholars, the most important one. Nothing was known about this during Husserl's life. He carefully formulated the idea for the first time in his final draft for the second part of *Krisis* which he was preparing for publication in the review *Philosophia*. The article, however, was not published because of Husserl's illness and death in 1938. The concept of life-world preoccupied Husserl for the last fifteen years of his life. We saw before how in 1925 he was busy with this theme,

20. *Ibid.*, pp. 222–223.

although at that time he never or at least very rarely used the term 'life-world' to refer to it. The first express mention of the term 'life-world' can be found in an article by Landgrebe which appeared in 1940.[21] The life-world concept acquired greater emphasis through the publications of Maurice Merleau-Ponty who used it in his own works on the basis of his study of Husserl's manuscripts in Louvain. After the publication of the relevant manuscripts by the Husserl archives this concept rapidly became public property.[22]

Merleau-Ponty's publications often gave the impression that Husserl's original studies concerning transcendental subjectivity had later on been replaced by his thoughts on the life-world. There is absolutely no truth in that contention. On the contrary, Husserl's study of the life-world is but one of four different approaches used to reveal the constituting activity of transcendental subjectivity. The life-world is not the deepest layer to which phenomenological analysis can penetrate. The life-world itself is also constituted, and it is a careful explanation of its original constitution which precisely should reveal to us the anonymous achievements of the transcendental ego. The transcendental reduction forms a necessary prerequisite for such a study. This becomes immediately clear when we read the title of the section in *Krisis* in which Husserl deals with the life-world: "The road toward phenomenological transcendental philosophy by means of a questioning back from the pre-given life-world." [23] The fact that his concept of the life-world has aroused so much interest in contemporary thinking should not blind us to the fact that it only occupies a definite and subordinate part in Husserl's transcendental philosophy.[24] We shall now try to give a short

21. L. Landgrebe, "World as a Phenomenological Problem", *Philosophy and Phenomenological Research*, 1 (1940) pp. 38–58; see also: L. Landgrebe, *Phänomenologie und Metaphysik*, pp. 83–131.

22. H. Spiegelberg, *op. cit.*, vol. I, p. 159.

23. Edmund Husserl, *Krisis*, p. 105. See also the remarks made by Fink (*Husserl: 1859–1959*, p. 108), as well as the discussion between Biemel, Kuypers, and Fink (*Husserl* (Cahiers de Royaumont), pp. 65, 85).

24. H. Spiegelberg, *op. cit.*, vol. I, pp. 159–160.

survey of Husserl's most important contributions to the concept
of the life-world as we find it in *Krisis*.[25]

A study of the history of our culture since Galileo will show
the gradual replacing of the world of our common, immediate,
lived experience (*Lebenswelt*) by an objectively true and valid
world of the sciences. This latter world passes for reality in the
strict sense in the opinion of modern Western scientists. It is not
difficult to show, however, that such a view is entirely untenable.
First of all, it obviously is impossible to consider any objective
entity of the sciences without recourse to our immediate experience of objects and relationships out of which this entity in
question arose. The life-world on the other hand manifests itself
actually or virtually in any perceptual experience whatsoever
and reappears in all acts which are derived from that experience.
It also becomes clear that the scientific universe is but a network
of interlocking ideal constructs. These constructs are but the
theoretico-logical substruction of the immediately given things
and relationships. Our conception and understanding of the network are of the same nature as the ideas of the mathematical
sciences. The construction of the universe of the sciences includes
certain typical procedures in which idealization and abstraction
occupy a central position. Abstraction and idealization clearly
point to something that is prior to these activities. It is in this
sense that the sciences rest on a foundation and this foundation
cannot be anything other than the life-world, the world of the
immediate evidence of our lived experience. When we speak
here of 'evidence' we refer to the immediate bodily presence of
the thing or to the immediate self-presentation of the object in
question. The whole of theoretical truth, including the logical
and mathematical truths of the positive sciences, finds its ultimate justification and validity in the type of evidence which
concerns events and occurrences of the life-world. Husserl with-
draws the privileged position from the evidences ruling objective
scientific theory and accords it to the evidences governing in the

25. See for the following in general: Aron Gurwitsch, "The Last Work
of Edmund Husserl," *Philosophy and Phenomenological Research*, 16 (1955–
1956) pp. 370–399.

life-world. This means that the theoretical scientific world must find its foundation in the life-world rather than the life-world finding its justification in scientific theory.

Underlying the mental activities which construct the objective world of the sciences are the acts through which the life-world appears to us as always present, as pre-given and as prior to and independent of any scientific activity. We therefore must in our search for the ultimate explanation of the world of the sciences return to the life-world.

A radical philosophical reflection therefore must start by shedding light on the universal presupposition which forms the basis for all our activities. This presupposition precisely is the unquestioned, unformulated acceptance of the world in which we find ourselves and with which we maintain a certain form of familiarity. There is not a moment in our life that we are not busy in some way with things, plants, animals, or fellow human beings. All these manifest themselves as worldly beings and we even understand ourselves as belonging to this world. No worldly being ever appears in complete isolation, without being surrounded by other worldly beings. Everything, whether stone or tree or man, points to a context from which it emerged and appears within an all-encompassing horizon, which we call the world. Worldly beings can appear to us and then disappear but the world remains always present to us as a universal field of all actual and possible activities of any kind whatsoever. The world is experienced as always already there because the world is announced in every single appearance of any worldly object whatsoever. The world announces itself in every one of my contacts with any particular worldly being. All our activities are permeated by an unclear consciousness of the world; and this silently accepted, presupposed world becomes the basis on which we accomplish our activities.

This world naturally includes nature. However, by nature is to be understood here that which is immediately and directly given in experience, not that nature which has been idealized and conceptualized by the physical sciences. Yet, the world is more than mere nature. The things which surround us are not only natural beings, which can be described in terms of color, form, size, etc., but include instruments, books, art-objects, etc. which are objects serving human purposes, needs, and desires. It is precisely the fact that the world contains these latter objects that we can think of this world as a world in which human life runs its course, thus as our life-world. We meet our fellow human beings in the life-world and we rest assured that they not only are *in* the world but are also aware of it, that they are confronted by the same things and objects as we are, even though these things may show themselves under different aspects and perspectives depending on the position of the observer. We all carry with us a never quite formulated conviction that the world is the same for everybody; the lived world is a common, intersubjective world.

While meeting our fellow-man in this common, intersubjective world we can assume the role of disinterested observers with respect to each other. We also can become involved with one another in a variety of ways. In that case we not only live in the same world but we live and work together in the same world. We saw that the world assumes the character of a life-world when it refers to human life. This human life must not only be understood as individual human life. The life-world also refers to an historically grown society whose social life consists in the interrelatedness of thought and action in different modalities. The life-world therefore has in the first place an historical and social meaning; a life-world is essentially related to a certain community at a certain moment in history; it should be viewed as it is taken by the people of that particular historically developed community. Husserl refers in this connection to some exemplary work of cultural anthropology in which the world of primitive people is clarified by an understanding of their mythical and magical world.

Whether we act alone or whether we cooperate with others, we never can escape the fact that all the objects with which we are confronted, that all our insights and plans, that ultimately the whole fabric of our world is interpreted in the light of the particular convictions, opinions, and attitudes which dominate the community in which we live. The word 'community' may be interpreted here as correlative to the culture at large to which we belong, or we may also see it in a more restricted meaning as referring to a special group within a larger community. In all these cases, the life-world forms the ground for our lives; a ground which is always accepted in an unquestioning way, which is understood as existing independent from and anterior to all our individual and collective activities. We can meet each other as worldly beings among other worldly beings only on the basis of this ground, this world, that we have in common.

Even though we are objects in the life-world we also are subjects in regard to this world insofar as it is our common, spiritual life that gives meaning and sense to this world. The collective accomplishments become a part of the life-world which not only is as it is taken to be by the respective society but also comprises all its innovations. The progressing, changing life of a community subjects its life-world to changes and affords continually new perspectives from which it is being interpreted. In reflecting upon this we can become aware of the life-world as something that continuously grows and develops, as something that carries the impress of the communal history.[26]

Scientific activity plays a very important role among the collective activities to which we have here referred. When a physicist refers to the work of another physicist he does not do this to point to some psychological peculiarity or some psychophysical reality of his colleague; he is not trying to reveal the objective true nature of the other physicist but rather refers to him as a colleague, as one who lives in the same world, who has the same interests, who works on the same plan, etc. When the first physicist meets the second physicist in the same life-world, when he feels in real contact with him on the basis of their common goal and general orientation, he will try to understand the ideas of his colleague. He appropriates his ideas, or transforms them into new ones, he uses his conclusions as a stepping-stone for further research. Then the first physicist may

26. Edmund Husserl, *Krisis*, pp. 105–116, 446–455. (Gurwitsch, *art. cit.,* 370–373).

talk about his own ideas and seek the opinion of the second physicist. Science proceeds in such a mutual exchange of spiritual activity by members of the same community, to which, of course, also belong the scientists of the past on whose insights a science in its present form is built. This community also opens up into the future in that the present state of science is to be carried to further completion by future generations. This mutual exchange of spiritual activity consists in the interchange of thought, in mutual criticizing of each other's ideas, and in the affirmation or the correction of other's thoughts. All this exchange tends toward the achievement of justifiable and satisfactory conclusions. Science appears here as a common, cultural achievement which basically does not differ too much from other cultural activities. Husserl therefore refers to the scientific enterprise as a praxis of a special type, as a 'theoretical praxis.'

In order to find an explanation and a fundamental understanding of science we need to analyze those 'spiritual' functions and operations which are themselves enclosed in the scientific enterprise. We also need to study the different ways in which mental activities become intersubjectively connected. We have already defined the human sciences as the study of the psychic life of human beings and of the products brought forth by this life. Newtonian physics certainly qualifies as a product of the mental life of human beings and therefore forms one of the topics to be included in the sciences of man. The objective nature which is studied by physics must not be regarded as some hidden reality lying beyond the life-world and which could only be revealed with the aid of certain methods and techniques. Rather we see this nature as the theme of an unending intersubjective effort, as an idea around which the members of a scientific community group their individual activities in an ever encircling yet never entirely encompassing movement. These results are actually the scientific theories which serve also to delineate the successive phases of science's history.

Just as any other cultural activity, scientific endeavor remains, as far as its point of departure is concerned, within the realm of the life-world. Each scientific problem arises in the life-world and relates to special aspects of that world which had been separated from others by means of abstraction. Abstraction reveals to us, for example, the spatio-temporal dimension of material being. The scientist over and over makes use of events of the *Lebenswelt* in which he performs his experiments, finds his apparatus, reads his dials, etc. The fact that the scientist makes use of these events in order to build his scientific theories does not yet mean that these are already interpreted and under stood in scientific concepts. The laboratory is for the man of science a place for work, for study, and research; it points to the specifically human activities in whose service this building stands. The scientist does not normally see this building in the light of a universal scientific theory of all phenomena, nor does he see his colleagues as physico-chemical systems. The goal to be reached through a scientific effort points also to human existence in the life-world. Scientific effort is one of the intersubjectively connected activities which we pursue in our common praxis. The goal of this effort has its own particular nature and structure just as any other goal that mobilizes and directs our culture. The goal of science is to expand the possibilities for prediction into the infinite, far beyond the possibilities of our pre-scientific life. It is the aim of science to replace that knowledge which generally suffices for our practical needs and for our orientation in the life-world, and put in its place a knowledge in the strict sense which is built around the ideas of 'objective truth' and 'being as it is in itself.' As is the case with all cultural projects, the products and results of scientific endeavour are added to the original structures of the life-world. We can easily see how science and scientific theories form an integral part of the historical cultural reality of modern Western man, i.e. his life-world. This is not to say, however, that the world of science reveals a truer world which must replace the life-world. Science gives us a possible view on the world of our every day living. In the West this view is quite dominant, and it implies, indeed, that nature, as it arises out of our common experience, appears to us as something that lends itself to possible scientific interpretation and explanation.

The life-world thus turns out to be the foundation underlying the world of science; the specific logico-mathematical evidence used in the sciences refers necessarily to evidences involving
common experience. It follows that we must not look upon the
life-world as solely a starting-point for the transition to another
realm of Being. One cannot argue for the existence of two types
of truths: one type one could call subjective and relative truth
which pertains to the practical situations of the life-world, and
another type would be the objective, scientific truth which, even
though it refers to the first type, nevertheless remains unaffected
by it. Husserl correctly points out that the life-world's real function is not only in the development of the sciences. The life-
world appears to us as given and we experience ourselves as
living in the midst of this world regardless of whether we
participate in some scientific research or other. Humanity existed for a long time in its respective life-worlds, long before
the emergence of science in the modern Western sense of the
word. Such ideas as 'objective truth' or 'being as it really is in
itself,' which are supposed to bring about the transcendence of
the subjectivity and relativity of ordinary experience, belong to
the specifically human activity which Husserl calls *theoretical
praxis*. However, inasfar as these ideas give direction and
coherence to this *theoretical praxis,* they themselves belong to
the domain of the psychical, the subjective, and the relative.

At the beginning of this discussion it may have appeared that
the problem of the life-world had been posed only in order to
give a philosophical explanation of the sciences. Now it becomes
clear, however, that the philosophy of science is preoccupied
with only a particular and partial theme; the life-world is not a
theme that only emerges when we talk about science, it forms an
important topic for study in its own right.[27]

A science of the life-world must start with respecting the
specific and unique character of this world as it emerges in our
immediate pre-scientific experience. This science cannot be a
science in the way Newton and Galileo defined it, in which a

27. Edmund Husserl, *Krisis*, pp. 123–138, 455–467. (Gurwitsch, *Ibid.*, pp.
373–375).

theoretical logico-mathematical superstructure replaces the life-world. A science of the life-world must start with a reduction concerning the objective sciences. This does not mean that we should act as if we did not know these sciences or that we should pretend to live in a world in which the objective sciences do not exist. The objective sciences, their results, and activities remain in this reduction what they always have been, namely cultural facts which as such belong to the life-world. We will not even go so far as to diminish our concern and our interest in the objective sciences. Our reduction implies only that we will place this interest between parentheses, that we will deny this interest a voice so to speak. We stay clear from an active involvement in the activity of the objective sciences and assume an attitude of disinterested observer in respect to it. Such an attitude implies not only that we will withhold our consent to any particular scientific theory; we will go further and deny ourselves both positive and negative judgment in respect to the truth or untruth of any scientific theory whatsoever. We must even in this attitude refrain from doubting any particular scientific position. Valid, objective, scientific theories remain valid theories for us. Under the impact of the reduction we consider scientific theories merely as valid positions being held by the scientists, without getting involved in the merit of these positions. We may not consider any objective scientific judgment as well-founded truth, nor may we use these judgments or statements as valid points of departure for our own investigation. The *epoché* not only covers particular scientific positions, it encloses the whole area of the objective sciences. And although we recognize objective science as a driving force in our cultural life, we nevertheless refrain from being motivated or determined by it.

This reduction will now enable us to experience the life-world as an historical, cultural reality without referring it to, or considering it as supplanted by 'being as it really is in itself.' Yet, the realization of the idea of a general science of the life-world meets with an almost inescapable difficulty. Such a science must itself possess a certain objectivity and validity of its own which cannot be the objectivity and validity of the Newtonian

science. Such a science must develop methods which will enable
it to verify true and well-founded statements, i.e., assertions
which will appear as conclusive and convincing to anyone who
makes use of the same methodology. This necessity seems at odds
with the essential relativity of the life-world, with the forms it
takes in the different communities in the various phases of their
development. Do we need a separate science for each life-world?
Is there really a place for a general science of the life-world as
such? Despite its essential relativity, each life-world shows an
invariant structure, or rather, an invariant framework within
which the relative and the changeable take their positions.

Each life-world appears as extended in time and space, and
this extention appears prior to the introduction of objective
science and is independent thereof. This space is the space
which we experience immediately and in which we live. This
space is not mathematical space, it does not contain ideal,
geometrical entities, it is not infinitely divisible, nor does it
form an infinitesimal continuum, etc. The same can be said
about time. We meet with corporeal things in the life-world but
these are not the same things about which geometry and physics
tell us. We also observe a certain causality operating in the life-
world, but we cannot understand this causality in terms of
physical laws or formulate it in equations expressing functional
dependency. Causality here rather refers to a certain regularity
and typical uniformity. Objects have a typical usual 'bearing'
which under the same circumstances makes them behave in a
typically similar way.

We want to note the fact that the categories expressing the
unchanging structures of the life-world and of the things which
we find there as immediately present, are also used in the *a
priori* sciences such as logic and the different branches of
mathematics. This terminological usage should not hide the
essential differences between the *a priori* of the life-world and
that of the objective sciences. This identity in terminology only
indicates the essential reference of the *a priori* of the objective
sciences to the *a priori* of the life-world. The *a priori* of the ob-

jective sciences is formed from the *a priori* of the life world by means of idealization. While discussing the origin of geometry Husserl insists upon the historico-intentional investigations which have their starting point in the invariable structure of perceptual space as lived in pre-geometrical experience, and not from the passing apperceptions of a specific historical period, such as the mythico-magical conceptions which, as a matter of recorded history, were involved in the rise of early geometry.

Husserl's general science of the life-world concerns itself with the general, unchanging, formal structure of the life-world, with its essential typical characteristics. This science need not be limited to the life-world of Western man but can include the life-worlds of other cultures. As a matter of fact we need not limit ourselves to actual existing cultures, or cultures that have actually existed at some time. We can even concern ourselves with possible life-worlds. While comparing one life-world with another we gradually can rid ourselves of the actual and factual aspects involved. We could try to approach purely possible life-worlds by means of the method of free variation and thus achieve an understanding of what are the essential and necessary aspects of any *Lebenswelt* whatsoever. In this approach we place all the cultural aspects of a given cultural community between brackets; we leave out of our consideration all those typical cultural aspects that give this culture its particular physiognomy; and thus we make the original world of our experience appear. We, therefore, could see this science as an ontology of the life-world as such, provided that we understand life-world to mean here a possible world of our immediate intersubjective experience. The structures which are revealed in this ontology, should be recognizable in any actual life-world whatsoever even though these life-worlds may differ markedly as far as the historical content of these formal structures is concerned.

The type of ontology which Husserl proposes in this connection differs markedly from the ontologies which have been developed throughout the last centuries. This difference can be traced to their respective points of origin. Husserl seeks an ontology that is concerned with the *a priori* of the life-world while previous ontologies focussed attention on the *a priori* of the worlds of the different sciences.[28]

Husserl never published a complete ontology of the life-world, even though we find valuable studies and analyses in his *Phänomenologische Psychologie,* as well as in his last work. In his own published work Husserl's interests assume another direction. As we have already noticed before, his first interest is in introducing us to transcendental phenomenology. Husserl brought to our attention the extent to which we are usually caught up in what he calls the *naive attitude.* This attitude is normally assumed by us in our normal everyday activities; there we are only interested in things and in their properties or behavior. We ask ourselves in this attitude about the 'what' and 'what for' of these objects and do not concern ourselves with the question of whether these things are taken as objects of the life-world or whether they are considered from an objective, scientific point of view. We are constantly overwhelmed by our theoretical and practical designs; we are constantly occupied by plans and purposes which involve the mundane realm in one way or another. In this natural attitude we pay no attention to how the world and worldly objects come to appear to us; all conscious acts which make the world accessible to us are experienced in an unreflective way. These acts do not become the actual focus of our experience and therefore remain hidden to us in a certain sense. If we want to reveal this mode we must break through the natural attitude and dispel temporarily our fascination with questions concerning the nature of things and instead seek to understand how objects do appear to us. We saw earlier that objects appear in and through a systematically connected synthesis of appearances. Our theme of research no longer concerns the world itself or the mundane objects contained in it, but rather turns to the fabric of our own conscious life, to the syntheses of the acts of consciousness in which and through which we have a persistent awareness of the world as always

28. Edmund Husserl, *Krisis,* pp. 138–151, 156–158, 176–177. (Gurwitsch, *Ibid.,* pp. 375–378).

already there. While systematically proceeding in our investigation in this way, we eventually come to the point where we pass beyond a phenomenology of the life-world into the transcendental study of transcendental subjectivity. For, as noted before, phenomenology finds its completion and its foundation only in such a transcendental study. In the same connection we explained that this study can be made only on the basis of a new transcendental reduction. This reduction transforms all the entities of the life-world into phenomena which essentially and necessarily refer to the acts of consciousness in which and through which they originally appeared.[29]

We want, finally, to note here that the original life-world as such is not immediately accessible to man, insofar as he has been influenced by the culture in which he lives. Modern Western man's scientific interpretations of the world easily work as an obstacle in this respect. If we want to elucidate the 'original' life-world as such, then we will need a special reduction involving the cultural world. Once this reduction is accomplished we acquire clear access to an ontology of the life-world which we could also label as a kind of phenomenology. Husserl speaks here of a *mundane phenomenology*. During the last period of his development he came to regard mundane phenomenology as a prerequisite for transcendental phenomenology. For it became clear, on the one hand, that the analysis of the mundane phenomenology is without *radical* meaning when this analysis is not supplemented with analyses taken from the transcendental sphere. But on the other hand, we see also that transcendental phenomenology can only find a good point of departure and adequate guidelines in a mundane phenomenology, i.e., a general ontology of the life-world as such. Thus we must first try to return from the world of culture to the original life-world by means of an initial reduction. After this is accomplished, a second transcendental reduction must lead us further back from the structures of the life-world to the hidden achievements of an original functioning intentionality. Only in this way do we find a radical foundation for our mundane phenomenology.[30]

29. Edmund Husserl, *Krisis*, pp. 178–193. (Gurwitsch, *Ibid.*, pp. 378–380).
30. H. Spiegelberg, *op. cit.*, vol. I, pp. 160–161.

When, finally, we make a comparison between the life-world with its correlative mundane phenomenology of *Krisis,* and the world of our immediate experience with its general ontology of the world of our immediate experience, which we met in Husserl's *Phänomenologische Psychologie,* we find a perfect correspondence. What Husserl calls 'original life-world' in *Krisis* is doubtless what he earlier referred to as world of our immediate experience. This observation should not blind us to the fact that the formulation in *Krisis* is by far the more comprehensive and desirable than his earlier attempts in *Phänomenologische Psychologie.*

The Psychologico-Phenomenological Reduction in 'Krisis'

HUSSERL STATES in his last work, *Krisis,* that every positive science including psychology, must start from the level of the life-world.[31] We encounter in the life-world human souls which we see as incarnated in human bodies. The question is how each one of us experiences his own body as a differentiated system of organs, how he experiences his 'functioning' in and his 'inhabiting' of this body. As examples of such organic functioning we can mention kinesthetic movements such as pushing, drawing, touching, typing, dancing, etc. Such functioning allows us to affect objects which are outside of us.

The movement of my body and its organs takes place in space; yet I cannot say that the functioning of my hand, for instance, and the kinesthetic movement represent real movements in space. My localization in space and time represents a universal form of the *Lebenswelt,* yet my soul can only indirectly possess such a localization in time and space. A human soul becomes spatially and temporally localized on the basis of its being incarnated in its body. This fact of being incarnated is originally experienced by everyone through his dwelling in a

31. See for what follows: Edmund Husserl, *Krisis,* pp. 194–276; H. Drüe, *Edmund Husserls System der phänomenologischen Psychologie,* pp. 181–223; Aron Gurwitsch, *art. cit.,* pp. 380–399.

body that within certain limits he finds at his disposal. We speak of human souls existing in the world. The word 'existing' has here a different meaning than in other cases where we speak about material or bodily things. It does not therefore make good sense to use the terms 'existence' and 'reality' in the same way for both material, inanimate things and besouled realities such as human beings. Spatio-temporal characteristics serve as the individuation principle of a material thing; the soul however has its own individuation principle and at least does not depend for its unique characteristics as this individual, on its temporal or spatial location. In analogous fashion we must differentiate between the relationships and interconnections characteristic of psychological or psychic and somatic events, and those characteristic of physical entities.

We must realize that every science originally starts from the life-world. The domain of physics is determined by means of an abstraction in which we freely focus our conscious attention exclusively on the purely bodily aspects of the objects which we meet in the life-world. This abstraction prepares the ground for further idealization and mathematization. We could ask ourselves whether psychology should not follow a similar procedure, namely that of a complementary abstraction. When we proceed with our thought in this direction we come to see the dualism of traditional psychology and especially the dualism necessarily connected with its theoretical praxis as entirely legitimate and accurate, at least as long as we leave the body-mind problems just mentioned out of consideration for the moment. On the other hand, however, we must maintain that there does not seem to be any possibility for our penetration of the realm of the psychical, except with the help of such a complementary abstraction. Everything therefore depends upon the nature and on the meaning of this complementary abstraction.

Even a superficial survey of our conscious life will help us see that we do not possess the sensory data of which traditional psychology speaks, at least not as long as we approach our conscious life as we actually and immediately experience it, and as long as we remain uninfluenced by all the *a priori* theories.

We find in our conscious life innumerable acts of consciousness which are most adequately described as "I observe a tree," "I remember my youth," "I feel like smoking a cigar," "I am sad because my friend is sick," etc. Every one of these acts is characterized by the fact that in and through this act I become conscious of something. We refer to this particular fact when we speak of the intentionality of consciousness. Research in the area of consciousness and in that of the subject matter of psychology must therefore start with a careful description of human beings in so far as they are tied up with objects, events, and happenings of the life-world.[32]

We can easily see that we are inadequately served by the traditional distinction between external and internal sensations as soon as we try to determine the subject-matter of psychology. This is not to say that there are no important differences between my experiences of stones, rivers, and flowers, and my experiences of my own feelings. Yet, both of these types of acts of consciousness are lived experiences. That is why both types of experiences belong to the subject-matter of psychology, if at least we see psychology as the general science of consciousness, of 'spiritual life,' or of subjectivity.

We must be careful at this point, not to see the intentionality of consciousness as a mere trait or characteristic of consciousness, or consider it as one human characteristic among many others. It is by means of a conscious act that an object makes its appearance, it is by means of this act that an object becomes present to an observing soul in a particular way. This object should be taken, exactly as it appears to us in this moment and in this particular act. When we observe a tree we see this tree as appearing in a certain perspective, as appearing far away, close by, or in a particular direction. We see the tree as something that presents itself in a certain respect and from a certain perspective. Although a real tree can be destroyed in a fire, such a fate cannot befall the perceptive appearance of the tree. Generally speaking, one can say that to every act of consciousness

32. Edmund Husserl, *Krisis*, pp. 219–224.

belongs that object of which the act makes us conscious exactly as it appears to us, as it presents itself to us, as it is meant and intended in and through that act. This we call the *cogitatum qua cogitatum,* the intentional object of the act. The intentional object belongs to the act as its correlate, as its sense and meaning. The full and concrete meaning of the words 'intentionality of consciousness' expresses this relationship of correspondence between the act and its intentional object. The intentional object is inseparable from the act as its correlate. No description of a conscious act can be called adequate if it does not clearly refer to its intentional correlate.[33]

Human beings maintain relationships with houses, flowers, animals, and fellow human beings by means of their conscious acts. Intentionality, therefore, represents a real relationship between a person and a certain worldly reality. Every description of any person's conscious acts therefore transcends the domain of psychology, if at least, we see this as the domain of that which, strictly speaking, belongs to the *pure* subjective life of human beings. No such description can be made without some reference to worldly reality with which the person concerns himself by means of his conscious acts. Husserl felt here that a phenomenological reduction would be required if we were to enter the domain of the psychical and purely subjective. The person whose behavior is being studied psychologically is always of necessity confronted with worldly realities which announce themselves as really existing or as probably existing. These realities appear as pregnant with values, possibilities, utility aspects. There is always a certain emotional tone accompanying the appearance of these realities.

The psychologist may or may not have certain convictions concerning these things, and these convictions may or may not correspond with those of the persons whom he studies. The phenomenological psychological reduction places between brackets all the psychologist's existential convictions and judgments concerning the object of study. Nor may these existential con-

33. *Ibid.,* pp. 229–235.

victions enter into any part of his research. He is required to
assume the position of that of a disinterested observer and wit-
ness to the spiritual life of his subjects. The psychologist notices
what it is that occupies his subjects and he will try to understand
this occupation, but he will not assume any position in regard
to this. He does not share in his subject's insights, nor does he
reject them. As soon as a subject is confronted with a particular
mundane object, the psychologist will take that object as it manifests itself to the subject, he will see this object for what it is in
the opinion of the subject. He will definitely not try to determine the relationship between what the client sees and what is
actually and 'objectively' true in the situation. Similarly, a psychologist who studies an act of perception must constantly remain present to the object as it appears in the actual perception.
He may not ask whether this object actually exists or not, or
whether the object really is as it appears to him. The psychologist
therefore concerns himself with intentional objects, not with
real objects. While trying to shed light on the conscious life of
his subjects, the psychologist comes across conscious acts and
intentional objects as their inseparable correlates. All other con-
templations must be left out of consideration. The psychologist
leaves the domain of his discipline as soon as he concerns himself with another reality from the one which is experienced and
intended taken just inasfar as it is experienced and 'meant.'[34]

The specific theme of the realm of descriptive psychology
concerns the typical essence of the human person seen as the
subject of an exclusively intentional life. Psychology studies the
person as an individual soul seen from the perspective of its
intentional life. Yet, every soul is intentionally connected with
other souls in a community, that is to say in a purely intentional
and typically closed interrelationship which we call intersubjectivity. Descriptive psychology has to deal with this topic, also.
We must realize, too, that phenomenological psychology needs
to concern itself with all psychical phenomena which can only
be explained in an indirect way. But among all these topics,

34. *Ibid.*, pp. 238–240, 235–237.

that which is given in immediate experience occupies the most important position. The phenomenological reduction remains an absolute claim in all these cases. Psychology usually chooses as its point of departure the real intentionalities such as they present themselves in the natural attitude. A psychological analysis and description which tries to rise to the realm of a purely descriptive phenomenological psychology will, however, need the universal *epochē* of the psychical. The *epochē* includes all souls, including the one of the research psychologist himself. The psychologist must also refrain from passing any judgment concerning entities which according to our natural and everyday life are to be taken as real beings belonging to the objective world.[35] He must become a disinterested observer and analyst of himself as well as of others. Unless he makes complete use of this *epochē* the phenomenological psychologist will never reach the essentially uniform and in itself absolutely closed 'inner-world' of subjects and the universal and total unity of intentional life which is supposed to be the subject matter of his investigation.[36]

It is of the greatest importance to realize that a subject can be thematically approached from two different directions, and in these two approaches we might find entirely different, although corresponding characteristics. On the one hand, we see the purely inner relationship which a person maintains with things of which he is conscious and which therefore are to be taken as intentional objects in a world which equally is to be taken as intentionally meant. On the other hand we observe a real relationship between this person as a reality in the real world and the real objects in this real world. Purely descriptive psychology approaches persons from a purely 'inner' attitude which is achieved by means of the *epochē*. And only by means of the *epochē* is its genuine subject matter revealed to it, that is to say the realm of the pure souls merely taken as such.[37]

In the preceding discussion we sometimes compared the phe-

35. *Ibid.*, p. 242.
36. *Ibid.*, p. 243.
37. *Ibid.*, pp. 240–244.

nomenological-psychological reduction with the universal abstraction which forms the basis for the physical sciences. If seen in this light, we could call this reduction a 'counter-abstraction.' It should have become clear in the meantime, however, that besides a certain similarity there remains also certain essential differences which we should not overlook. The pure subject-matter of physics makes its appearance after a universal abstraction which disregards the dimension of the psychical. If we address ourselves to the life-world and disregard all the manifestations of the realm of the psychical, we end up in the presence of pure matter. It should not be difficult to see that a phenomenological-psychological reduction could not be brought about by a mere abstraction of the material aspects of the life-world. The psychologist is enjoined, instead, not to disregard any material thing or aspects of mundane things which actually appear in experience in any form whatsoever. Precisely as intentional objects of one or another conscious act, material things remain to belong to the subject matter of psychology.

Neither may the psychologist disregard the manner in which the object is given in the act nor the attitude assumed by the subject in respect to his object. For the reduction does not only open up the realm of our intentional experiences but also it makes it possible to focus attention on their intentional objects and, in particular, on the way in which these objects are constituted in and by those intentional experiences.[38] Psychology studies primarily the intentional act and this act cannot be studied separately from that which was intended by this act. Both aspects necessarily belong to the realm studied by psychology. Husserl asks the psychologist to refrain only from ascribing the 'real Being in the real world' to all that which may manifest itself in original experience; he may not ascribe real and worldly reality to the objects intended by acts of consciousness, but he must, instead, view these as pure phenomena. In a pure and genuinely descriptive psychology the reduction is a necessary means to experience and thematize in essential purity the sub-

38. *Ibid.,* p. 244.

jects which in our natural life in the world are experienced and also experience themselves as maintaining real relationships to real, mundane things. By means of the reduction these subjects in a typically new way become 'phenomena' for the psychologist as disinterested observer. This change of attitude is what we call the phenomenological-psychological reduction.[39]

We now must try to focus attention on a few very important points made by Husserl, and to elucidate them with the help of a deeper understanding of the meaning of the reduction. Although we have already touched on most of the important points we might not have been too successful in making these points clear enough for most psychologists to achieve a good understanding of them. Also we may have failed up to now to clearly overcome the many objections of contemporary psychologists. To achieve any understanding at all of Husserl's phenomenology we must be, first of all, thoroughly familiar with Husserl's view on intentionality. As Brentano had remarked before, the purely psychical which forms the subject matter of psychology is indeed to be characterized by intentionality. The phenomenological reduction is the one necessary and sufficient condition by means of which we can achieve access to the essentially intentional psychical reality. For only by means of the universal reduction does it become possible to see the genuine meaning of the life of the pure ego as an independent theme of investigation. Only within the sphere of the reduction can this life of the ego be seen as intentional life in which this ego in various forms and modalities is directed toward and concerned with purely intentional objects. The task of psychology consists precisely in descriptively and adequately uncovering these manifold intentional relationships in all their immediate and mediate implications as far at least as all this belongs to the immanence of this pure ego.[40] But even though a psychologist may see this view on psychology as an essentially correct one, even though he may accept the necessity for a phenomenological-psychological reduction, he may nevertheless find great difficulty

39. *Ibid.,* pp. 247, 244–247.
40. *Ibid.,* p. 248.

in proceeding from there, in reviewing his earlier convictions, and in taking all that which was valuable in his former approach in order to integrate it into this new way of thinking.[41]

Even under ideal circumstances we might find it difficult to achieve a complete phenomenological reduction. To illustrate this we will pause here and point to a few typical difficulties. The reduction applies to any conscious act of any concrete person seen by the psychologist. We could take this to mean that we should proceed after the reduction of a particular act of a particular person to the next act and then from one person to the other. In this manner we would build up a complete reduction with the help of a whole series of individual reductions. Such a view is unacceptable and it is not difficult to show why. It is certainly true that to live in the world means to be affected by particular individual things and this gives rise in the sphere of the reduction to individual representations, individual feelings, and individual acts. Yet, it is also clear that the individual acts which are directed to certain worldly things, nevertheless, manifest themselves within a perceptual horizon. However wide or narrow this horizon may be, it appears as a segment of the world. It is on the basis of this reference to the world as a whole that each worldly object is experienced as *mundane* object. A reduction aimed at a particular object must therefore necessarily include the whole of the life-world. This change of attitude implied in the reduction transforms the life-world and all that which appears therein into a phenomenon in the strict sense of the word. This reduction transforms all human subjects, including the psychologist in question who applies this phenomenological-psychological reduction. All persons, including the observing phenomenologist, are transformed into phenomena insofar as they see and experience themselves as human and mundane beings. This transformation into phenomena itself reveals those persons as pure subjects of a pure, intentional, conscious life. The phenomenological reduction is therefore not something that can be achieved step by step; it needs to be applied in such a way

41. *Ibid.,* pp. 247–254.

that it includes the totality of the life-world, even when a psychologist has only interest in a specific act of a particular mundane person.[42]

The phenomenological reduction, when applied to ourselves as psychologists, reveals that our consciousness is of necessity related to the conscious life of others. Within the sphere of the reduction my own Being undergoes a change: my own Being-man acquires the meaning of an experienced phenomenon. Yet, the psychologist cannot experience himself as a human being without experiencing himself as living in a particularly historical *now,* which in turn implies a connection with the past and the future. The experiencing of oneself as a human being also contains references to other people, to an open horizon of mankind, to intersubjectivity. The experience of myself proves inseparable from the experience of others. The phenomenological-psychological reduction reduces all human beings to pure subjects of conscious life so that within the sphere of the reduction every historical, social group appears as a community of pure subjects. The investigator who applies the reduction now belongs himself to this group; thus, also, he becomes the pure subject of intentional life.

This reference, this pointing to such a community of subjects forms one of the essential and constituting components of the experience of the life-world. Although this world is reduced to a pure phenomenon, it nevertheless maintains its meaning of one and the same world for everybody. Everyone experiences this common world from his own point of view, his own particular orientation. This implies that other subjects can experience this same world from other points of view and in different orientations. We should be fully aware of the fact that my experience of this common world can be affirmed, corrected, expanded, and enriched by others. Such affirmation or correction is effected in actual contact with other conscious subjects. A phenomenological psychology of intentionality eventually must deal with the phenomenon of intersubjectivity in its full concreteness. We

42. *Ibid.,* pp. 254–257.

must not subscribe therefore to the notion of human souls as isolated, separate spheres which are isolated because of the fact that they necessarily are connected with bodies which are 'external' to each other. On the contrary, descriptive psychology of intentionality shows us how each ego and everybody's conscious life implies other egos and the conscious lives of others. Implied in each ego we even find a quasi-infinite multitude of such egos. The life-world common to everybody is the intentional correlate of a pure intersubjectivity; it is ultimately constituted in the intersubjective synthesis of pure intersubjectivity.[43]

All that which we said concerning the *Lebenswelt* and intersubjectivity needs further clarification, and more detailed descriptions. It should have become clear up to now however that a full treatment of these ideas would lead phenomenological psychology towards transcendental phenomenology. "In astonishment we see in this way that in the pure elaboration of the idea of a descriptive psychology which tries to bring to light the very essence of souls, the phenomenological-psychological reduction necessarily turns over in the transcendental *epochē* . . ."[44] For, descriptive psychology of intentionality brought us to the problem of the world as an intersubjective and common 'product' of a quasi-infinite, open community of pure subjects whose lives are mutually interconnected; a logical development of this problem now requires us to take in addition the last step in the form of a transcendental reduction. Ultimately we want to solve the problem arising from those acts and systems of acts by means of which an absolutely isolated, pure psychologist, who by means of a transcendental reduction experiences himself as a purely transcendental ego, is able to experience other egos, and enter into contact with them so that in their intersubjective cooperation a common, identical world can emerge. The phenomenological-psychological reduction applies, strictly speaking, only to the subject matter of psychology, e.g., to all acts and to all subjects which are to be considered in psychol-

43. *Ibid.,* pp. 257–259.
44. *Ibid.,* p. 259. See for the following explanation also: H. Drüe, *op. cit.,* pp. 227–245.

ogy and, therefore, ultimately to the whole of the life-world. A *radical* consideration of the problems connected with the life-world ultimately convinces the psychologist that he himself as the subject of knowledge needs to be reduced in this reduction. The phenomenological-psychological reduction then is transformed into the transcendental reduction. "However when I perform the reduction in regard to myself and my consciousness of world, then this reduction extends itself necessarily to all other human beings and the world itself; all this is for me now only an intentional phenomenon. A radical and consequent reduction thus leads to the absolute sole ego of the pure psychologist who in this way becomes absolutely lonely and does no longer have the meaning of a real human being in the real world; instead he is now merely to be taken as the pure subject of his own intentionality and all its intentional implications which themselves owe their universal and pure character to the reduction. This is the apodictic ego, which is apodictic in all its intentionalities which apodictically are inclosed in himself and now are to be uncovered." [45]

The surprising results of this research can be briefly summarized as follows. A *pure* psychology as a *positive* science seems to be impossible; there is only a transcendental psychology and this psychology is completely identical with transcendental philosophy. When we look more closely we can see that this conclusion contains a good deal of truth but that it cannot be entirely correct. It is clear, in the first place, that it is possible to have an empirical psychology as a science which studies human beings and animals within the natural attitude. We even have such a science in actuality, or at least we have the beginnings of such a science in empirical psychology. It is also clear that such a psychology requires a pure phenomenological psychology for the establishment of its foundation. We also can be sure that such a psychology will need a universal reduction. The radical and consequent application of this universal reduction eventually leads phenomenological psychology into tran-

45. Edmund Husserl, *Krisis*, p. 260.

scendental philosophy. We therefore must say: "Thus pure psychology is in itself identical with transcendental philosophy as the science of transcendental subjectivity. That is definitely settled now." [46]

Thus while Husserl pursues this thought he seems again to end up by identifying phenomenological psychology *entirely* with transcendental philosophy. He assumes expressly that a consequent and radical execution of the phenomenological-psychological reduction necessarily leads to a transcendental subjectivity which must be studied within the context of transcendental philosophy: "And in this way pure psychology is nothing else and even cannot be anything else but that which from a philosophical point of view was sought after in advance as absolutely founding philosophy, and can be materialized only in the form of a phenomenological, transcendental philosophy." [47] But it seems that when we consider psychology in this light we are still able to maintain a certain link with empirical, natural psychology, because as a pure psychologist or as a transcendental philosopher, I never stop being a human being in the same way that people, animals, and objects of the world do not cease to be real under the influence of the reduction. And within the reduction I do not cease to have this particular mundane interest in this universal science of man as a psychical being. Thus I return to the natural attitude, as it were by change of profession, by taking my work as a psychologist again in hand on the basis of my belief in the reality of the world. Precisely as a psychologist I was forced to decide to develop a pure psychology. We therefore must conclude that for a genuine psychology and for the exactness which is essential to this science only transcendental philosophy can take the part of the aprioric science which will give to psychology its absolute and radical foundation.[48]

Seen from this viewpoint Husserl seems to have gone further in *Krisis* than in any of his books and manuscripts written

46. *Ibid.,* p. 261.
47. *Ibid.,* p. 263.
48. *Ibid.,* p. 263.

between the years 1913 and 1931. Also we cannot deny that there exists a certain similarity between the view proposed in *Logische Untersuchungen* and the ideas presented here, despite the great difference in formulation and even in motivation of the two conceptions. We feel, however, that paragraph 72 of *Krisis* can be brought into harmony with Husserl's earlier writing if we adopt, with Gurwitsch and Fink, the following interpretation.[49]

Even though a radical and consequently executed phenomenological psychology necessarily leads to a transcendental philosophy, it nevertheless is a mistake to equate the two sciences *completely* with each other. The phenomenological-psychological reduction as such does not encompass the subjectivity of the psychologist himself while the transcendental reduction does. In *Krisis* Husserl tries to emphasize the fact that phenomenological psychology as a theoretical science is of necessity directed toward a transcendental phenomenology. In other words Husserl tries to show clearly that a phenomenological psychology cannot be thought apart from a transcendental philosophy. The striving toward more fundamental insights which characterizes all sciences, inexorably propels psychology as the study of consciousness' intentionality toward transcendental philosophy. In actual psychological praxis, however, the psychologist must return to the life-world in order to apply there his insights on real people living in real mundane situations.[50] Phenomenological psychology therefore is a *scientia media* between pure empirical psychology and transcendental philosophy.

49. *Ibid.*, pp. 515–516 (Gurwitsch, *art. cit.*, pp. 387–396).
50. *Ibid.*, pp. 266–269.

VII SUMMARY, EVALUATION, AND CONCLUSION

Basic Issues in Husserl's Phenomenological Psychology

In the previous chapters we have tried to give a brief survey of Husserl's view on phenomenological psychology and also of the development which he underwent in this respect. Now that we are near the end of this historical study we must try to evaluate what has been said so far. To this end we will use a brief survey of the insights Husserl had achieved at the end of his career. Following Drüe [1] we wish also to introduce a few distinctions which were not mentioned explicitly in the preceding pages. These distinctions, however, definitely specify Husserl's position and will consequently help us to gain a firmer hold on the whole of his thought as far as phenomenological psychology is concerned.

Contemporary psychology as the science of the psychical, taken inasfar as this is concretely involved in spatio-temporal reality, considers as its subject matter all that is present in the world as living subject which perceives, strives, wills, thinks, etc. We, therefore, could call this concrete psychology a *psychophysical psychology* since it seeks to study psychic life as it manifests itself in the plenitude of our immediate experience and, therefore, as it appears in the concrete connectedness with a living body. This psychophysical psychology often degenerated into naturalism when it tried to explain the psychical exclu-

1. H. Drüe, *Edmund Husserls System der phänomenologischen Psychologie*, pp. 55–62.

sively on the basis of material bodily happenings as for instance in classical behaviorism. The unacceptability of this naturalism has already been the topic of previous chapters, so we will not deal with it here again. The psychophysical psychology which we want to discuss now, simply accepts the fact that the psychical never occurs in the world without a foundation in the physical. But this psychology, at the same time, maintains the insight that the psychical has its own typically essential characteristics and that it therefore commands its own realm of lawfulness.[2]

The first problem arising out of this consideration concerns the question of whether the *purely* psychical can be sufficiently separated from the physical to form the basis of a pure psychology which would operate in addition to psychophysical psychology.

Before answering this question we must first clarify the characteristics of psychical experience itself and of the psychical data which it brings to light. To that end we must concentrate our attention on our *immediate* experiences. These experiences allow us to discover the psychical only by means of reflection, i.e., by means of a change in our normal, natural attitude. In the natural attitude we usually concentrate on objects, on their characteristics, their values, etc., but bypass the psychical acts of experience through which we get to know these objects. The act itself cannot be revealed except through reflection, and such a reflection can be applied to every experience. In this reflection we turn away from things, from their values, purposes, or usefulness. Instead we try to contemplate the experiences in which things and their different aspects stand revealed. These appearances we call *phenomena*. The essential characteristic of a phenomenon consists in the fact that it is a consciousness-of-its-object. *Pure psychology* is concerned with these phenomena. Since these phenomena are essentially intentional we can speak also here of *intentional psychology*.

It is possible to assume two different theoretical positions in

2. *Ibid.*, pp. 56–57.

respect to these pure psychical phenomena: we can accept them as psychical facts and stop there, or we can shift our position and concentrate on the very essence which, at the same time, manifests itself in these facts. In the first instance we achieve a *pure, factual scientific psychology* or a psychology which investigates only psychical facts after removal of those components which in reality are always connected with the psychical. The object of such a psychology is the study of human experiences seen apart from all bodily and physical components. Actually this pure, factual scientific psychology is often closely related to psychophysical psychology. Together these sciences form what usually is called *empirical psychology*.[3]

The investigations of this pure, factual scientific psychology need to have as their foundation a pure eidetic and also an aprioric psychology. This latter psychology also restricts its activities to the realm of the purely psychical, and concentrates then on the very essence of the psychical phenomena rather than on their factual aspects. The best avenue of approach to this eidetic or *phenomenological psychology* is through a deeper understanding of intentionality.[4]

In the natural, non-reflective attitude we direct our attention to objects which we know or toward which we strive. Reflection reveals to us that this intentionally being-directed-toward is an immanent process characteristic of all forms of experience. This process can assume any number of concrete forms or modalities. 'To be conscious of something' does not mean simply to possess this something in consciousness. Each phenomenon has its own intentional structure which in analysis can be shown to be an ever expanding system of individual, intentional and intentionally connected components. The perception of a house turns out to be a manifold synthesized intention: a continuous diversity of appearances of this house which answers the different points

3. *Ibid.*, p. 57. See also: Edmund Husserl, *Ideen*, vol. I, p. 395; *Phän. Psych.*, pp. 217–222, 285, 324–328; *Krisis*, pp. 215–219, 227–229.
4. H. Drüe, *op. cit.*, pp. 58–61. See also: E. Husserl, *Ideen*, vol. I, p. 395; *Ideen*, vol. III, pp. 37–53, 70–75; *Phän. Psych.*, pp. 46–51, 217–222, 222–234, 278–287, 303–324; *Krisis*, pp. 235–260; *Cart. Med.*, pp. 72–76, 107, 159, 168–174.

of view from which it is seen. This diversity of appearances also answers the different corresponding perspectives which are revealed when we observe the sides and the rear of the house after we have seen the front part. These latter perspectives originally remained hidden, were also relatively undetermined, and yet were always already presupposed. Seeing the front of the house already contains expectations concerning the side and the back of the house. When we observe closely this stream of appearances and the manner in which they form a unity, we come to see that each phase of the total process is already by itself a consciousness of something although these different acts of consciousness do not disrupt our distinct consciousness of dealing with one and the same thing. The intentional structure of a complete perceptual act must conform to a certain type if a certain physical object is to be perceived as an actually present, perceived thing. Something analogous to this must take place if we are to remember, to imagine, to judge, to value or to strive for a particular object.[5]

The task of phenomenological psychology is to systematically investigate these types and forms of intentional experiences and to reduce their structures to a primary intention. The ultimate purpose is thus to explicitate the very essence of the psychical and to come to an understanding of the Being proper to and characteristic of the 'soul' itself. The validity of this research reaches beyond the particular life of the investigating psychologist because psychic life is not only manifested in his own self-consciousness but also in his consciousness of other people. This last source of experience, which concerns other people, does not offer us merely a repetition of what we already found to be present in our own consciousness; to the contrary, this source shows us the difference between what we experience as belonging to us and belonging to others, and confronts us with the characteristics of social life. A further task of phenomenological psychology therefore directs itself to the intentionality operative in and constitutive of social life.[6]

5. Edmund Husserl, *Phän. Psych.*, pp. 279–281.
6. *Ibid.*, p. 281.

Phenomenological psychology therefore shares with pure, factual scientific psychology an interest in the conscious life of ourselves, and the experience of others and of community which are derived from it. Its subject matter comes to light as soon as we remove all the non-psychical aspects of a given reality by means of abstraction. Now it is not immediately clear how such an abstraction can be realized, how it can be consistently performed and how it can be maintained without getting caught up time and again in physical and psychophysical considerations. It is this fundamental problem that, notwithstanding Brentano's discovery of intentionality as the fundamental characteristic of the physical, has made the psychologists turn their backs to the many possibilities inherent in phenomenological psychology. The psychologist always finds his consciousness of himself mixed with non-psychical ingredients. That which is experienced as external does not belong to the intentional, internal experience even though our experience of the external just as experience belongs to the intentional internal. The phenomenologist who only seeks to get a clear view of his own life, therefore, needs to apply an additional reduction. He must refrain from any ordinary, objective point of view. He must also forego any particular point of view concerning any judgment applied to the objective world. In his investigation the experience must remain what it genuinely is: it must remain this experience of this house, this body, of the world in general or seen under this particular aspect. It is impossible to describe an intentional experience without first noting all that is contained in this experience, thus, without dealing with the objects of consciousness.

This all encompassing *epochē* places the world between parentheses, it excludes from our field of study the world which always is present as self-evidently pre-given. This world must be "bracketed" so that we may clearly see the particularly experienced, perceived, remembered, judged, and valued world. We can only gain full access to a phenomenological experience if we are prepared to forego the objects as they appear in the natural world. Instead we must direct our attention to the manifold ways in which they appear in the subject as reduced objects, as phenomena.

The phenomenological reduction of natural objects, or the transformation of natural objects into purely psychical phenomena requires two separate steps: 1) the systematic and radical *epochē* of any objectifying point of view, both in regard to the object and with respect to the entire attitude of the subject; 2) a careful analysis and description of the manifold appearances of that which now no longer can be called objects but which rather should be named 'unities of meaning.' Phenomenological description as such always has two sides, namely the description of the 'noetic' aspects *and* the 'noematic' aspects of the total phenomenon. We want to remind the reader again at this point that the analysis and description are not directed towards uncovering factual facts but rather seek to shed light on the essences of phenomena. This is why the *epochē*, the analysis, and the description need to be accompanied by an eidetic reduction. The eidetic reduction essentially consists in the execution of free variation, the noticing of overlapping areas in all that which has been realized in free variation, and the active grasping of the *eidos* in an original intuition.[7]

We can apply a similar *epochē*, analysis, and description, to the lives of other human subjects; the reductive method can be applied beyond my own experience of myself to include my experience of other human subjects. Also the social group which we experience in our ordinary conscious life can be reduced not only to the intentional fields of the individual conscious subjects, but also to the field which connects all these individual fields, namely the phenomenological unity of social life. This form of reduction could be described as the intersubjective phenomenological reduction. This reduction also contains an implicit invitation for a noetic-noematic, eidetic description analogous to the one we mentioned before.

What we have described thus far is not sufficient to penetrate

7. *Ibid.,* pp. 281–283.

intentional life with its inseparable components, its 'unities of meaning', toward an understanding of the 'soul'. Individual life can never be completely separated from the "I-subject" which constantly persists as the continuously identical ego and as the pole of all the particular intentions and the consequent habitualities.[8]

It should be clear thus far that phenomenological psychology can be freed of any and all empirical and psychophysical elements by means of a phenomenological-psychological reduction. Thus purified phenomenological psychology no longer speaks of facts but of essences, of *eide*. This psychology therefore takes up an eidetic position insofar as it looks for the unchanging aspects of psychic life; it thus tries to uncover the typical layer of the *a priori* which underlies the realm of the factual. Phenomenological psychology essentially is an eidetic phenomenology.[9]

Phenomenological, pure psychology forms the absolutely indispensible foundation upon which the 'exact' empirical psychology must rest, much as pure physics rests on pure mathematics. For the psychologist demanded that empirical psychology should be as 'exact' as modern physics. In this connection we do well to remember that physics started as a vague inductive empirical discipline and that it owes its present-day character to an aprioric system of forms which has been worked out by the pure auxiliary sciences of physics such as pure geometry, pure phoronomy, and a pure science of time. The methods of the natural sciences and those of psychology differ considerably but neither one can really be an exact science without the radical uncovering of the very essence of the subject matter with which it deals. The exactness of empirical psychology, therefore, must build on the essence of psychical reality. It is the task of phenomenological psychology to uncover the essences in the realm of the psychical. However, this psychology itself must, in turn, be rooted in a transcendental-phenomenological philosophy.

A typical problem arises here for the psychophysical psy-

8. *Ibid.*, pp. 283–284.
9. *Ibid.*, pp. 284–285.

chology to which we referred above. The *a priori* of psycho-physical psychology is much more encompassing than the *a priori* which can be revealed by phenomenological psychology. Psychophysical psychology, as the study of the psychical as it manifests itself in the pre-given world as a real moment of a besouled body, deals with psychophysical entities which are part of the natural world. Psychophysical psychology therefore finds its foundation also in the *a priori* of physical nature as it is revealed by the pure natural sciences. The necessary consequence of all this is that this psychology needs also to be founded upon the empirical and aprioric sciences of nature. This psychology is ultimately based on its own *a priori* that belongs to the realm of the psychophysical as such. In other words, a psychophysical psychology concerns itself with more than the psychical to which phenomenology directs itself because this psychology does not *solely* depend on the essence of the psychical but also on the essence of physical and even on the essence of organic nature as such. Very little, however, is known up till now about the essence of organic nature.[10]

Returning to our original topic, phenomenological psychology, we note that its proper development can take place only when the following requirements are met: 1) A description of all characteristic traits belonging to the essence of each and every intentional experience and, in particular, of the universal law of synthesis. 2) The explanation of all characteristic traits and forms of the different kinds of experiences which are necessarily found in the psychic life of any person whatsoever, together with a description of all the typical syntheses involved. 3) An explanation of the essence of the universal stream of consciousness as such. 4) An exploration into the ego seen as center of all experiences and as pole of all actualities and potentialities of consciousness. 5) Following this static description an attempt must be made at describing the genesis of life of the ego, in particular, as far as the universal and eidetic laws involved are concerned. Besides the static phenomenology which we dis-

10. *Ibid.,* p. 285.

cussed thus far, there is need thus for a genetic phenomenological psychology in which the different forms of active and passive genesis are explored. As far as passive genesis is concerned we will need an entirely new phenomenological approach to association.[11]

We must now try to determine more accurately the relationship between phenomenological psychology and transcendental phenomenology. Both the eidetic and the pure empirical psychology are "positive" sciences insofar as both start from a world which in the natural attitude is presupposed as pre-given. Transcendental phenomenology, however, is the highest and the absolutely unworldly science. Although phenomenological psychology is a completely new science insofar as it makes use of an intentional analysis, yet, this science can easily be approached from any positive science. Once this science is discovered and built up it becomes possible to attempt more radical forms of reduction and analyses and, in this way, to enter the realm of transcendental phenomenology which exclusively occupies itself with transcendental phenomena. Phenomenological psychology can thus be seen as a good introduction to transcendental philosophy, although it is possible, of course, to build up this philosophy without the assistance of phenomenological psychology. The discovery that consciousness is relative in two entirely different manners in respect to 'that which is other than itself' suggests to us a two-fold reduction, namely the phenomenological-psychological and the transcendental reduction. The psychological reduction does not reach beyond the psychical of the living reality. Psychology precisely seeks to render service to real beings and limits itself therefore to the possibilities inherent in the real world. Every psychologist, even the phenomenological psychologist, is, seen from a transcendental point of view, still naive, insofar as he occupies himself with souls which are conceived of as belonging at least to possible men and animals in a possible space-world.[12] The transcendental problem, however, implies the entire world with all its sciences including phe-

11. *Ibid.*, pp. 285–286.
12. *Ibid.*, pp. 290–291.

nomenological psychology. The world comes into being through us as Descartes already was able to show. The general meaning of the world is something of which we become aware only in our perception, in our thinking, and our valuing life. That is why the world is something that is "constituted" in a subjective genesis.

The world with its characteristic of 'Being-in-itself' is there and it also is what it is independently of my being conscious of it. But once this world appears to us as 'the' world it enters into an essential relationship with the subjective. Then the world acquires a whole new dimension and it is this dimension that poses such great problems for us. What namely is this 'Being-for-us'? What is this 'appearing' of the world, which only can acquire its significance from the side of the subject? We could call the world 'internal' insofar as it is related to human consciousness. Yet, how is it possible that this 'general' world whose immanence is as ephemeral as that consciousness in which it appears, manifests itself in a multiplicity of aspects, whereas immediate experience apodictically assures us that they are the aspects of a world which exists independently by itself. We meet this same problem when we consider all the ideal worlds such as the 'world of mathematics' and the 'world of truths that are in and by themselves true.' Not a single existing being and no mode of Being is more completely understandable than our own existence. We ourselves and all the subjects for whom this world *is,* nevertheless, also belong to this world. Is it necessary for us to relate to ourselves in order to gain a worldly meaning and mundane being? Is it true that we are, on the one hand, subjects of psychic life, while on the other, we are precisely as subjects of a transcendental and world-constituting life, transcendental beings in regard to the world and, therefore, also in regard to ourselves? Psychical subjectivity, the 'I' and the 'we' of everyday life can be experienced such as they are even within the realm of the phenomenological-psychological reduction. In the same way this subjectivity can also be considered from an eidetic point of view and be made the object of phenomenological psychology. Transcendental subjectivity, however, cannot be studied from the natural attitude because it is not part of the world. For transcendental subjectivity precisely is that subjective conscious life in which the world with all its contents is constituted into a 'world-for-me.' As human beings who are present in the world in a psychic and bodily way, we are 'for us'; we are the phenomenon of a very manifold intentional life, 'our' life in which what is present apperceptively constitutes itself 'for us.' This apperceived 'I' and 'We' presupposes an apperceiving 'I' and 'We' for which they can be present, but such an apperceiving 'I' and 'We' are not present in the same way. We can encounter this transcendental subjectivity only by means of a transcendental experience. And just as the psychical experience can be a pure experience only on the basis of a reduction, so also does this transcendental experience require a special reduction.[13] This transcendental reduction can be considered as a further purification and radicalization of the psychological which leads to a universality of a still higher order since the *epochē* not only encompasses the world but also the pure souls and the phenomenological psychologist who studies them. This reduction transforms all this into transcendental phenomena. Whereas, therefore, the psychologist, within the world as it is given in our natural attitude, reduces the subjectivity which is met there, into a purely psychic subjectivity in the world, the transcendental phenomenologist reduces this psychologically pure subjectivity into the transcendentally pure subjectivity by means of his absolutely universal *epochē*. It is this transcendental subjectivity which executes the apperception of the world and also the objectifying apperception of 'souls which belong to animal realities.' [14]

As a transcendental phenomenologist I no longer contemplate my perceptual experiences, my imagination, or the psychical data revealed by my psychological experience. Instead I try to get an overview of my transcendental experience. I am no longer interested in my own existence but seek, instead, access to the purely intentional field in which my psychical real experi-

13. *Ibid.*, pp. 292–293.
14. *Ibid.*, p. 293.

ences took place. At this point the transcendental problem reaches its high point. We must realize here that the relativity with respect to consciousness is not only an actual quality of our world, but is, by eidetic necessity, a typical quality of any imaginable world whatsoever. For we can subject our actual world to changes by means of the method of free variation and transform it into any other world we can imagine. In this process we ourselves need to undergo analogous transformations although we are limited here by the boundaries set by the nature of subjectivity itself. We also can change this world in any manner we please, as long as it remains a world that we can continue to experience as such. Transcendental phenomenology thus proves to be a real eidetic science in which psychological experiences remain what they are as far as form and content are concerned. Yet, these experiences are seen as structures which find their ultimate explanation only in the last structures of transcendental consciousness itself.

It now becomes clear that the transcendental problem, like any other problem, can be solved only when we dip into a layer of Being which is presupposed by the problem and thus remains outside the problem. This layer of Being is nothing but the pure subjectivity of consciousness in general whereas the domain of research precisely consists in any sphere that somehow can be called 'objective' and now must be studied in its generality and its ultimate root. Nobody can claim to solve the transcendental problem by means of empirical, or even phenomenological psychology without becoming guilty of a *petitio principii*. Subjectivity and consciousness as seen by the psychologist are not the same as the subjectivity and consciousness studied by the philosopher. The transcendental reduction which replaces the phenomenological psychological reduction, transforms the psychical 'I' and 'we' into a transcendental 'I' and 'we' which now must be understood from the point of view of the concreteness of transcendental consciousness itself.

It is, of course, possible to shift positions in such a way that a transcendental self-experience is immediately transformed into a psychological self-experience. While shifting positions we ascertain a certain identity between the transcendental and the psychological 'I.' That which in psychological reflection I see as my objectivation, I see in the transcendental reflection as objectified by the transcendental 'I.' The psychological and the transcendental spheres can make their appearances in a parallel fashion insofar as there exists an 'identity' in meaning between the two, even though they differ from each other in radicality. Psychological subjectivity is transformed into transcendental subjectivity and psychological intersubjectivity is transformed into transcendental intersubjectivity by means of a more radical *epoché*. This transcendental intersubjectivity provides the ultimate soil from which all that which transcends consciousness, receives its ultimate meaning.[15]

Husserl's Phenomenological Philosophy in the Light of Contemporary Criticism

No MORE than forty years after Husserl's course in *phenomenological psychology* at the University of Freiburg, we find a wide-spread phenomenological psychological movement with strong support in many countries. Although all contemporary phenomenologists honor Husserl as the founder of this movement, we nevertheless find very few psychologists who accept Husserl's view without major modifications. It is not possible to discuss here all the divergent points of view which have been developed over the last 40 years. Many writers occupy themselves with phenomenological themes without having a clear understanding of the real problems involved, and without a sufficient background in the history of phenomenology itself. This is quite understandable if we realize that Husserl's later thought on the subject remained inaccessible to most scholars until just a few years ago. The insights of his disciples and of those who had access to his manuscripts, were generally available but their views seemed to differ considerably. We therefore

15. *Ibid.,* pp. 287–296.

see in contemporary writings a lack in differentiation between the views of such phenomenologists as Scheler, Heidegger, Sartre, Jaspers and Merleau-Ponty and the views of Husserl himself. A general confusion concerning what we are to understand by phenomenological psychology ensued.

Strasser very aptly remarks that we cannot get out of this confusion by merely looking for the largest common denominator of all famous phenomenologists and to thus arrive at an adequate description of what we are to understand by phenomenological psychology. Instead we must turn to a careful historical study of the problem in which we can clarify the essential aspects of the different points of view. Only after this has been done is it possible for us to critically determine our own point of view. Only then will we have a secure basis from which to judge the typical and essential of phenomenological psychology. It is also possible, of course, to arrive at a justified definition of phenomenological psychology by means of an exposition and critical justification of that which we ourselves think of phenomenology. Yet, by far, the majority of psychologists have neither done one nor the other. This seems to be the most important reason why most of the studies dealing with phenomenological psychology are less than convincing.[16]

One thing becomes abundantly clear when we look through the contemporary literature on the subject: most phenomenological psychologists direct their criticism of Husserl not so much to his views on phenomenological psychology as to his views concerning the transcendental phenomenological philosophy. This is why we will approach our evaluation of Husserl's views on phenomenological psychology from a critical investigation of his transcendental phenomenology.

Landgrebe has often dealt with the many difficulties one must overcome in order to come to an understanding of Husserl's transcendental phenomenology. We must first of all remember that much of Husserl's writing is not yet published or has only recently become available, and that the readily avail-

16. S. Strasser, *Phenomenology and the Human Sciences*, pp. 245–248.

able publications mostly concern themselves with elaborating an ideal program rather than with patiently worked out detailed analyses. It seems that Husserl, without quite being aware of it, cut the ground from under this ideal program in these detailed analyses. In *Ideen* and *Cartesianische Meditationen* Husserl understands his work as an attempt to radicalize the Cartesian demand for an absolutely certain basis for philosophy as a strict science. The numerous, detailed, and unpublished analyses, however, are often quite at odds with this quest. In these analyses the attempt to radically comprehend the modern subject problem turns out to be forever in vain: these analyses reveal that that problem is a pseudo-problem.[17]

In his systematic treatments of phenomenological philosophy Husserl intends a philosophy as a strict science. He sees the idea of an all encompassing rational knowledge of all that is, as the proper and characteristic intention of all philosophy since its early inception in Greece. The phenomenological and transcendental reductions make it possible for us to take the decisive step in the direction of this old ideal. These reductions do not destroy the world in which we live, nor do they deny it; they only put this world between parentheses. What remains after this reduction is nothing but the transcendental ego with its transcendental life. Once we have gained access to the transcendental sphere with the help of the reductions we can start the task of clarifying the essence of what we find there by means of the intentional and constitutive analyses.[18] The phenomenological-transcendental reduction and the theory concerning constitution form the two pillars upon which the rest of Husserl's phenomenology rests.[19] The phenomenological reduction makes it possible for the mind to discover its own nature; originally lost in the world, the mind can find itself again by means of these reductions. The moment of that discovery opens up the possibility for an entirely new task. Only at this moment

17. L. Landgrebe, *Philosophie der Gegenwart*, Bonn, 1952, pp. 31–32.
18. G. Berger, *Le Cogito dans la philosophie de Husserl*, Paris, 1941, pp. 67–74.
19. *Ibid.*, pp. 16, 94.

is the mind capable of interpreting the world as a coherent system which is constituted by it itself. The coherence and unity of the world are ultimately founded in the unity of the ego to which all elements of the world necessarily refer. The task of constitutive analyses is to clarify how the ego constitutes worldly Being and the world itself.[20]

What exactly does Husserl mean by the word "constitution"? Husserl uses this word to indicate the original relationship between I and the world, between the ego and any worldly structure whatsoever. We must not forget here that any worldly Being as well as the world itself, when analyzed in terms of *meaning,* will necessarily refer to the transcendental ego. The explanation of the constitution of the world concerns itself with how the ego gives *meaning* to whatever is present to it; it also highlights how this ego grants certain aspects of the world an *existential meaning.* To fully understand Husserl's concept of constitution we must place ourselves on the level of sense and meaning. We must be thoughtful of the fact that: "the whole Being of the world consists in a certain meaning which presupposes an absolute consciousness as the domain in and by which all meaning is given." [21] Phenomenology does not deny the real existence of the world, but only tries radically to explain its meaning. The same is true for the ego itself. Ultimately the ego, too, is a certain meaning that needs to be explained. The constitution problem thus includes the ego itself. Transcendental phenomenology tries to make explicit and to radically ground the meaning of any possible being.[22]

This original view can be further interpreted in different ways, and it will depend upon the particular interpretation as to whether or not Husserl's vision is acceptable to us. Husserl's own interpretation is rooted in the conviction that a consistent phenomenology must turn its back on every established theory, on all traditional, prejudiced, and 'metaphysical' views in order to gain access to a pure and primordial experience in which the

20. *Ibid.,* p. 94.
21. Edmund Husserl, *Ideen,* vol. I, p. 135.
22. G. Berger, *op. cit.,* pp. 94–95.

'things themselves' appear to us in a genuinely original way. We must ask ourselves what might be the criteria for such an experience and what position we must assume in order to be able to judge the originality of such an experience. Experience is a manner of possessing something in a conscious way; only consciousness itself can therefore distinguish between an original and real experience and an improper one. But as adult and educated people we already have a number of views on a great many of things. The question, then, is to work through these derivative views on things and problems, back toward the original experiences in which any being whatsoever emerges originally as it itself.[23]

This is the task of the intentional analysis in which we question each and every being concerning the conscious modes and the conscious achievements in which it made its original appearance. The phenomenological reduction is of the greatest importance here since it enables us to reach the data in their purity, and in the original form in which they appear in consciousness, to the exclusion of every conception and view which transcend the original data. Consciousness itself cannot be described nor is it possible to distinguish the separate acts of consciousness, without our first becoming aware of the distinction between consciousness and that of which we are conscious, and without also noticing the particular manner in which each act is oriented toward its object. The object of the analysis of consciousness therefore includes the different manners in which acts of consciousness are directed toward objects; thus, this analysis basically interrogates the different ways in which intentionality can manifest itself. All questions concerning the very essence of each being are referred back to questions concerning the different modes of consciousness and, therefore, to the experiences in which this being manifests itself in its originality as 'this here.' The essence of any being whatsoever thus can be revealed by means of an intentional analysis of the acts of consciousness in which this particular being is constituted as such. In this way Being and consciousness appear as strongly

23. L. Landgrebe, *op. cit.*, pp. 32–34.

interwoven: there exists no object nor any quality of any object that does not find its correlate in the constituting acts of consciousness, in which it is originally given as this or that thing or quality.

Intentional analysis uses the essential differences between all possible objects of consciousness as a guiding clue when it inquires into the modes of consciousness in which these objects are given originally. The phenomenological reduction which up to this point had manifested itself as a mere suspension of all unfounded opinions concerning objects, now assumes a more radical form. This reduction now appears as that process which leads us to the ultimate and irreducible point to which all our knowing and speaking of the world, things, and their essential structures, refer; this point is the certainty of myself as a being who is conscious of himself and the world. This *ego cogito* does not serve as a point of departure for a deductive philosophical system. The discovering of this *ego cogito* merely frees an *original* field of description. The analyses of phenomenology can thus be seen as always moving in two different directions; on the one hand these analyses are noematic descriptions which take as a guiding clue the essential differences between species, regions, etc.; on the other hand they are noetic descriptions of conscious acts which intend a being of this or that type.[24]

Originally the ego understands itself also as a mundane being over and against other egos. A more radical analysis reveals that this understanding is based on an already constituted world in which this, my ego, appears over and against other egos. This analysis can be pursued one step further; we then discover in ourselves a center of intentional acts through which each being is what it is and through which alone it can appear as this particular being. The analysis thus reveals an absolute consciousness through which all that which is, is what it actually is.[25]

In Husserl's view this methodic conviction implies a particular way of raising and answering the fundamental metaphysical questions concerning Being, concerning the meaning of Being

24. *Ibid.,* pp. 34–35.
25. *Ibid.,* pp. 35–37.

and the different modes of Being. To Husserl, Being *a priori* is the correlate of consciousness. 'Being' means 'being an object for consciousness.' Each object is originally revealed in consciousness according to its own essence. True, absolute constituting consciousness ultimately is a stream of constituting achievements which as stream forms itself, but it can understand itself and unveil itself according to its essence in the products of its own achievements, that is to say in the objective unities: the things. This process of uncovering again implies the disclosure of the essential correlation between any being whatsoever and the corresponding conscious achievement. Every factual being, including man himself, loses its real meaning in this analysis of the absolute constituting consciousness. Particular objects are seen in this perspective as mere examples of this or that class, as guiding clues in the question concerning the discovery of the universal and necessary conscious achievements associated with a certain class of beings. Idealism cannot be avoided here, however.[26]

The weak points in Husserl's position become more evident when we compare him with Heidegger. It is unfortunate that we do not possess any documents in which these two men explain their points of view as far as each other's philosophy is concerned. We know, however, that Husserl rejects Heidegger's interpretation of phenomenology in his *Nachwort*[27] and that in *Sein und Zeit* Heidegger explains only his own vision on penomenology.[28] A comparison between the two views is further complicated by the fact that neither thinker ever had access to the complete works of the other. Their critical observations therefore sometimes are based on faulty interpretations of each other. This is particularly true in Husserl. Yet, despite all this, it is quite evident that both thinkers essentially differ from each other even though they agreed on some basic issues.[29]

26. *Ibid.*, pp. 37–38.
27. Edmund Husserl, *Ideen*, vol. III, p. 140.
28. M. Heidegger, *Sein und Zeit*, Tübingen, 1953, pp. 27–39.
29. L. Landgrebe, *Phänomenologie und Metaphysik*, Hamburg, 1949, pp. 83–84.

Husserl's method demands that we doubt every being what-soever. In this way we must ultimately arrive at the 'unquestion-able' which constitutes the ground of all beings. Husserl finds this root in the transcendental ego. If this ego be the ultimate ground for all that is, we must find that everything is ultimately constituted in this ego. Thus, all beings ultimately must be dissolved in consciousness of those beings; the transcendental ego becomes the only absolute and real being. The whole of Husserl's method is characterized by the transcendental reduc-tion in which the whole realm of Being is placed between parentheses in order to yield the transcendental ego. Heidegger makes no use of these reductions. The relationship between *Dasein* and other beings precisely belongs to the essence of *Dasein* itself.[30] While Husserl tries to free the transcendental ego from the world by means of his reductions, Heidegger sees *Dasein* precisely as that being which discloses the world. The relationship of *Dasein* and world is of such importance in Heidegger that he defines *Dasein* as Being-in-the-world. Husserl's 'pure I' is an abomination to Heidegger, a mere artificial ab-straction which only hampers our understanding of man as concrete ek-sistence.[31] Let us try to clarify this possibly over-stated difference between the two thinkers.

Both Husserl and Heidegger, start out from the idea that each kind of Being gives and manifests itself in a way which is characteristic only of this kind of Being. On the basis of this self-presentation only are meaningful philosophical statements about that kind of Being possible.[32] Husserl as well as Heidegger brings this basic principle in connection with the demand concerning a re-instatement of a 'natural world-concept.' The function of this concept is not the same in both philosophers. Husserl gives the following explanation. Intentional analysis as the universal disclosure of conscious achievements owes its guid-

---

30. W. Biemel, "Husserls Encyclopaedia-Britannica Artikel und Heideggers Anmerkungen dazu," *Tijdschrift voor Philosophie*, 12 (1950), 246–289, pp. 273–276.

31. *Ibid.*, pp. 276–280.

32. L. Landgrebe, *op. cit.*, p. 85.

ing clue to objects; that is to say to the ever changing ontological status of the objects which continuously requires a particular type of conscious achievements in which these objects can be presented. The true point of departure for any investigation into conscious achievements therefore cannot be found without insight into the structure of objectivity itself. Only thus can we gain insight into the original and genuine object of our experience; and only thus can we correlatively find the deepest and most primary achievements of our consciousness in which this object is given originally. The contemporary exact, scientific tradition imposes upon us certain prejudices concerning the original object of our experience. For the exact sciences claim that the original Being consists in the object as this manifests itself in the exact determination of science. Actually, however, the object with which the sciences deal is an abstraction, and a construction in regard to the world of our immediate and original experience. We, therefore, must renounce the prejudices of science if we are to discover the real original structure of the objects of the different realms of beings and their correlative conscious achievements. Instead, we must penetrate Being as it announces itself, prior to every scientific investigation, in the immediacy and primacy of our original experience. We must leave the cultural world of the sciences and try to find our way back to the original *Lebenswelt.* A special reduction is an essential condition without which this return never can be successful. However, the link between this reduction and the phenomenological-transcendental reduction is an essential one according to Husserl.[33]

This reduction from the scientific, cultural world toward a *Lebenswelt,* is also found in Heidegger. His Being-in-the-world forms one of the basic structures of *Dasein.* Yet, to understand the world in its relationship to *Dasein* and also *Dasein* itself inasfar as it originally *is* mundane and *has* world, that is the main theme of fundamental ontology in which Heidegger wants

33. *Ibid.,* pp. 85–87.

to bring to light what Husserl called 'the natural world-concept.' [34] Heidegger rejects the phenomenological reduction even though in many respects he is much more faithful to Husserl than the most important other disciples. With Husserl, Heidegger protests against those who try to interpret phenomenology in the classical realistic sense and fail to see it as a 'going back into the depths of subjectivity.' [35]

One of the most noticeable differences between Husserl and Heidegger is found in their different interpretation of what is a phenomenon. Heidegger defines phenomenon as "that which shows itself in itself" or concretely "the Being of beings, its meaning, its modifications and derivatives." [36] Heidegger came to this interpretation because he chose a point of view concerning intentionality that differed from Husserl's. Heidegger sees intentionality as a relating to that which is, as a relation to the world. This is directly evident from his description of *Dasein* as Being-in-the-world.[37] With this in mind we can easily understand that the intentional analysis of Heidegger can never take the form of a constitutive analysis as we find it in Husserl. This is also the reason why Heidegger will have nothing to do with a transcendental subjectivity or a theory of the ego as a 'disinterested observer' nor with a complete and universal reflection.[38]

Summarizing this we can say that Heidegger rejects Husserl's method because it did not take sufficient note of *Dasein's* original experience of itself as *Being-in-the-world*. Husserl's method cannot fully penetrate *Dasein* in the originality of its ek-sistence. It can only lead to an idealized subject never to *Dasein's* essence, to its ek-sistence. The subjectivity in its most essential meaning is thus by-passed.[39] Once the true meaning of subjectivity is revealed, we immediately become convinced of the impossibility of a statement which equates Being with object (*Sein-Gegen-*

---

34. *Ibid.*, p. 87; Heidegger, *op. cit.*, p. 52.
35. L. Landgrebe, *op. cit.*, p. 87.
36. M. Heidegger, *op. cit.*, pp. 28, 35.
37. *Ibid.*, pp. 52–62.
38. L. Landgrebe, *op. cit.*, pp. 87–94.
39. *Ibid.*, p. 94.

stand) . With this insight the possibility of Husserl's transcendental idealism comes to an end.[40]

Ricoeur forcefully summarizes all this in his study of Husserl's *Cartesianische Meditationen*,[41] taking his starting point in
the following quotation: "Since the monadically concrete ego
includes also the whole of actual and potential conscious life,
it is clear that the problem of explicating this monadic ego
phenomenologically (the problem of his constitution for himself) must include all constitutional problems without exception. Consequently the phenomenology of this self-constitution
coincides with phenomenology as a whole." [42] Referring to this
passage of the *Cartesianische Meditationen* Ricoeur explains
Husserl's final view as follows. If the whole of transcendental
reality is limited to that of the ego, the problem of the constitution of reality coincides with the problem of the self-constitution of this ego. Phenomenology becomes a self-explanation
of the ego, even there where the original interest was in the
constitution of the object, the realm of the psychical or the
cultural. The ego is here no longer the subject-pole placed
opposite an object-pole; it instead becomes that which encompasses everything. Everything now becomes a *constructum* of
and for transcendental subjectivity; the whole world of reality
becomes a mere product of its activity. Phenomenology as a
whole becomes a "self-explanation of my own ego taken as subject of every possible knowledge." [43] Husserl's definitive view
on the ego links phenomenology inseparably with idealism, a
conclusion which, otherwise, is fully accepted by Husserl
himself.[44]

The thing about which phenomenology speaks, therefore, is
not Being itself; it rather is a being which is essentially an
object. Husserl maintains that the question which asks about the
link between Being and Being-object is a pseudo-question. He

40. *Ibid.*, pp. 99–100.
41. P. Ricocur, "Etude sur les 'Méditations Cartésiennes' de Husserl,"
Revue Philosophique de Louvain, 52 (1954), 75–109.
42. Edmund Husserl, *Cart. Med.*, pp. 102–103.
43. *Ibid.*, p. 118.
44. P. Ricoeur, *art. cit.*, pp. 107–109.

thus dodges the problems which are connected with this question primarily because he *a priori* refuses to make use of speculation. He decrees without further explanation that Being is phenomenon and that phenomenon is Being. The basic mistake that Husserl makes in this *a priori* decision is that he understands the appearance of the object only as an appearing before a *knowing* subject, whereas this appearing of the object must originally be grasped in its metaphysical dimensions as an ontological relationship between two beings. Husserl does not realize that the self-presentation of a being encompasses more than the presentation of that same being in and through man's theoretical knowledge. As far as its ontological possibility is concerned man's knowledge is grounded on the general Being of things for other things.[45] Husserl's phenomenology sees intentionality purely as relationship of knowledge. This ties in with the fact that he practically always interprets substance as subject as this generally has been done in the metaphysical tradition since Descartes and Leibnitz. This view sees the phenomenon as indeed identical to a represented object for a representing ego. Without being fully aware of it, and even without explicitly subscribing to this view, Husserl places himself on the same foundation as modern metaphysics.

Heidegger tries to overcome the difficulties inherent in Husserl's vision by replacing the idealized and abstract subject of modern philosophy with the concretely human ek-sistence. He feels that we can bypass certain pitfalls in Husserl's theory only when we understand man's Being as a Being-in-the-world. At the same time this vision does not basically conflict with the rest of Husserl's insights.

In this connection we must mention another important factor. More than once have commentators pointed to Husserl's onesided interest in analysis as an important source of errors and prejudices. Heidegger was one of the first to notice this factor and it is useful to compare him to Husserl in this respect,

45. E. Fink, "L'analyse intentionnelle et le problème de la pensée spéculative," in *Problèmes actuels de la phénoménologie.* (Ed. H. L. Van Breda), Brugge-Paris, 1952, pp. 53–87, p. 70.

also. Jaspers, Marcel, Merleau-Ponty, De Waelhens, and Strasser have shown a great deal of interest in this aspect of phenomenology.[46] We also want to mention Gadamer's *Wahrheit und Methode*.[47] Strasser in his *Phenomenology and the Human Sciences* [48] arrived at a particularly fortunate systhesis of the most important aspects of this point. Strasser characterizes contemporary phenomenological philosophy as hermeneutic, intuitive and dialectical.[49] The hermeneutic postulate has its origin in the fact that in the phenomenology of the post-war period the Cartesian ideal of an absolute beginning which Husserl always maintained, had been rejected. Contemporary phenomenologists turned their backs on this ideal because it implies a *regressus in infinitum*. It is felt also that such an ideal runs counter to the phenomenological situation. A philosopher's thought is always situated; in particular, this thought always presupposes his concrete ek-sistence. Ultimately our thinking is a thinking together with others, including the great philosophers of the past. That is why philosophy must be conceived of as an hermeneutic interpretation of man's concrete ek-sistence in which his social and historical situation is fully recognized. The Greek world used the word *to ἑρμήνευμα* to indicate such an interpretive explanation of something that remained opaque in and of itself. The hermeneutical attitude can be negatively described as that attitude in which the philosopher no longer maintains the pretenses of being an a-cosmic, a-historic and a-social consciousness. The attitude can be positively defined as one in which the philosopher must consider his own ek-sistence and all its essential characteristics as already previously given. He then must try to clarify the essential structures of this ek-sistence and to understand them in their metaphysical meaning.

---

46 Joseph J. Kockelmans, "Over de methode der wijsbegeerte," in *Algemeen Nederlands Tijdschrift voor Wijsbegeerte en Psychologie*, 54 (1962) 201–218, pp. 208–215 and the literature quoted there.

47. H.-G. Gadamer, *Wahrheit und Methode. Grundzüge einer philosophischen Hermeneutik*, Tübingen, 1960.

48. S. Strasser, *Phenomenology and the Human Sciences*, pp. 245–276.

49. *Ibid.*, p. 249.

Heidegger's research in this matter is now generally recognized as correct, at least in principle.[50]

An explanation of the intuitive character of phenomenology must choose as its point of departure a description of the concept of 'phenomenon.' A physicist uses this concept to indicate a 'merely subjective appearance'; the physicist is likely to forget here that all mediate and experimental evidences necessarily presuppose an immediate evidence based on original phenomena. These original and immediate phenomena are characterized by Heidegger as 'that which manifests itself in itself, the manifest.'[51] Such a phenomenon places us in immediate contact with the thing itself. Since Husserl we speak of 'evidence' to designate such an immediate contact with things. In addition to a thing in its self-givenness one must distinguish a thing as merely intended (*bloss Vermeintes*). Intuition now is that act of knowledge which corresponds to the Being-evident of real Being. Intuition is therefore not identical with sensory perception, although it is true that all intuitive grasping and understanding reaches back to a perceptual intuition. We thus see emerge a very important methodological insight, namely that all that which presents itself to us in obvious evidence need not be subjected to proof and cannot be subjected to proof either. The task of the philosopher is to bring evidences to light and to incorporate all his other insights into these evidences.[52]

This evidence-principle has certain typical limitations however. These arise primarily from the perspectivity to which every perception and all subsequent derivative acts are subjected. These limitations also follow from the fact that one object can be covered by another. We must finally remember in this context that the horizon-phenomenon makes all 'seeing' into a 'conceiving-as.'[53]

Phenomenologists usually are least explicit when it comes to

50. *Ibid.,* pp. 249–251.
51. M. Heidegger, *op. cit.,* p. 28.
52. S. Strasser, *op. cit.,* pp. 251–254.
53. *Ibid.,* pp. 254–256.

the dialectic character of phenomenology. Yet, it is clear from what we said above, that the principle of intuition is incomplete without a dialectic principle. The fact that there is nothing *behind* the phenomena does not exclude the possibility that a phenomenon may be partly hidden. It is even true that the phenomena do not originally present themselves in their entirety in intuition. It is precisely because of the fact that phenomena are both clear as well as obscure (*Verdecktheit*) that we are in need of a phenomenology.[54] The dialectical method now plays an essential part in the process of uncovering phenomena. By dialectics we understand here: any orderly change in perspectives which enables human beings in search of meaning to overcome the limitations of one-sided perspectives and limited horizons in a systematic manner. Mute experiences and the 'incarnated' dialectics are further in need of a language which has an intersubjectively valid meaning. Besides the pre-predicative dialectics, we are, therefore, also in need of a predicative dialectics which in a community of persons materializes itself necessarily in the form of a dialogue. The word dialogue points here to the mutual effort of the 'we' in which truth, goodness and beauty are brought to light by means of language. This dialectical-dialogical effort is and forever remains an attempt which seeks to rescue things from their darkness and brings them to light.[55]

Husserl overestimated at first the value of the evidence-principle. In the years following the second World War one began to see some of the limitations of this principle, particularly under the influence of Merleau-Ponty's contention that philosophical evidence is valid only within a certain sphere of thinking. Philosophical evidence is furthermore determined by social, historical and cultural horizons. These evidences do not make themselves come true but rather *we* must make them come true from the perspective of our own social and cultural situation.

To understand these words correctly we must distinguish

54. M. Heidegger, *op. cit.*, p. 36.
55. S. Strasser, *op. cit.*, pp. 256–259.

between the formal evidences of logic and mathematics and the material evidences of pre-scientific and scientific life. It is then easy to see that formal evidences arise out of material evidences of an intuitive nature, by means of abstraction and idealization. Intuitive evidence arises out of immediate experience. These experiences are not to be understood as the 'sensory perceptions' of empiricism but rather as the original, existential orientations toward beings insofar as they include insight and lead to knowledge. Experience, then, is the origin of all forms of consciousness; thinking in concepts and categories is then the continuation of this very same orientation toward beings on an essentially higher level. We can state, therefore, that every evidence corresponds to the result of a certain experience. But what are we precisely to think of the intuitive evidence?

We should note first of all that not every experience leads to evidence. Only after all the different intentionalities which are included in one particular experience are fulfilled can we speak of evidence. We speak of evidence then, only when the data of all the partial experiences agree with each other and when all the intentions of knowledge have been at least relatively satisfied. A further requirement is that we express in language the complete concordance that exists between that which we saw and that which is given.

It is possible that a situation arises in which something is held to be evident while it is not. When this happens it may be due either to mistakes made in the observation, to gaps in the process of fulfillment, or because of some mistakes made in the process of verbalization. This does not detract from the fact that there are evidences which are unshakeable. Strasser speaks here of primordial evidences.[56] These refer to those obvious aspects which make this concrete dialectical process itself possible, regardless of the question whether it elicits a truth or a mistake in a particular instance. These aspects include my ek-sistence, your ek-sistence, our mutual openness, the world, time and space, etc. Primordial evidences are relatively small in number.

56. *Ibid.,* pp. 268–270.

Even when we accept this view in its general outline we nevertheless run into a difficult problem, namely the one of differentiating between primordial evidences and others, especially the naive evidences on the level of the existential dialectic itself. Most phenomenologists, including Husserl, underestimated this problem. It seems that we will need a special method in order to keep these evidences apart. In our search for such a method we would probably do well to start with the following questions: what are the methods used by the philosopher that permit him to discover 'universality' and 'necessity'? how are these two categories related? It seems clear that necessity cannot simply be derived from universality on the basis of empirical observations. Universality is the consequence of necessity and not vice versa. Existential necessity can be discovered only by dialectics, by which we mean here a systematic choosing and discarding of determinate horizons. The desired method is then found to consist in postponing our judgment concerning a particular experiential fact, to formulate an antithesis out of this fact and to then see whether the thesis can be destroyed by the antithesis. If this does not happen we are facing a primordial evidence. If the antithesis turns out to be not only thinkable but liveable and capable of forming part of our ek-sistence, we are not faced with a primordial evidence, but, instead, with a limited evidence.

Phenomenology, then, is a philosphy concerned with human ek-sistence in its dialectical interwovenness with other beings. The philosopher gives an analytic and a hermeneutics of his ek-sistence and of his original interwovenness with other ek-sistences. His existential orientation toward and his dealing with other people and things forms the starting point for his philosophical work. The evidences which relate to this orientation are spontaneous and naive experiential evidences. The philosopher is required to point out their universal and essential structures and he uses the dialectical method to that end. A methodical and critical sifting all the natural evidences results then in the primordial evidences. When we view phenomenology from this perspective we see it as a methodically developed 'wisdom' of man's ek-sistence, as a strict philosophy rather than a strict science. Starting from this philosophical anthropology the philosopher must try to rise above the world while remaining in it in his search for a real metaphysics.[57]

The phenomenological philosopher finds his starting point in the thought that human experience manifests a meaningful structure. He wants to uncover this structure, rescue it from the multitude of human experiences in which it lies buried. He wants to describe these structures with the help of an analytic-explicitating method which is essentially distinguished from the methods of the sciences. In the dialectical method he finds a tool that makes it possible to demonstrate the universality and necessity of his description of essences. Through this revelation of the basic structures of man's experience the philosopher at the same time furnishes the foundation of empirical research. He is capable of stating in general terms the particular dimension of intelligibility to which certain phenomena belong. The phenomenologist, therefore, can be of real service to the empirical scientist. His independence as a thinker makes it possible for him to make orienting, interpretive, and supplementary contributions to the empirical sciences. The philosopher cannot base his explanation of man and world on the facts and concepts developed by science since all scientific theories implicitly presuppose man and world. Starting from the fact of man's Being-in-the-world the philosopher must interpret all forms of man's ek-sistence including the ek-sistence of the scientist. Although the phenomenologist does not start out with the facts of the empirical sciences of man, he nevertheless makes use of these in order to concretize, to illustrate, and to enrich his primordial evidences.[58] This places the relationship between phenomenological psychology and phenomenological philosophy in an entirily new perspective. We must try to further clarify this relationship.

57. *Ibid.,* pp. 260–276 (passim).
58. *Ibid.,* pp. 277–280.

Phenomenological Psychology and Existential Phenomenology

WE NOW want to ask ourselves whether we can still speak of a phenomenological psychology within the context of an existential phenomenology as briefly described in the foregoing. And if our answer turns out to be affirmative we still must question ourselves concerning the possible content which is to attributed to the term 'phenomenological psychology' in this context.

First of all, one could adopt the point of view that phenomenological psychology as it was understood by Husserl does not seem to fit into an existential phenomenology. In the context of the latter this psychology becomes superfluous, even impossible. For Husserl had based the distinction between transcendental phenomenology and phenomenological psychology on his view on the meaning of the transcendental reduction. Since the transcendental reduction is explicitly rejected by existential phenomenology, it seems that phenomenological psychology becomes a part of what Heidegger refers to as fundamental ontology (*Fundamentalontologie*) and what with certain reservations could also be called a philosophical anthropology.[59] All this becomes clear as soon as we realize that in existential phenomenology we no longer see man as 'pure consciousness' but rather as ek-sistence, as *Dasein*, as Being-in-the-world. Although it still remains possible to think about man in the abstract as a pure consciousness, this possibility is not sought by contemporary psychology. This psychology is precisely interested in the existential orientation of man toward his world. This world is a cultural, scientific, historical, economic, social and religious world.[60] This existential orientation toward the world can first be studied in the positive sciences, such as far instance empirical psychology. This orientation can also be studied from a philosophical perspective; this phenomenological, interpretive, and

59. M. Heidegger, *op. cit.*, pp. 13–14, 182–183, 200–202, 405–406, 436–437.
60. S. Strasser, *op. cit.*, p. 3.

dialectical approach to the study of man's existential orientation toward the world is called philosophical anthropology. We see, therefore, that there is no room for a phenomenological psychology between empirical psychology and philosophical anthropology. This presses all the more when we realize that the proponents of existential phenomenology maintain that the hermeneutic and dialectic character of the phenomenological method are indispensable to philosophy.

Yet, it seems possible to speak in this context of a phenomenological psychology in a meaningful way, when we understand it to mean the usual empirical psychology which, however, orients itself in its view on man towards an anthropology as this is developed in existential phenomenology. Strasser's thinking has moved along these lines; he even no longer wants to speak of phenomenological psychology. Instead he uses the term 'empirical psychology on a phenomenological basis,' a truly apt expression describing precisely what is intended.[61] He develops the relationship between such a psychology and existential phenomenology in the following manner. In the development of an empirical psychology based on phenomenological insights our first task is to study the empirical basis of this science and to free it of all pseudo-philosophical prejudices which lead psychology into objectivism, scientism, and empiricism. This task cannot be accomplished by the empirical scientist alone; he needs to cooperate here with the philosopher. The phenomenologist in the role of advisor should not disparage the results of empirical investigations, he only can point to the particular limitations of this mode of inquiry. His task is to restrain and delimit the meaning of this 'form of experience.' This restraining criticism must apply to both the point of beginning in empirical experience and to the further development of everything that is implicitly contained in this experience. The point of departure for any psychological work must be founded on and nourished by a real experience of man and the human realm. Working our way up from such a starting point we should gain access to real

61. *Ibid.*, pp. 307–313.

evidences, even though these evidences be not absolute and eternal. Theories, models, philosophical notions, etc., can never form a true basis for empirical research. True, the further development of every empirical science requires these theories, notions, hypotheses and models, but we should be careful by these methodical tools to introduce nothing which will contaminate our original experience. Also the complete scientific 'apparatus' should remain intact in psychology. Experimental techniques, tests, questionnaires, etc., are neither phenomenological nor anti-phenomenological. They remain valid provided they are employed according to the current critical-technical rules. These methods must be reviewed only in so far as they contain physical prejudices. Science ultimately must develop a more adequate overall picture and this can only be done when the scientist is ready to accept the hermeneutic horizon of the philosopher. Phenomenological philosophy as a fundamental philosophy of man's ek-sistence and as a real rigorous philosophy seems to be able to provide us with such a horizon.

In Strasser's view many empirical psychologists have recently stopped the old practice of forcing the 'facts' belonging to the realm of the human into the schemes of the natural and physical sciences which are clearly unsuitable for this purpose. He feels that phenomenological philosophy could provide the needed theoretical justification of a new ideal of scientific rigor.

We find another possible perspective in the writings of Sartre [62] and Buytendijk.[63] Sartre refers on numerous occasions to phenomenological psychology. One of the most valuable treatments of this theme can be found in the introduction and in the conclusion of his *Esquisse d'une théorie des émotions*. He maintains that psychology has always tried to pretend to be a positive science, by which is meant that it tries to be a science in which all insights are based on experience. We no longer live in the reigning period of associationism, and today it is generally

62. See for instance: J.-P. Sartre, *Esquisse d'une théorie des émotions*, Paris, 1939.
63. F. J. J. Buytendijk, "Die Bedeutung der Phänomenologie Husserls für die Psychologie der Gegenwart," in *Husserl et la pensée moderne*, pp. 98–114.

agreed that the psychologist may ask real questions and genuinely interpret data. Yet, every psychologist still wants to confront the object of his investigation in very much the same
manner as the physicist does with his. In psychology we need to
define 'experience' with much greater accuracy than is the case
in the physical sciences. One used to recognize in psychology
only two types of experience, namely those produced by the
spatio-temporal perception of organized bodies, and the intuitive knowledge of man himself. This latter is also referred to as
reflective experience. However, from a methodological point of
view we must ask ourselves whether in psychology these two
types of information complement each other. Or must one be
subordinate to the other? In the dispute that arose around this
question all participants seem to agree that we must start with
the facts if we are to come to any valid conclusions. By 'facts'
are here to be understood everything that during the research is
encountered as an unexpected enrichment, as something new
in regard to earlier observed facts. Such facts do not by themselves constitute a synthetic whole, nor does this whole by itself
communicate its own meaning. Nor is there here *a priori* a
guiding idea. If we understand by anthropology a science in
which the essence of man and his existential conditions are
studied, then, we cannot possibly call psychology of man an
anthropology since psychology refuses to determine its object
a priori. The concept of man to which human psychology refers, is purely empirical; it refers to a certain number of beings,
spread out over the world who in experience manifest analogous
characteristics. The psychologist learns from physiology and
from sociology that there are certain objective relationships
which are maintained among these creatures. He will restrict his
research to this group of beings as a matter of hypothesis, but he
does not feel fully committed to this. The question as to whether
this concept of man is adequate or true or at least not arbitrary
is left open. He feels that it is the task of empirical research to
eventually define *man*. If this psychology would ever achieve a
carefully circumscribed concept of man, which is rather doubtful
anyhow, this description would only be the result and the crown-

ing piece of an already constituted science. Such a concept of man can be no more than an *idea* in the Kantian sense of the word. In the meantime the psychologist uses as a working-hypothesis a preliminary concept of man and he is guided in this use by expediency, by what seems useful or successful. Peirce states that the worth of an hypothesis is no more than the sum total of the experimental results to which it leads. From that perspective the concept of man would be nothing but the sum of all established facts which it is able to unify.[64]

The result of such views is that psychology can do no better than present us with a sum of heterogeneous elements and facts, most of which remain entirely unconnected. This chaos is not the result of chance but rather follows from the basic principles underlying that science. To focus exclusively on facts means by definition to attend to that which is isolated. It means to place the accidental above the essence, that which is contingent above that which is necessary, to prefer chaos above order, to push in principle all that which is genuinely fundamental and vital toward some indeterminate future. An anthropological synthesis is then out of the question. One could evidently say that this precisely represents the ambition and the method of the physical sciences. We must remind ourselves here, however, that the natural sciences as such never make the world understandable to us. These sciences only explain the necessary conditions which make it possible for us to understand certain universal phenomena. 'Man' however, is a concept of the same order as 'world' and according to Heidegger it is impossible to separate the human reality or *Dasein* from the world. A psychology which uses purely empirical methods can therefore never reach this human reality, nor shed light on it.[65]

Psychologism is a logical consequence of this view on the meaning of psychology and we can see phenomenology as a reaction against both of these conceptions. Husserl's work is above all permeated with thoughts about the essential incommensurability between essence and fact. When we start a scientific in-

64. J.-P. Sartre, *op. cit.*, pp. 3–5.
65. *Ibid.*, pp. 5–6.

vestigation with facts we will never be able genuinely to grasp the essential aspects of whatever we are studying. Husserl further maintains that it is possible to have an original intuitive experience of essences and that this experience is not inferior in any respect to our experience of concrete facts. Only the intuitively grasped essences make it possible for us to further classify and order facts. All psychological generalizations are meaningless as long as we continue to work in the dark without an essential *a priori* about man's Being; and this essential *a priori* can only be grasped in an original intuition. Husserl finally maintains that psychology as the science of certain human facts can never be the original science of man in the radical meaning of that word. *The essential structure of human facts discloses these facts as human reactions against the world.* These human facts presuppose man and world. Psychological facts therefore do not ever become meaningful in their true sense without a thorough enlightenment concerning the meaning of these two fundamental concepts. In our attempt to find a true foundation for psychology we must delve beyond the realm of psychological facts, beyond the situation of man in the world, toward the source of man, the world, and the psychical, that is to say toward transcendental, constituting subjectivity. This latter realm of Being can only be approached by means of the transcendental reduction in which the 'world' is placed between parentheses. Thus it is transcendental subjectivity which must be questioned. And what in doing so endows its answer with the strength to support the edifice of my thought is precisely the fact that this answer is *my* answer. Husserl thus was able to derive advantage from the absolute closeness of consciousness to itself; a fact that psychology never had used to advantage. Also on this transcendental level we are not concerned with facts but with the transcendental essences of psychic phenomena.[66]

Heidegger has also succeeded in taking advantage from the closeness between the investigator and that which he investigates. Research on man is to be distinguished from all other

66. *Ibid.,* pp. 7-8.

research, precisely because we ourselves are the beings which are
to be discovered. "The Being of any such being is in each case
mine." [67] The fact that I study this human reality and that I am
this human reality is not a mere accidental happening. For man
to ek-sist precisely means to take his ek-sistence upon himself and
to take responsibility for this human ek-sistence rather than to
look upon it as an outsider. "And because *Dasein* is in each case
essentially its own possibility, it can, in its very Being choose
itself and win itself; it can also lose itself and never win itself." [68]
This commitment to itself which is characteristic of man's Being
implies at least some understanding of *Dasein* of itself in no
matter how vague a manner. "In its Being this being comports
itself toward its own Being . . ." [69] This understanding of oneself is not something that comes from the outside as it were; it is
rather the mode of Being characteristic of this being. The human reality which I myself am thus takes its own Being upon
itself by understanding it. This understanding is also *my* understanding. I make myself being man through understanding
myself. I can question myself. This questioning can grow into
an analysis of the human reality and this analysis in turn can
serve as the basis of an anthropology. We are not speaking here
of introspection because introspection reaches only for facts;
moreover the ontological understanding of my own being is
vague and inauthentic. It must be explicated and formulated
anew. Such an hermeneutics of ek-sistence can form the genuine
basis of anthropology and this in turn can serve as a real basis
for a truly adequate psychology. We can see here with exceptional clarity the divergent situations in which both, phenomenology and traditional psychology, find themselves. For
traditional psychology takes its starting point in heterogeneous
facts and hopes that these facts will ultimately yield a synthetic
totality and an harmonious picture of the human reality. Phenomenology, on the other hand, wants to start with a determina-

67. M. Heidegger, *op. cit.*, p. 41.
68. *Ibid.*, p. 42.
69. *Ibid.*, p. 42.

tion of the very essence of man; only after this task is accomplished can one start with a true psychology of man.[70]

Phenomenology then is the study of phenomena, not of facts. A phenomenon is that which announces itself to us; its reality is precisely its spontaneous appearance. This spontaneous appearance itself must be questioned and described as it appears. It does not further 'stand for' anything else; it does not hide or represent any deeper reality. The whole of man can be found in any particular human attitude. We therefore see emotion, for example, as the human reality itself which gathers itself and directs itself emotionally to the world. A phenomenologist therefore can question man about his emotions and also can question the emotions concerning man's essence. For man to ek-sist means to take one's own Being upon oneself in some existential mode, in some or other orientation toward the world.[71]

When we consider this background it becomes clear to us why the old psychology has been so distrustful of phenomenology. The first concern of the practitioner of the old psychology has been to consider a particular psychical situation in such a way so as to denude it of all *meaning*. This psychical situation is to him a *fact* and as such, something incidental. Following in the footsteps of the physicist he empties himself of all interest in *what this is* and *why this is*. When we ask him concerning *meaning* he answers: "A fact means nothing, it simply is." He only wants to observe without attaching any meaning to what is observed. To the phenomenologist, on the other hand, each and every human fact is essentially meaningful; to cut the fact loose from its meaning means to him to reduce this fact to incoherence and to deprive it of its nature as a *human* fact. A phenomenologist wants to study the meaning of the different forms of man's existential orientation toward the world. Emotion as such has no meaning to a traditional psychologist since he studies emotion as a fact which is cut loose from its living,

70. J.-P. Sartre, *op. cit.*, pp. 8–9.
71. *Ibid.*, pp. 9–10.

meaning-giving matrix. A phenomenologist, on the other hand, says that the fact *is* only insofar as it means something. And emotions, in their own way, mean the whole of 'human consciousness,' of human reality. An emotion is not a mere accident nor is it an effect of human reality, but, on the contrary, it is this reality itself which now realizes itself as emotion. It therefore makes no sense to consider emotion as a psychophysical disorganization. On the contrary, it has its own structure, its own laws, its own meaning, and its own sense. It does not arrive on the scene of human reality from the outside, so to say. It is man himself who realizes himself in emotion. Emotion is 'an organized form of human existence.' [72]

Phenomenological psychology does not make man problematic, nor does it place the world between parentheses. It precisely directs itself to man-in-the-world, to the multitude of situations in which man realizes himself in the family, in the theater, in the war, etc. As such this psychology is subordinate to phenomenological philosophy. Only after the latter has explained such ideas as 'man,' 'world,' 'Being-in-the-world,' and 'situation' can we start the work of a strictly positive study of man-in-situation. Such a phenomenological philosophy, and specifically a phenomenological anthropology, has not yet been completely developed. Does this mean therefore that psychology must wait till all this work has been done. It is obvious that psychology will and must advance in the meantime. Yet, we must be aware that such an anthropology is actually in the process of being realized, and psychology should consult with this budding source of information wherever this is possible. Psychology should stop collecting mere facts but instead should turn its questioning attitude toward phenomena in so far as they are meaningful. It will be necessary to see that an emotion, for example, does not exist as a mere bodily phenomenon, because a mere body cannot be affected nor can it give meaning to its own manifestations. Psychology should look beyond respiratory irreg-

72. *Ibid.*, pp. 10–11.

ularities or reflex-patterns toward the meaning of joy and sadness. An this meaning is not some quality which is *attached* to joy or sadness; this meaning rather exists insofar as these emotions are seen within the context of human reality. It is this reality itself which must be questioned. Since such a psychology does not look for facts, but rather for meaning, it rejects both inductive introspection and empirical observation in order to apply itself to the task of describing the essential aspects of phenomena. Phenomenological psychology is therefore also an eidetic science. Yet, it does not reach beyond the psychic phenomena toward human reality as such in the manner of phenomenological anthropology. It limits its interest and scope to phenomena so far as they are meaningful.

Phenomenological psychology interests itself in the emotions and asks concerning their meaning. It seems, however, that this meaning of the emotions consists in their constant referring to the human reality as a whole. To be moved in an emotional sense involves a total modification of my Being-in-the-world. The psychological description of the meaning of emotion has its own limits, however: it already presupposes a description of affectivity insofar as it constitutes the very Being of *Dasein* itself, insofar as it is constitutive of our human reality as affective reality. Phenomenological psychology starts out with emotionality; phenomenological anthropology starts out with man as Being-in-the-world. The first represents a regressive discipline, the latter a progressive one.

The question arises here as to whether phenomenological anthropology would not suffice to provide us with all the needed understanding of human reality. Why would we want to also have recourse to a phenomenological psychology? Phenomenological anthropology can explain to us that emotionality is a realization of the essence of *Dasein* insofar as this *Dasein is* affection. It cannot come to grips with why this *Dasein* necessarily realizes itself in *this* emotion and not in another. The fact that *Dasein* has only these emotions brings us into contact with the facticity of human existence. This facticity makes it mandatory that we remain in constant touch with empirical reality, and it is this aspect that will forever separate psychological regression and anthropological progression.

What we have said up to now should not be interpreted to mean that the existing empirical psychology would become superfluous. There also is a place for this type of psychology. One has to realize, however, that if we limit our perspective exclusively to what is offered within this discipline as such, we will meet only with a chaos of facts. Phenomenological psychology therefore must move away from facts toward a description of phenomena seen as meaningful. These phenomena, however, can only find their radical explanation in a phenomenological anthropology where they are seen within the context of human reality as such.[73]

Now that we have summarized Sartre's view it becomes evident that he came to conclusions which are quite different from those of Husserl, yet, these views diverge less from the original Husserlian conceptionalization than the one we described earlier. Sartre remains faithful to the idea of a phenomenological psychology which occupies a position halfway between empirical psychology and philosophical anthropology. He objects, however, to Husserl's transcendental philosophy and seeks closer alliance with Heidegger on this point.

It seems then that Husserl's original views lead, via Heidegger's philosophy, to two entirely different conceptionalizations of the role and function of phenomenological psychology. From one perspective phenomenological psychology as a separate discipline becomes superfluous. Instead we have an empirical psychology on an existential-phenomenological basis and this psychology could be termed "phenomenological psychology." The name here indicates only a certain direction, trend or movement of empirical psychology. It is that trend of empirical psychology which as far as philosophical and in particular anthropological presuppositions are concerned is founded in Heidegger and Husserl. However, one also can maintain with

73. *Ibid.*, pp. 11–13; 51–52.

Sartre that there is a place for phenomenological psychology as a distinct and separate discipline. This psychology is not only possible but indeed necessary because existential anthropology cannot provide empirical psychology with the insights which prove to be necessary for empirical and positive scientific efforts. Which of these two points of view must be considered superior in respect to the adequacy of its foundation? This is a question with which we occupy ourselves in the last section of this book.

CONCLUSION

The proponents of phenomenological psychology originally seem to have felt that this psychology, although closely connected with empirical psychology, was nevertheless a separate science. Such thinkers as Sartre, Merleau-Ponty, Buytendijk, Gurwitsch, and others exerted influence in this direction. Although, as far as I know, there is little explicit information on this point, it seems, nevertheless, that the distinction between phenomenological psychology and empirical psychology was maintained on the basis of methodological differences in the two disciplines. Yet, the term 'phenomenological psychology' was often used in such a way as to include both the empirical and the phenomenological psychology. This usage stressed the unity existing between the two disciplines.

Recently, however, we find more and more thinkers who maintain that a separate and distinct phenomenological-psychological discipline is superfluous. Empirical psychology has to develop with the direct help of the existential-phenomenological anthropology and without the mediacy of phenomenological psychology. Still one hears the word 'phenomenological psychology' used in this context but only to refer to an empirical psychology based on phenomenology. We have here, then, an 'ordinary' empirical psychology which, as far as its foundation is concerned, directs itself to existential anthropology as found in the works of Heidegger, Sartre, Merleau-Ponty, Jaspers, and others.[74]

74. Literature which explicitly deals with phenomenological psychology is relatively rare. The following publications seem to be of importance: H. Drüe, *Edmund Husserls System der phänomenologischen Psychologie,*

Both ways of approaching the matter have something substantial to offer and we will not be so bold as to attempt a definite solution of the matter. Yet, it seems that Sartre's view appears to be the more acceptable because Husserl's phenomenological psychology has a meaningful function which is in certain ways not compatible with the function of existential-phenomenological anthropology. To dissolve the phenomenological psychology in this anthropology would therefore amount to a definite loss. In our attempt to distinguish between phenomenological psychology and philosophical anthropology we can no longer make use of the transcendental reduction since in existential phenomenology this reduction does not make any sense. Possibly we might differentiate the two sciences in the following manner.

Sartre sees philosophical anthropology as primarily progressive and phenomenological psychology as regressive.[75] This vision seems to contain a good deal of truth since it is the first task of anthropology to understand the very essence of man. From that central preoccupation it approaches emotionality, for instance,

---

Berlin, 1963; F. J. J. Buytendijk, "Die Bedeutung der Phänomenologie Husserls für die Psychologie der Gegenwart," in *Husserl et la pensée moderne*, pp. 78–98; C. Lannoy, "Phenomenologie, ontologie en psychologie in het werk van Edmund Husserl," *Tijdschrift voor Philosophie*, 11 (1949) 391–416; J. van den Berg, and J. Linschoten, *Persoon en wereld*, Utrecht, 1953; B. Delfgaauw, "Verantwoording der phaenomenologische psychologie," *Nederlands Tijdschrift voor Psychologie en haar Grensgebieden*, 9 (1954) 78–83; J.-P. Sartre, *Esquisse d'une théorie des émotions*, Paris, 1939; S. Strasser, *Phenomenology and the Human Sciences*, Pittsburgh, 1964; Maurice Merleau-Ponty, "Phenomenology and the Sciences of Man," in *The Primacy of Perception*, Evanston, Ill., 1964, pp. 42–95; Joseph J. Kockelmans, *Over fenomenologische psychologie*, Den Bosch, 1964.
Phenomenological-psychological considerations are for instance found in: E. Minkowski, *Vers une cosmologie*, Paris, 1936; F. J. J. Buytendijk, *Over de pijn*, Utrecht, 1943; M. Merleau-Ponty, *Phénoménologie de la perception*, Paris, 1945; G. Bachelard, *La psychanalyse du feu*, Paris, 1949; *L'eau et les rêves*, Paris, 1947; *L'air et les songes*, Paris, 1943; *La terre et les rêveries de la volonté*, Paris, 1948; A. Gurwitsch, *The Field of Consciousness*, Pittsburgh, 1964; C. Graumann, *Grundlagen einer Phänomenologie und Psychologie der Perspektivität*, Berlin, 1960; J.-P. Sartre, *L'imaginaire. Psychologie phénoménologique de l'imagination*, Paris, 1948; L. Binswanger, *Grundformen und Erkenntnis menschlichen Daseins*, München-Basel, 1962.
75. J.-P. Sartre, *Esquisse d'une théorie des émotions*, pp. 51–52.

as the concrete realization of the Being characteristic of man in so far as this being *already* is affection. Phenomenological psychology, on the other hand, is especially interested in the different concrete forms which are assumed by our existential orientation toward the world. In this orientation, we see the clear manifestation of the facticity of man's ek-sistence. This facticity forces us to keep in touch with the factual aspects of human ek-sistence and with empirical psychology in which these facts are dealt with in a scientific manner. The description and explanation of a particular form of existential orientation toward the world is, of course, permeated with essential insights concerning man brought to the fore by philosophical anthropology; yet, these insights themselves are here not the objects of investigation. It is the task of philosophy to investigate the general characteristics of the ontological dimensions of beings in a radical manner. That is why Heidegger sees philosophy as ultimately an ontological discipline [76]; and most of the proponents of phenomenological psychology are in agreement with this. De Waelhens describes this ontology as a scientific investigation which tries to understand and comprehend the Being of the 'ontic' entities which themselves are to be described by phenomenology.[77] This perspective allows us to differentiate between phenomenological description and ontological, interpretive, dialectical explanation. When we apply this insight to the realm of our existential orientation toward the world we find it possible to distinguish between a phenomenological psychology and a philosophical anthropology.

Maybe we could clarify this still further in the following manner. It is possible for us to inquire into the nature of memory, perception, emotion, etc., without paying attention to the ontological dimensions and the ontological problems which, no doubt, announce themselves in that realm. It is true that no *definitive* insight can be gained without taking the ontological dimension as such into consideration, yet, for methodological

76. M. Heidegger, *op. cit.,* pp. 11, 12, 15–16, 27, 35, 38, 231–232, 248, 303–333.
77. A. De Waelhens, *Existence et signification,* Louvain-Paris, 1958, p. 115.

reasons we might refrain from pursuing this dimension in depth. In the perspective mentioned philosophical anthropology, however, is not only the necessary first step in the direction of a genuine ontology, but such an ontology, in turn, also must form a necessary and harmoniously concluding part of anthropology. Anthropology only acquires real meaning within this perspective when it inquires into the relationship of man to Being.[78] It remains possible, on the other hand, to give analytic descriptions of the different forms of human behavior without explicitly referring to the underlying ontological aspects, even though these descriptions, therefore, cannot be held to be 'radical' descriptions from an ontological point of view.

Furthermore, we should not neglect to mention here that one of the major factors which have made Husserl's philosophy as a whole unacceptable must be sought in his tendency to solve philosophical problems exclusively by means of analyses. Almost all phenomenological philosophers of today seem to agree that it is impossible to build a philosophical anthropology entirely on pure eidetic, intentional analyses. To the method of analysis we need to add a hermeneutic and dialectic method.[79] It nevertheless seems possible to restrict ourselves to the use of intentional analyses in our description of the concrete forms of man's behavior and to then understand these descriptions, either implicitly or explicitly, from the perspectives afforded by a philosophical anthropology.[80] We can point to numerous examples in modern psychological literature to make this point clear. A survey of the publications of Sartre, Merleau-Ponty, Minkowski, Bachelard, Buytendijk, Linschoten and others will bring us in contact with a great number of pure analyses and descriptions. We do not intend to deny the fact that these analyses require a further philosophical basis, and no phenomenological psychologist would disagree with that. We also often find analyses in psychological literature which are recognized as

78. M. Heidegger, *op. cit.*, pp. 8–15, 15–19, 231–232.
79. See Chapter VII, second section.
80. P. Ricoeur, "Méthode et tâches d'une phénoménologie de la volonté," in *Problèmes actuels*, 111–140, pp. 115–117.

correct and valuable by many psychologists even though these psychologists approach these analyses from different anthropological perspectives. One and the same phenomenological description apparently can be interpreted from different philosophical backgrounds as long as these backgrounds are not antagonistic to the general phenomenological perspective.

Finally, it seems that the proponents of phenomenological psychology are often in trouble when they try to deal with questions concerning the methodology of psychology. One of the difficulties centers around the intentional analysis as it is used in psychology. On the one hand, the value of this method cannot be denied while, on the other hand, it is difficult to see how such a method could go hand in hand with empirical and experimental methods. Should we not see this ambiguity as an indication that there are two distinct psychological sciences which nevertheless remain essentially related? Does this not mean that we should recognize both an empirical *and* a phenomenological psychology? We previously mentioned in this connection how Husserl made this matter clear by using physics as an example. The *a priori* and the methods of the positive natural sciences are explained in the pure natural sciences. Empirical psychology must analogously find its methodological basis and its content in phenomenological psychology. This phenomenological psychology as an eidetic, descriptive, intentional, and aprioric science is distinct from philosophy. Even though this comparison is defective for reasons which we will mention later, we nevertheless find that there is some truth in it. Would it not be possible to see phenomenological psychology as a general theoretical part of empirical psychology, analogous to theoretical physics? A general discipline dealing with man's functions and founded on a phenomenological basis is from a *methodic* point of view neither strictly philosophical nor purely empirical. Be this as it may, it remains true that a distinction between a phenomenological and an empirical psychology in the strict sense of the word, would facilitate our view of the methodology of psychology.

We might summarize all this by saying that a phenomenological psychology remains possible when conceived of as an eidetic science of the psychical with the help of noetico-noematic analyses of our typical human behavior. This human behavior consists of the concrete forms assumed by our existential orientation toward wordly beings and the world. It also seems that such an eidetic study would be meaningful only when it is accompanied by a special reduction which leads us from our cultural world back to the original *Lebenswelt*. Husserl tried to develop such a reduction in his later works but his involvement in the transcendental reduction interfered with these attempts. It seems that Heidegger and Merleau-Ponty succeeded better than Husserl himself in developing his original conception of that reduction. A phenomenological-transcendental reduction in the sense of Husserl has no meaningful function in either philosophy or psychology.

In conclusion, we want to say that the difference between phenomenological and empirical psychology is not so much in the object of study as in the manner in which this object is approached. Phenomenology is an eidetic, aprioric science and empirical psychology is a science of facts. This difference manifests itself clearly in the entirely different methods used by the two sciences. Yet, despite this essential difference, the two sciences nevertheless form a solid unity. Husserl saw correctly the relationship between empirical and phenomenological psychology, but he did not succeed in a complete description of this relationship. As we noted before, the difference between phenomenological psychology and philosophical anthropology must not be sought in a phenomenological-psychological and a transcendental reduction but only in the presence or the absence of an ontological perspective. We do not mean to imply here that psychology can do without an ontology and without a philosophical anthropology. On the contrary, psychology should orient itself to anthropological insights concerning the general fundamental structures of man's Being-in-the-world. Following Husserl we can even assume a point where phenomenological psychology and philosophical anthropology overlap each other. This suggests also that philosophical anthropology would be well advised to look at what phenomenological psychology is doing in order to enrich itself. Merleau-Ponty remarks in this connection that a science without philosophy cannot know what it really is doing, and a philosophy without science tends to lose itself in vague and endless horizons of purely formal considerations.[81]

When we now overlook from this perspective Husserl's investigations concerning phenomenological psychology as a whole, we are forced to conclude that his views are unacceptable in many respects. We are thinking here in particular about his approach to epistemological problems, about the phenomenological-psychological reduction, and his description of the subject-matter of psychology. We have already dealt in some detail with the problems involved in the Husserlian reductions. We want to focus here briefly on the other two problems mentioned. It seems clear that the epistemological status of phenomenological psychology can be clarified only with the help of a general theory of science. Husserl insisted that this theory of science should lead in the direction of a pure study of the *Lebenswelt*. Only from the viewpoint afforded by the "ontology" of the *Lebenswelt* would the meaning and function of the method and the object of phenomenological psychology become truly visible. This position is unacceptable to us because this "ontology" of the *Lebenswelt* is an eidetic, phenomenological, *non-philosophical* (because a non-transcendental) discipline. Also the further elaborations of this philosophy of science in Lotze, Bolzano and ultimately Leibnitz carry little conviction. In this respect, too, we find ourselves in closer agreement with Heidegger who bases his philosophy of science on a fundamental ontology.[82]

81. M. Merleau-Ponty, *Sens et Non-Sens*, Paris, 1948, pp. 194–195; A. De Waelhens, *Une philosophie de l'ambiguité. L'existentialisme de Maurice Merleau-Ponty*, Louvain, 1951, p. 391; R. C. Kwant, "Het phenomenologisch wetenschapsideaal," *Tijdschrift voor Zielkunde en Opvoedingsleer*, 41 (1955) 20–43, pp. 38–39.
82. See for instance: Joseph J. Kockelmans, *Phenomenology and Physical Science*, Pittsburgh, 1966, pp. 48–91 and the literature quoted these; A. De Waelhens, *Existence et signification*, pp. 105–121 and pp. 233–261.

Furthermore, Husserl's contention that phenomenological psychology should concern itself with the realm of the purely psychical as distinct from the realm of the physical and the psychophysical seems correct insofar as the object of psychology is essentially different from the object of physics, biology or physiology. Yet, the description of the object of psychology as "the purely psychical" is not only insufficient, but positively unacceptable. The fact that Husserl has struggled with this problem becomes clear when we realize that he maintains in several places that the *a priori* of empirical psychology is not purely physical, nor purely psychical, but psychophysical. He abandoned further speculation on the problem with the remark that further work is needed in this area.[83] It seems, however, that precisely this question is of importance for a phenomenological psychology which seeks in a pure eidetic study to approach the different modes of our existential orientation toward the world. We should not neglect to mention that Husserl made little or no effort to follow the trends of empirical psychology which developed after the year 1900. Several of these modern trends have contributed many valuable insights, especially from the methodological point of view. If Husserl had paid more attention to this matter he might have come up with an entirely different conception of psychology as has indirectly become manifest in the recent investigations of Merleau-Ponty, Minkowski, Bachelard, Sartre, Buytendijk, Gurwitsch, and many others.

Despite these objections, Husserl's investigations concerning psychology are of tremendous importance for contemporary positive scientific thinking about man. Together with Dilthey, Husserl was one of the first to assert that 'science' is not to be equated with 'natural science' or with 'physics.' Husserl saw that each science must use the methods of investigation which concord with the typical and essential *a priori* of that science without, however, losing sight of the general demands which issue from methodology, logic and mathematics. Husserl further has stressed throughout his works that psychology should orient

83. Edmund Husserl, *Phän. Psych.*, pp. 285, 325–326.

itself towards philosophy rather than towards physics. To give this orientation concrete form he devised a new form of psychology. This phenomenological psychology should remain in contact with empirical psychology as a 'natural' empirical science and should be tied to philosophy as an eidetic, aprioric science. His research into the object, the method, and the function of this phenomenological psychology opened the door to entirely new methodological perspectives. We want to mention in this connection especially the intentional analyses and the reduction which leads from our world of culture toward the *Lebenswelt*. In so doing, Husserl leaves untouched the typical methods of empirical psychology, at least insofar as these methods are truly adapted to the specific demands of its particular subject matter. Husserl, finally has stated several times that not only could psychology profit from further contact with philosophy, but that philosophy, in turn, can profit from a closer association with psychology. This Husserlian insight is interpreted today from a somewhat different philosophical perspective. We do well to remember, however, that these newer perspectives could only come into being as a result of Husserl's pioneering investigation in this area.

BIBLIOGRAPHY

For a complete list of Husserl's works quoted in this book see: pp. 12–14.

G. Bachelard, *La psychanalyse du feu,* Paris, 1949.

———*L'eau et les rêves,* Paris, 1947.

———*L'air et les songes,* Paris, 1943.

———*La terre et les rêveries de la volonté,* Paris, 1948.

S. Bachelard, *La logique de Husserl. Etude sur logique formelle et logique transcendentale,* Paris, 1957.

R. Bacon, *Novum Organum Scientiarum* (Ed. C.W. Kitchin), Oxford, 1855.

O. Becker, *Die Philosophie Edmund Husserls,* in *Kantst.,* 35 (1929) 119–150.

G. Berger, *Le cogito dans la philosophie de Husserl,* Paris, 1941.

———*Les thèmes principaux de la phénoménologie de Husserl,* in *Revue de Métaphysique et de Morale,* 49 (1944) 22–43.

W. Biemel, *Husserls Encyclopaedia–Britannica Artikel und Heideggers Anmerkungen dazu,* in *Tijdschrift voor Philosophie,* 12 (1950) 246–280.

L. Binswanger, *Grundformen und Erkenntnis menschlichen Daseins,* München, 1962.

———*On the relationship between Husserl's Phenomenology and Psychological insight,* in *Philosophy and Phenomenological Research,* 2 (1941–1942) 199–210.

R. Boehm, *Husserl et l'idéalisme classique,* in *Revue Philosophique de Louvain,* 57 (1959) 351–396.

H. Boelaars, *De intentionaliteit der kennis by Edmund Husserl,* in *Bijdragen,* 3 (1940), 111–161, 221–264.

———*Husserls reducties en haar betekenis voor het Tho-*

misme, in *Tijdschrift voor Philosophie,* 6 (1944) 333–376.
E. Boring, *A History of Experimental Psychology,* New York, 1957.
G. Brandt, *Welt, Ich und Zeit,* Den Haag, 1955.
F. Brentano, *Psychologie vom empirischen Standpunkt,* 2 vol. (Hrsg. v. O. Kraus), Hamburg, 1955.
F. Buytendijk, *De psychologie van de roman,* Utrecht, 1950.
———*De vrouw; een existentieel-psychologische studie,* Utrecht; 1950.
———*Over de pijn,* Utrecht, 1943.
B. Delfgaauw, *Verantwoording der phaenomenologische psychologie,* in *N. Tijdschr. v. Psychol. en haar grensgeb.* 9 (1954) 78–83.
A. De Muralt, *L'idée de la phénoménologie. L'exemplarisme husserlien,* Paris, 1956.
D.M. De Petter, *Het tweede international colloquim over de phenomenologie, Krefeld, 1—3 November 1956,* in *Tijdschr. v. Philos.* 18 (1956) 726—739.
R. Descartes, *Oeuvres complètes* (Ed. Adam-Tannery), 12 vol., Paris, 1897–1910.
A. De Waelhens, *De la phénoménologie à l'existentialisme,* in *La choix, le monde, l'existence,* Paris, 1947, 37–82.
———*Existence et signification,* Louvain-Paris, 1958.
———*La philosophie et les expériences naturelles,* Den Haag, 1961.
———*Phénoménologie et dialectique,* in *Ordre, désordre, lumière,* Paris, 1952, 1–23.
———*Phénoménologie et métaphysique.* in *Rev. Philos. de Louv.,* 47 (1949) 366—376.
———*Phénoménologie et vérité,* Paris 1953.
———*Phénoménologie husserlienne et phénoménologie hégélienne,* in *Rev. Philos. de Louv.,* 52 (1954) 234—249.
———*Une philosophie de l'ambiguïté. L'existentialisme de Maurice Merleau-Ponty,* Paris, 1951.
A. Diemer, *Edmund Husserl. Versuch einer systematischen Darstellung seiner Phänomenologie,* Meisenheim a. Glan, 1956.

H. Drüe, *Edmund Husserls System der phänomenologischen Psychologie,* 1963.

H. Ebbinghaus, *Über erklärende und beschreibende Psychologie, Zeitschr. f. Psych. u. Phys.* 9 (1896).

M. Farber, *The foundation of phenomenology. Edmund Husserl and the quest for a rigorous science of philosophy,* Cambridge Ma., 1943.

————*Philosophical essays in memory of Edmund Husserl,* Cambridge Ma., 1940.

E. Fink, *Die phänomenologische Philosophie Edmund Husserls in der gegenwärtigen Kritik,* in *Kantst,* 38 (1933) 319–383.

————*Was will die Phänomenologie Edmund Husserls?,* in *Tatwelt,* 10 (1934) 14–32.

————*Das Problem der Phänomenologie Edmund Husserls,* in *Rev. intern. de philos.,* 1 (1938) 226–270.

————*Operative Begriffe in Husserls Phänomenologie,* in *Zeitschr. f. philos. Forsch.,* 11 (1957) 321–337.

J. Flugel, *A hundred years of psychology: 1833–1933,* Edinburgh, 1945.

G. Funke, *Zur transzendentalen Phänomenologie,* Bonn, 1957.

H.-G. Gadamer, *Wahrheit und Methode. Grundzüge einer philosophischen Hermeneutik,* Tübingen, 1960.

C. Graumann, *Grundlagen einer Phänomenologie und Psychologie der Perspektivität,* Berlin, 1960.

A. Gurwitsch, *Théorie du champ de la conscience,* Brugge-Paris, 1957.

————*The last work of Edmund Husserl,* in *Philos. and phenom. research,* 16 (1955–1956) 370–399.

G. Gusdorf, *Introduction aux sciences humaines. Essai critique sur leurs origines et leur développement,* Paris, 1960.

M. Heidegger, *Sein und Zeit,* Tübingen, 1953.

D. Hume, *A treatise on human nature* (Ed. Selby-Bigge), London, 1896.

W. James, *Principles of psychology,* New York, 1891.

A. Janse De Jonge, *De mens en zijn verhoudingen. Hoofdstukken uit de phaenomenologische psychologie,* Utrecht, 1956.

K. Jaspers, *Die phänomenologische Forschungsrichtung in der Psychopathologie,* in *Zeitschr. f. Psychol.,* 9 (1912).

F. Jeanson, *La signification humaine du rire,* Paris, 1950.

Joseph. J. Kockelmans, *Realisme-idealisme en Husserl's phenomenologie,* in *Tijdschrift voor Philosophie,* 20 (1958) 395–442.

———*Over de methode der wijsbegeerte, A.N.T.W.Ps.,* 54 (1962) 201–218.

———*Over fenomenologische psychologie,* Den Bosch, 1964.

———*Phenomenology and Physical Science,* Pittsburgh, 1966.

———*Edmund Husserl. An Introduction to his Phenomenology,* Pittsburgh, 1967.

———*Phenomenology and the Sciences of Man,* on *Social Research,* 15 (1966) 433–467.

Ph. Kohnstamam, J. Linschoten, M. Langeveld, B. Kouwer, D. Van Lennep, en P. Balland, *Inleiding in de psychologie,* Groningen-Djakarta, 1955.

B. Kouwer en J. Linschotten. *Inleiding tot de psychologie,* Assen-Amsterdam, 1938.

J. Kraft, *Von Husserl zu Heidegger. Kritik der phänomenologischen Philosophie,* Frankfurt a. M., 1957.

H. Kunz, *Über Sinn und Grenzen psychologischen Erkennens,* Stuttgart, 1957.

R. Kwant, *Het phenomenologisch wetenschapsideaal,* in *Tijdschr. v Zielk. en Opvoedingsl,* 41 (1955) 20–43.

L. Landgrebe, *Husserls Phänomenologie und die Motive zu ihrer Umbildung,* in *Rev. intern. de philos.,* 1 (1938) 277–316.

———*Phänomenologie und Metaphysik,* Hamburg, 1949.

———*Philosophie der Gegenwart,* Bonn, 1952.

———*Seinsregionen und regionale Ontologien in Husserls Phänomenologie,* in *Studium Generale,* 9 (1956) 313–324.

———*World as a phenomenological problem,* in *Philos. and phenom. research,* 1 (1940) 38–58.

M. Langeveld, Ph. Kohnstamm, C. Van Parreren, J. Linschoten, B. Kouwer, D. Van Lennep, A. Oldendorff, B. Palland, *Inleiding in de psychologie,* Groningen-Djakarta, 1957.

C. Lannoy, *Phenomenologie, ontologie en psychologie in het werk van Edmund Husserl*, in *Tijdschr. v. Philos.*, 11 (1949) 391–416.

E. Lévinas, *La théorie de l'intuition dans la phénoménologie de Husserl*, Paris, 1930.

————*L'œuvre d'Edmond Husserl*, in *Rev. philos. de France et de l'Etranger*, 129 (1940) 33–85.

————*En découvrant l'existence avec Husserl et Heidegger*, Paris, 1949.

————*Totalité et infini. Essai sur l'extériorité*, Den Haag, 1961.

J. Linschoten, *Op weg naar een fenomenologische psychologie. De psychologie van William James*, Utrecht, 1959.

B. Lorscheid, *Max Schelers Phänomenologie des Psychischen*, Bonn, 1957.

J. Maréchal, *Le point de départ de la métaphysique*, 5 Cahiers, Bruxelles-Paris, 1944–1949.

M. Merleau-Ponty, *Eloge de la philosophie*, Paris, 1953.

————*La structure du comportement*, Paris, 1942.

————*Les sciences de l'homme et la phénoménologie*, Cours de Sorbonne, 1951–1952, Paris, s.a.

————*Phénomenologie de la perception*, Paris, 1945.

————*Sens et Non-Sens*, Paris, 1948.

————*Signes*, Paris, 1960.

E. Minkowski, *Vers une cosmologie*, Paris, 1936.

E. Mounier, *Introduction aux existentialismes*, Paris, 1947.

M. Müller, *Crise de la métaphysique*, Paris, 1953.

R. Müller-Freienfels, *De voornaamste richtingen in de hedendaagse psychologie* (Vert. P. Ronge), Utrecht, 1938.

J. Nota, *Phaenomenologie als methode*, in *Tijdschr. v. Philos.*, 3 (1941), 203–260.

F. Nuyens, *Ontwikkelingsmomenten in de zielkunde van Aristoteles. Een historisch-philosophische studie*, Nijmegen-Utrecht, 1939.

A. Osborn, *The philosophy of Edmund Husserl in its development from his mathematical interests to his first conception of phenomenology in 'Logical Investigations'*, New York, 1934.

G. Pedoli, *La fenomenologia di Husserl*, Torino, 1958.

J. Prick en H. Van der Waals, *Nederlands handboek der psychiatrie*, Arnhem, 1957.

P. Ricœur, *Analyses et problèmes dans 'Ideen II' de Husserl*, in *Phénoménologie—Existence*, 23–76.

———*Etude sur les 'Méditations Cartésiennes' de Husserl*, in *Rev. Philos de Louv.*, 52 (1954), 75–109.

———*Idées directrices pour une phénoménologie*, Paris, 1950.

J. P. Sartre, *Esquisse d'une théorie des émotions*, Paris, 1939.

———*L'être et le néant. Essai d'ontologie phénoménologique*, Paris, 1948.

———*L'imaginaire. Psychologie phénoménologique de l'imagination*, Paris, 1948.

M. Scheler, *Die transzendentale und die psychologische Methode*, Leipzig, 1920.

———*Wesen und Formen der Sympathie*, Frankfurt a.M., 1948.

K. Schneider, *Psychiatrie heute*, Heidelberg, 1955.

H. Schümmer, *Die Wahrnehmungs- und Erkenntnismetaphysik Max Schelers in den Stadien ihrer Entwicklung*, Bonn, 1954.

L. Schuwer, *Het derde international colloquium over de phenomenologie: Royaumont, 23–30 april 1957*, in *Tijdschr. v. philos.*, 19 (1957) 524–544.

H. Spiegelberg, *The phenomenological movement. A historical introduction*, 2 vol., Den Haag, 1960.

E. Stein, *Beiträge zur philosophischen Begründung der Psychologie und der Geisteswissenschaften*, in *Jahrb. f. Philos. und phänom. Forschung*, 5 (1922) 1–116.

S. Strasser, *Beschouwingen over het vraagstuk van de apodiciteit en de kritische verantwoording van de phenomenologie*, in *Tijdschr. v. Philos.*, 8 (1946) 226–270.

———*Das Gemüt. Grundgedanken zu einer phänomenologischen Philosophie und Theorie des menschlichen Gemütslebens*, Utrecht-Antwerpen-Freiburg 1956.

———*Phenomenology and the Human Sciences*, Pittsburgh, 1963.

P. Thévenaz, *Qu'est-ce que la phénoménologie?*, in *Rev. de Théol et de Philos.*, 42 (1952) 9–30, 126–140, 294–316.

————*L'homme et sa raison*, 2 vol., Neuchâtel, 1956.

Ueberweg-Moog, *Grundriss der Geschichte der Philosophie. Die Philosophie der Neuzeit bis zum Ende des XVIII. Jahrhunderts*, Berlin, 1924.

Ueberweg-Oesterreich, *Grundriss der Geschichte der Philosophie. Die deutsche Philosophie des XIX. Jahrhunderts und der Gegenwart*, Berlin, 1923.

H. Van Breda, *Het 'zuivere phaenomeen' volgens Edmund Husserl*, in *Tijdschr. v. Philos.*, 3 (1941) 447–498.

J. Van den Berg, *The phenomenological approach to psychopathology. An introduction to recent phenomenological psychopathology*, Springfield. 1955.

J. Van den Berg en J. Linschoten, *Persoon en wereld*, Utrecht, 1953.

C. Van Peursen, *Lichaam - ziel - geest. De mens als oriëntatie vanuit zijn wereld*, Utrecht, 1956.

G. Van Riet, *Réalisme thomiste et phénoménologie husserlienne*, in *Rev. Philos de Louv.*, 55 (1957) 58–92.

J. Wahl, *Notes sur la première partie de 'Erfahrung und Urteil' de Husserl*, in *Phénoménologie - Existence*, 77–105.

————*Note sur quelques aspects empiristes de la pensée de Husserl*, in *Phénoménologie - Existence*, 107–135.

————*L'ouvrage posthume de Husserl: la Krisis. La crise des sciences européennes et la phénoménologie transcendentale*, Cours de Sorbonne, Paris, 1957.

Problèmes actuels de la Phénoménologie. Actes du premier Colloque international de phénoménologie. Bruxelles, Avril 1951. Edités par H. L. Van Breda, Brugge-Paris, 1952.

Husserl et la pensèe moderne. Actes du deuxième Colloque international de phénoménologie. Krefeld, 1–3 novembre 1956. Edités par H. L. Van Breda et J. Taminiaux, Den Haag, 1959.

Husserl, [Actes du troisième Colloque international de phénoménologie. Royaumont, 23 au 30 avril 1957. Edités par M.-A. Bera] Cahiers de Royaumont, Philosophie no. III, Paris, 1959.

Edmund Husserl: 1859–1959. Recueil commémoratif publié à

l'occasion du centenaire de la naissance du philosophe. Edité par les soins de H. L. Van Breda et J. Taminiaux, Den Haag, 1959.

La phénoménologie. Juvisy, 12 septembre 1932, Juvisy, 1932.

Phénoménologie - Existence. Recueil d'études par H. Birault, H. Van Breda, A. Gurwitsch, E. Lévinas, P. Ricœur et J. Wahl, Paris, 1953.

Fascicule consarcé à Husserl. Rev. intern. de philosophie, 1 (1939).

For a more complete Bibliography see the following literature:

H. Van Breda, *Bibliographie der bis zum 30, Juni 1959 veröffentlichten Schriften Edmund Husserls,* in *Edmund Husserl: 1859–1959,* 289–306.

L. Eley, *Husserl-Bibliographie* (1945–1959), in *Zeitschr. f. philos. Forschung,* 13 (1959) 357–367.

J. Patocka, *Husserl-Bibliographie,* in *Rev. intern. de Philos.,* 1 (1939) 374–397.

J. Raes, *Supplément à la Bibliographie de Husserl, Revue intern. de Philos.,* 4 (1950) 469–475.

H. Spiegelberg, *The phenomenological movement,* vol. I, 163–167.

Q. Lauer, *Phénoménologie de Husserl. Essai sur la genèse de l'intentionnalité,* Paris, 1955, 341–441.

J.-D. Robert, *Eléments de bibliographie Husserlienne,* in *Tijdschr. v. Philos.,* 20 (1958) 534–544.

S. Strasser, *Fenomenologie en empirische menskunde,* 309–327:

H. Drüe, *Edmund Husserls System der phänomenologischen Psychologie,* 318–324.